⌂ SUCCESSFUL HOMEOWNER'S TOOLS

⌂ SUCCESSFUL HOMEOWNER'S TOOLS

James D. Ritchie

Structures Publishing Company
Farmington, Michigan

Manufactured in the United States of America

Edited by Peggy Frohn

Text design by Linda A. Zitzewitz

Cover design by Carey Jean Ferchland

Cover photograph by Dave Knox,
Ann Arbor Photographic, Inc.

Current Printing (last digit)

10 9 8 7 6 5 4 3 2 1

Structures Publishing Co.
24277 Indoplex Circle
Box 1002, Farmington, Mich. 48024

Library of Congress Cataloging in Publication Data

Ritchie, James D
    Successful homeowner's tools.

    Includes index.
    1. Tools.   I. Title
TJ1195.R57   621.9′08   79-28667
ISBN 0-912336-85-4
ISBN 0-912336-86-2 pbk.

Contents

Wood turning lathe, circa 1860's, is itself made largely of wood parts.

Introduction

A Brief History of Tools

From the time some primitive man first used a large rock to give himself mechanical advantage as he pounded a post (or a neighbor) into the ground, the progress of civilization can be charted by man's development of tools and implements to extend the force, speed and precision of his own two hands.

We can only guess how long the more basic tools have been around. Archaeologists place the first tool making at more than 400,000 years ago. No drawing of a caveman is complete without a stone axe or hammer. Many museums feature examples of sharpened blades and flint saws made by Neanderthal man some 100,000 years ago—some of them designed remarkably like saws still in use.

Copper tools have been found dating back to about 4,500 B.C. Implements of the Bronze Age included saws, awls, gouges, hammers, anvils and axes. The composition of most prehistoric bronze implements was 90 percent copper to 10 percent tin.

As man gradually gained knowledge of metallurgy, the use of softer metals gave way to the Iron Age, and for the first time, a metal was abundant and cheap enough to be put into wide use. From about 1,200 B.C., iron tools were used in Palestine, Syria and Greece. Metal saws have been around, in pretty much the same design, for at least 3,500 years.

Early Egyptian saws had teeth slanted backward, to cut on the pull stroke, to lessen the chance of bending the soft metal blades. In some Oriental countries, virtually all saws are still made this way; while here in the West, only hacksaws and coping saws are generally designed this way.

Egyptians pioneered the use of spirit levels and other measuring implements, too. As early as 1,600 B.C., Egyptian builders were using water levels to indicate truly horizontal surfaces. Bits, braces, chisels and claw hammers also were used by ancient Egyptians.

Some versatile tools have a more recent history. Take the steel framing square, the carpenter's "computer." Near the end of the War of 1812, a Vermont blacksmith, Silas Hawes, decided that steel squares might be more useful and long-lasting than the wooden ones then in common use. He made a few squares from worn-out saw blades. Demand quickly outstripped Hawes' ability to make squares by hand, so he patented his invention and opened a factory to turn out the new steel squares.

Formerly, natural abrasives, such as emery, pumice, quartz, sand or diatomaceous earth were used to smooth and polish wood and other materials. Since the 1890's, most commercial abrasives are made of synthetics such as carbides, borides or nitrides—substances almost as hard as diamond.

The development and wide distribution of electrical power has brought about the invention of time—and worksaving implements for virtually all building and household chores. Today, we are heirs to an almost infinite variety of ingenious and efficient hand and power tools.

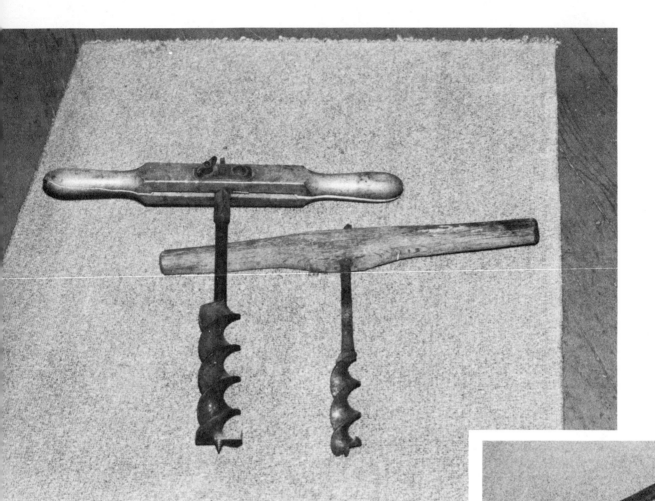

Boring augers were forerunners of modern hole making equipment. Auger at left has a chuck in the handle for interchanging bits.

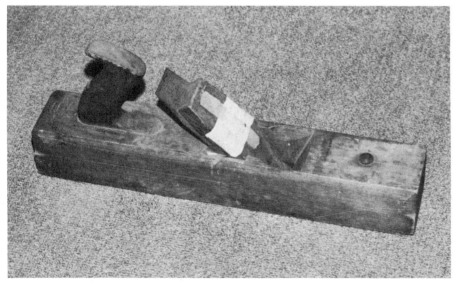

Chisels and gouges have not changed substantially. These are more than 100 years old.

This maple-bodied plane did the job 120 years ago.

Preface

This book is for tool *users*, rather than for tool *collectors*—although the two may often be combined in the same reader. But, here's the principal difference: A tool *collector* goes to the hardware store to buy a drill, primarily because he wants to own a drill. A tool *user* goes to the store to buy holes of a certain size, at the best compromise of time, effort and money.

A $50 electric drill might be a sound purchase for a tool collector. After all, collecting hand and power tools is as legitimate an enterprise as collecting stamps, firearms, Egyptian pottery or anything else; it's a perfectly good reason to buy and own tools. And, an electric drill might be a good investment for a tool user who needs the speed and efficiency of a power drill. But for a person who needs only a couple of holes in a board, that $50 drill represents a cost of $25 per hole.

It's that kind of economic distinction that guides the content and tone of much of this book. *Successful Homeowner's Tools* is written specifically for readers who utilize tools to let them perform tasks—from simple home repairs to complete construction projects—easier, quicker and with greater precision.

From the time man began walking upright, he has used tools to increase his strength, skill and speed. As man's intellect grew, so did the quality and complexity of the tools he built and put to use. It's interesting that the stages of man's civilization are often identified with the materials from which he fashioned implements: Stone Age, Bronze Age, Iron Age, etc.

Look around the room where you now sit. Few, if any, of the objects in view would be possible without the tools and machines devised and put to use by man. We humans are blessed with ten strong, dexterous fingers connected to an ingenious brain. We live in a world filled with raw materials from which we can fashion almost anything our minds can conceive, but only because those same facile minds can create tools to extend the force and skill of our hands many times over.

Bare hands cannot make much headway against wood, stone and metal. You can't make much progress at driving a nail with your fist. Hands, even hands guided by an ingenious brain, need tools. With no hammers, drills, saws, wrenches and other tools, our living standard would still be that of the caveman.

But again, merely *owning* tools is no guarantee of skill and craftsmanship; any more than the ownership of a Stradivarius makes one a concert violinist. It's possible to possess the finest saws made and still be unable to make a straight cut with any of them.

First, you must understand the tools you will use, how they are designed, what they can do and what they cannot do. Each tool, by its designed function, demands a specific application to the work to be done and a specific technique in its use. You can whack away at a nail with a hammer, without giving much thought as to how the hammer is designed to be used. But, unless you know enough about hammers to know how to hold and swing them, the result is likely to be bent nails and half-moon dents in the woodwork, rather than a smooth, professional finished job.

It's hard to over-emphasize the use of the proper tool for the job. Knowing which tool to use for which task—and how to use it properly—is a large part of craftsmanship in any trade or profession. An Oregon lumberjack and his axe are a marvelous team in the woods. But even the most skillful axeman cannot chop a satisfactory miter joint in a piece of milled trimwork. A screwdriver serves very well for the purpose of its design, but makes a poor chisel or crowbar.

The kind and amount of work you do is an important factor governing the quantity and kind of tools you'll need. There are literally thousands of tools—hundreds of them may be similar in design and use. For instance, how many different kinds of wrenches have you noticed? Each is designed for a specific use.

For your own purposes, you will need to weigh the investment in tools against the amount of use you will make of different implements. Many householders and home handypersons with a basic kit of well chosen tools are probably more productive—and more professional—

than some "tool bugs" who own an inventory that could set them up in the hardware business.

And, finally, to get the most out of a tool, the user needs to learn the technique of using it. Anyone with a moderate amount of dexterity and coordination can learn to use most tools efficiently. Tools are no discriminators of age or sex. They perform equally well for men and woman. Teenagers and retirees alike can learn the satisfying skills that come from good tools properly used.

Whether you will buy, borrow, rent or lease tools, choose them wisely and learn to use them well. In the chapters ahead, you will find a complete guide to selecting, using and caring for modern hand and power tools with skill and confidence; tools used in building, woodworking, masonry, plumbing, electrical work and other home care and maintenance chores.

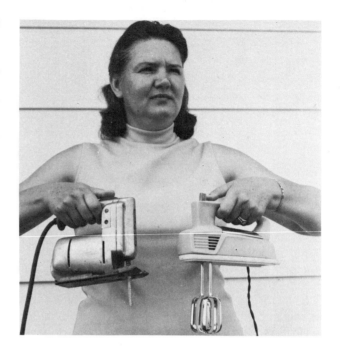

Power mixer's handle and switch match those of a sabre saw—don't forget the ladies of the house when choosing tools.

1
Tool Selection

The kind of jobs you do will dictate the kind of tools you'll need. Do you live in an apartment or rental house? Or do you own your home—a possession that calls for a wide range of skills and tools that go with them? Do you perform minor maintenance on the family car? Or, do you undertake all but major repairs and overhauls?

In every family, there are toys that need mending, shelves to be installed, leaky faucets that need new washers, lawnmower blades that need sharpening. You can save money—and often time as well—by doing your own repairs and household maintenance chores. And, as a bonus, there's a warm personal satisfaction that comes from completing a project yourself.

The correct starting place is to know which tool is needed for which job, and that is the purpose of proper tool selection. Later, you'll learn how to use each tool correctly and how to maintain, care for and repair the tools you use.

The Tools You Need

Which tools you *need* depends upon your intended use of them. Which tools you *buy* not only depends on your intended use and application, but also on the frequency you will use the tool, its cost and what you can afford. How often will you use a tool? Will it be daily, monthly, only occasionally, or once in a lifetime?

The tools you buy first depend foremost on the work you plan to do. A 12 or 16 oz. claw hammer, a pair of combination pliers, a 6 inch screwdriver and a 22 inch crosscut saw with 10 to 12 teeth per inch (points) is a good starter for most household jobs. In addition, you may want to add an awl, a small compass saw, a model maker's plane and a folding rule. With this mini-kit of tools, you can cut wood, smooth it, nail it or fasten it with screws. You can take measurements, cut wire, tighten nuts, pull nails and loosen screws.

You'd be surprised at the number of household projects you can complete with this basic set of tools. Suppose you want to install a shelf in the entry closet of your home or apartment. Tap the back wall of the closet with the

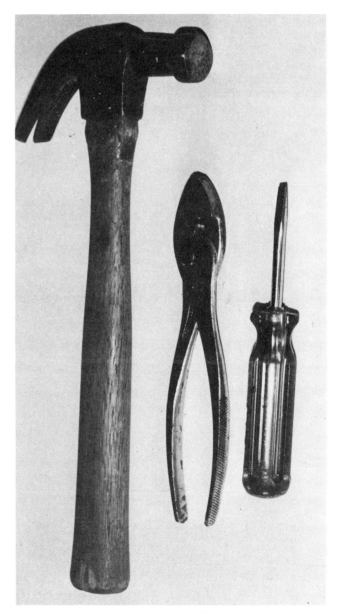

The simplest starting kit is pliers, hammer and screwdriver. These tools, plus an awl and saw can handle many small fix-it jobs.

hammer to locate the 2x4 studs inside the wall. (The wall over the stud will sound solid; wall spaces between studs echo a "hollow" sound.) Once you have located a stud—or think you have—you can confirm your discovery by pushing the awl through the wall board into the stud. The awl makes a smaller, less noticeable hole than a nail or screw, should you miss the stud.

Once you've located a stud, measure both ways to find adjacent studs. Most buildings have wall studs spaced every 16 inches. Then, mount shelf brackets (either those you have made or brackets purchased at the store) along the back wall of the closet at the desired height, inserting long wood screws through the wallboard and into the studs. You should decide beforehand how wide the shelf

should be, and have a board (about 1x8 or 1x10) of that width on hand. Measure the board to suit the width of the closet, saw it squarely and round the sharp corners with the plane. Attach the shelf board to the brackets with short wood screws, using the awl to make "pilot" holes for the screws. With a modest investment in tools and time, you have accomplished a project that needed doing— and you did it yourself.

The table below lists tools needed for common tasks. The least expensive tools and supplies needed to do the job are listed under the heading "Basic Equipment." Other practical equipment that may make the job faster or easier is listed under the column heading "Handy-to-Have Equipment."

Job Planned	Basic Equipment	Handy-to-Have Equipment
Measure and space items.	Ruler; yardstick.	6-ft. folding rule; 10-25 ft. retractable steel tape.
Attach objects to wall.	Hangers with nails or screws; 12-oz. claw hammer; hand drill and bits; screwdriver.	Hollow-wall screw anchors or toggle bolts; electric drill and twist drills; magnetic stud finder.
Attach objects to masonry wall.	Screw anchors and screws; proper size star drill and shop hammer.	Electric drill and tungsten carbide masonry drill.
Level items; plumb items.	Pan of water to level appliances; string with attached weight.	Spirit level or level on combination square; plumb bob.
Tighten or loosen screws.	4- and 6-inch conventional screwdriver; Nos. 1 and 2 Phillips screwdrivers.	Ratchet screwdriver; screwdriver attachment for electric drill.
Tighten nuts; hold small objects.	6-in. combination pliers; adjustable open-end wrench.	Locking wrench pliers; open-end or box-end wrenches.
Drive and pull nails.	12-oz. curved claw hammer.	16-oz. claw hammer; nail bar ("cat's paw").
Replace faucet washers.	Adjustable open-end wrench; screwdriver.	Pipewrench; adjustable spanner wrench.
Open drains and pipes.	Force cup ("Plumber's friend").	Flexible drain auger; compressed air flask.
Measure and mark wood.	No. 2 or 2½ common pencil; ruler or yardstick; drafting triangle or other square object.	Try square; combination square; dividers.
Cut small pieces of wood.	Coping saw; friction vise or bench hook to hold stock.	Handsaw, C-clamps; miter box.
Smooth wood.	Coarse, medium and fine sandpaper.	Block plane, rasps and scrapers; electric sander.
Assemble wood pieces.	Assorted nails and brads; 12-oz. claw hammer; $1/16$-in. nail set; glue.	Woodscrews; countersink; screwdriver; hand drills; gluing clamps; resorcinol glue.

Buy, Rent or Borrow?

Whether you will buy, rent or borrow a specific tool depends upon your immediate needs, longer range needs and your budget. The jobs you plan to do, the money you wish to spend and the storage space you have available are all matters to keep in mind when you consider buying a tool.

If you will be doing repair or maintenance work on a more or less continuous basis, you probably will want to own a basic set of tools for the purpose. Likewise, if you are a do-it-yourselfer or hobbyist, if you regularly perform automobile repairs and maintenance, buy first the tools you will use most often. Choose well. If you can get along with a hammer, pliers and screwdriver, why buy more than that? But if you can justify a wider selection of implements, consider one of the home maintenance kits that some tool manufacturers offer in a handy carrying case. Again, choose carefully to evaluate the tools included against your needs.

If you are planning to add a room, build a garage—or a house—you'll need more than a basic starter set of tools. Even so, you may want to rent or lease some power tools, rather than buy them. Obviously, you aren't likely to invest in a $500 table saw if you only have a few boards to cut—unless you just like the way an expensive saw sets off your workshop.

If you plan to use a tool regularly, for its intended purpose and keep it as a part of your permanent tool inven-

Job Planned	Basic Equipment	Handy-to-Have Equipment
Cut metal.	Utility saw or hacksaw.	Tin snips; cold chisel; power grinder and safety goggles.
Drill holes in metal.	Hand drill with twist drills.	Electric drill with twist drills; drill press with high-speed bits.
Smooth or sharpen metal.	8-in. mill file; whetstone.	8-in. half-round file; grinder and safety goggles.
Repair metal objects.	Epoxy resin.	Soldering equipment; gas or electric welder.
Install paneling.	Folding rule; 22-in. handsaw; 12-oz. claw hammer.	Saw horses; retractable metal tape; power handsaw with panel blade; glue gun.
Install plaster board.	Utility knife; claw hammer; putty knife.	Dry-wall jacks (for ceilings); taping machine; saber saw.
Install or replace plastic pipe.	Handsaw; medium sandpaper; solvent cement.	Miter box; spirit level.
Change engine oil.	Adjustable open-end wrench; can opener; oil filter wrench.	Socket wrenches; oil filler spout.
Repair concrete walks; driveways.	Wheelbarrow; square-end shovel; trowel.	Electric concrete mixer; tamper; float; concrete edgers and groovers.
Unstick doors; drawers.	Sandpaper.	Smoothing plane; electric sander.
Build picture frames.	Miter box; handsaw; small nails and brads; 12-oz. claw hammer.	Miter clamps; backsaw; glue gun.
Wood carving.	Pen knife; sandpaper.	Coping saw; woodcarver's knife set; modeler's tool; rasps.
Replace electrical outlets and switches.	Screwdriver; combination pliers; electrician's tape; solderless connectors.	Soldering gun and solder; wire stripper; diagonal cutter; needlenose pliers.

tory, buy quality tools from reputable manufacturers. Premium-quality tools are not necessary, unless you plan to use them a great deal. But cheap tools—especially edge tools such as saws, planes and chisels—are often a poor bargain. Learn which manufacturers make tools of enduring quality and watch for them in special sales and discount stores.

Price alone is no guarantee of quality, but well made tools constructed of quality materials cost more than poorly made tools of inferior materials. However, if you need a tool that will be subjected to abusive or infrequent use, inexpensive lower quality tools may be a smarter buy. For example, you may want to purchase a cheap "throw-away" power saw blade to use when cutting lumber that has been used in concrete forms, when the bits of concrete and sand would likely damage the blade. But for long-term service, tools of better quality are the best buy.

Keep in mind that some tools—notably screwdrivers, wrenches and socket-wrench outfits—are usually cheaper to buy in sets. That's also true, at times, of power tools. You may be able to buy an electric drill and a complete set of twist drills for little more than you'd normally pay for the drill alone.

However, plan your buying to avoid unnecessary overlaps. If you don't expect to own a power saw in the near future, buy the best handsaw you can afford. If you do plan to acquire a power saw, a good quality but less expensive handsaw will probably do until the power saw arrives—and you'll always have uses for the handsaw.

Tool sets come in a variety of sizes and assortments —and prices. If you only make now-and-then repairs around the house or apartment, you may get along with a low priced assortment of home maintenance tools, rather than buy single tools for individual jobs. At the opposite end of the deal, you can buy a set of several hundred tools for several hundreds of dollars. Again, determine which tools you will need and use more or less regularly.

If the set or kit of tools contains tools you would use fairly often, you may save money to buy an assortment of tools in one package. You can also scout classified newspaper ads and auctions for sets of used tools that suit your needs—and save even more money. Several mail order firms and U.S. General Supply offer name brand tools and tool sets by major manufacturers at a fairly good discount from the shelf price in the store.

But be careful when buying tools and tool sets sight-unseen through the mail. A tool assortment that looks like a bargain may not be such a good deal when you unwrap it. Be sure the tool assortment is described completely in the catalog or advertisement. For example, a 75 tool package deal may contain only 40 or 50 real tools, plus 25 or 35 hacksaw blades or sheets of sandpaper; and the total price may make the sandpaper pretty expensive.

Keep this in mind when buying sets of hand tools, also: If a set contains many tools that you already own, the lower price may not be much of a savings. Suppose you own a fairly complete set of standard wrenches—open-ends, box-ends and sockets—but need a set of metrics to work on your imported automobile. You spot a major brand metric socket set on sale that includes the wrenches you need, but also includes many of the wrenches you already own. Figure the cost of the set to see if you might not buy metric sockets separately and save money in the process.

Better quality tools—particularly power tools—often come equipped with attachments and accessories that help you get professional results with less skill and experience—another argument for buying quality equipment. For example, with a drill guide attachment, an electric drill bores holes exactly perpendicular to the work surface, whether the user is particularly skilled at drilling holes or not. By adjusting the guides on most brand-name power saws, you can cut a board to exact width, bevel the edge to a precise angle and cut the ends for a close-fitting miter joint. In other words, it's possible to buy a degree of skill along with the tool.

High priced but seldom used tools are hard to justify strictly on the basis of need. In most areas, you can rent power sanders, routers, cement mixers, ladders, scaffolding and other such specialized equipment. In many localities, individual tools, tool sets and other equipment can also be rented or leased.

If you will be using a tool for only a short time, or need a specialized tool for a short-term job, consider renting—

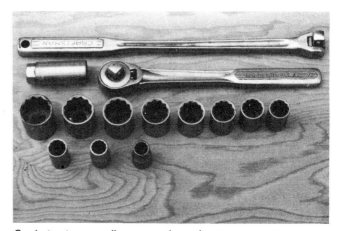

Socket sets normally are purchased complete, rather than by individual pieces.

even if you plan to buy the tool at a latter date. Perhaps you need an automatic nailer to install hardwood flooring as part of a house remodeling project. The job will last only a day or two, and you'd have little use for the equipment after it is completed. Renting is a wise way to go.

Another possibility for getting the temporary use of a tool is to borrow it. But borrowing tools—even from close friends—can be fraught with social hazards. If you need a spark plug wrench to finish an engine tune-up on a Sunday afternoon, however, borrowing may be the only solution open to you.

The old admonition for the care of borrowed tools says: "Treat it as if you owned it." But some people don't take very good care of their own tools. A better "Golden Rule" for borrowing is to take as good or better care of the equipment than the owner himself would.

Return a borrowed tool promptly after you've finished with it—clean and in good repair. The borrowing pest who never returns anything is popular with cartoonists, but not with neighbors.

Speaking of neighbors, two of them with the same interests and about the same level of skill can cooperate to finance tools and equipment together that neither might afford individually. For example, one neighbor might buy a radial-arm saw for his workshop, while the other purchases a wood-turning lathe—then both neighbors use both pieces of equipment.

This kind of individual ownership often is a more satisfactory arrangement than joint ownership of the same tools. Neighbors do move away, or have fallings out with each other, and a drill press is difficult to divide fifty-fifty.

Care and Storage of Tools

Keep tools in good condition. Tools that are used properly for the purpose intended seldom need a great deal of maintenance. Teeth of a crosscut saw should be nearly as sharp as a needle. Chisels and plane irons should be razor sharp. Tools should be kept clean and dry. Put a light coat of oil on sharp-edged tools before storing them—especially if they are kept in a place that may be damp.

Tools should be stored as closely as possible to the site of most frequent use. Some tools that are used often about the house—screwdrivers, pliers, measuring tapes—you may want to store close at hand, in a closet or drawer in the kitchen. Larger and less frequently used tools can be stored in one common area, such as a basement, garage or workshop. Storage in a specific place makes it easier to find a tool when you need it.

Well planned storage also provides protection for the edges of cutting tools—and protects the user from accidentally cutting himself on one tool while reaching for

Some power tools let you buy a degree of operating skill along with the tool—as this ripping guide on the sabre saw. (Courtesy of Black & Decker)

another. Cutting edges of saws, auger bits, planes, chisels and rasps should be protected so they will not bump other metal.

Tool storage can be as simple or elaborate as your space, interest and finances will allow. Pegboard or shelves installed in an existing area—such as a closet or corner of the basement—may be the simplest arrangement.

A specially built tool cabinet can be an improvement.

Or, depending on how many tools you own, a toolbox makes for neat, portable storage.

A workbench in a well defined area of a workshop is the ideal, most useable means of providing both a work area and tool storage. Workbenches and workshop layouts are discussed in Chapter 20.

The right tool for the job, used only for its designed purpose, kept clean and stored properly is a servant always ready to perform.

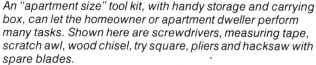

A more complete tool kit, with claw hammer, block plane, adjustable and open-end wrenches, crosscut handsaw and power drill with twist drills, can handle most household fix-it jobs.

An "apartment size" tool kit, with handy storage and carrying box, can let the homeowner or apartment dweller perform many tasks. Shown here are screwdrivers, measuring tape, scratch awl, wood chisel, try square, pliers and hacksaw with spare blades.

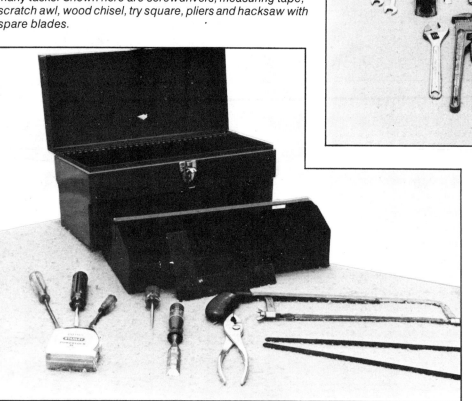

CARPENTRY, BUILDING & WOODWORKING TOOLS

For most of us, there is always a need to know something about repairing and constructing things of wood. We live in houses constructed largely of wood. We sit or lie on furniture made at least partly of wood. Wood is the common denominator of building.

While you may not wish to become a journeyman carpenter or a fulltime woodcraftperson, it's easy to gain proficiency in the use of woods and woodworking tools. Carpentry and woodworking are based on a relatively few basic tool processes and operations—measuring, sawing, smoothing, fastening. Once these basics are mastered, it's an easy step to constructing toys, furniture, buildings and other objects with professional results. Chapters 2 through 7 discuss carpentry and woodworking tools; how to choose them, use them and take care of them.

2
Tools To
Fasten Things

This chapter is about the materials and tools you will use to fasten one piece of material to another—nails, screws, bolts, nuts, staples, rivets and glues; as well as about the hammers, screwdrivers, wrenches and other implements needed to install them.

Strictly speaking, fasteners are not *tools*, but building materials that become part of the finished work. However, your mastery of the tools used to drive and install fastening devices depends to some extent on a knowledge of those fasteners. You'll get the best finished results by using the correct fastener for the job, and by using the proper tool to install it.

Hammers

As with any tool, your hammer (or hammers) will be chosen pretty much by the kind of job you need to do. Hammers are designed for various uses—nailing, ripping, driving chisels and punches, tacking, breaking rocks, spreading rivets and beating metal into shape—just to name a few functions. But, a large part of this discussion will feature the claw or nail hammer. It's the most commonly used tool for most householders.

Everyone knows how to drive a nail with a hammer right? Well, almost anyone can get a nail pounded into a

Types of hammers

board, after a fashion. But the right way to use a hammer, and the right hammer to use for a particular job, is knowledge that comes with experience and practice.

The claw (or nail) hammer is a tool used principally to drive nails, wedges, dowels and other fasteners into wood. A claw hammer is not designed to break rocks, drive punches or split kindling. There are specific tools designed for these jobs.

Claw hammers are made in head weights from 6 to 22 ounces. They are made in two general types—curved claw and straight claw. The curved claw hammer is designed for nailing and nail pulling. The straight claw, often called a ripping claw hammer, is used more often for dismantling woodwork.

Your best bet for an initial hammer purchase is a 14 or 16 ounce hammer with a curved claw and a slight bell face. Lighter hammers are better suited for cabinet making, bench work and other such jobs. For house framing, fencing and other heavy work, you might prefer a 20 or 22 ounce hammer.

Buy a hammer with a drop-forged, steel alloy head. The choice of handle—whether hickory, fiber glass, solid steel or tubular steel with hard rubber grip—is mainly a matter of personal preference. Many users like the spring and "feel" of a wooden handle, and claim that a hickory haft gives better control and eases the strain on muscles. The important things about a hammer handle are that the head stays on it and at a proper angle for efficient nail driving.

The hammer head is a matter for more careful consideration. A dime store variety hammer often has a cast head, rather than a forged one. The face of a cheaper hammer may not be hardened and ground. It's a good tool for bending nails and smashing fingers.

The face (the part of the hammer that makes contact with the nail) of a quality hammer, not necessarily expensive, is accurately ground to shape, after the head has been made by forcing red-hot steel into a metal die. The hammer face usually is ground smooth and slightly beveled at the edge to prevent chipping. It may be ground slightly convex, called a "bell" face, or ground flat, called a "plain" face. Some hammer faces have a cross-checkering sort of tread; particularly heavier hammers used for nailing together the frame of a building.

The first choice of most professional carpenters is a hammer face that is ground slightly convex. Although be-

Parts of a claw hammer.

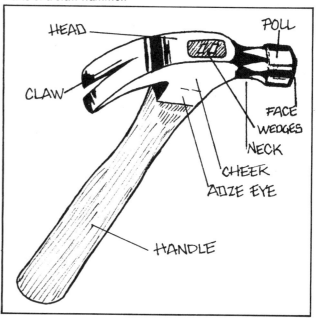

Various hammer handles.

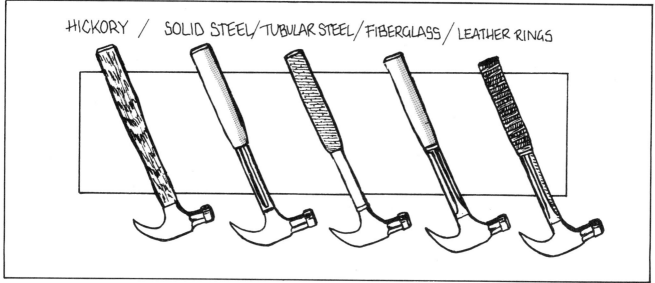

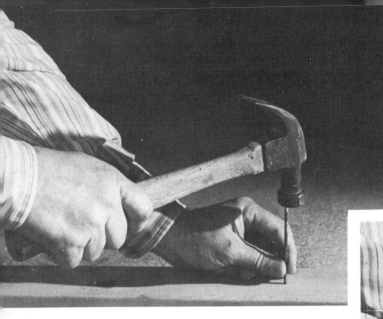

Start a nail straight into the wood by tapping on it lightly with the hammer, then hold the hammer near the end to give a more efficient swing.

To pull a nail with claw hammer, seat the nail head well down in the claw and pry up. For longer nails and to protect woodwork, use a block under the hammer.

ginners cannot drive nails straight quite as easily with it, the bell face hammer lets a craftsman drive a nail flush, or even slightly below the surface of the wood, without leaving hammer marks on the wood. Also, the bell face is not as likely to deflect nail heads, once the user acquires a measure of skill in swinging it.

To use a claw hammer, hold the handle near the end. This provides a full swinging arc that delivers the most force in the proper direction. "Choking up" on the handle nearer the head results in a smaller arc and glancing blows that bend nails. It also wastes much of the potential power in the swing, and tires the wrist, arm and shoulder more quickly.

When starting a nail into wood, hold the nail with the thumb and index finger of the left hand near the point. Position the nail at exactly the point you want to drive it and tap it lightly a couple of times to fix the nail in the wood and adjust your swing. Then, move your left hand out of the way (send it back into the nail apron for another nail) and firmly drive the nail in as far as you want it to go. (Note: unless you are a confirmed southpaw; learn to use the hammer in your right hand.)

With practice, you'll learn to adjust the wrist and arm power of your hammer swing to the size of the nail you're driving. Smaller nails naturally require less force; use lighter blows struck mostly with a wrist motion. Longer nails driven into two-inch softwoods require more force; put both wrist and forearm into the swing. For driving large nails and spikes, let the power come from wrist, forearm and shoulder.

Unless you have some reason to drive a nail at an angle (as in toe-nailing), the nail should be started perpendicular to the surface of the wood. Strike the nail with the center of the hardened hammer face, not with the side or "cheek" of the hammer. While driving a nail, hold the end of the hammer handle on the same plane as the nailhead, so that at the instant the hammer hits the nail, the nail head is flush with the hammer face. Striking the nail with the hammer at an angle can force the nail sidewise and bend it. (With experience, however, you will learn to use this trick of angling the hammer to straighten up a nail that has started going crooked.)

If a nail bends when it is being driven—unless it is your last nail—pull it out and throw it away. Start a new nail in the place. If that nail also bends, check to find out why. You may be trying to drive the nail into a knot, another nail or a piece of metal.

When pulling nails, be sure the hammer claw is set snugly against the nail before pulling. The sharp groove between the claws can be used to grip even headless nails. If the nail is a long one, don't try to pull it all the way out in a single operation. Instead, pull the nail until it starts to bend, then slip a small block of wood scrap under the hammer head for better leverage, so that the nail is pulled

straight up and out of the wood. Using a block under the hammer also prevents marring the wood.

Claw hammers require little care, other than proper use and what common sense and pride of ownership dictate. Keep the hammer face clean; dirt or grease can cause the hammer to slip. Grease or oil also causes hard rubber and leather ring grips to soften and deteriorate. Don't store wood handled hammers in damp or in hot locations. Moisture can cause the wood of a handle to swell and crush wood fibers, so that the handle will loosen when the wood dries out again. Heat can shrink the handle in the head and cause it to loosen.

If a hammer head becomes loose, tighten it by tapping the end of the handle squarely against a firm surface, then reseat the wedges that hold the handle against the adze eye in the head. Soak the head of the hammer in linseed oil. Be sure to wipe the head and face dry before using the hammer again.

Other hammers you may need for specific jobs: A "mash" or hand driller's hammer, for driving hardened masonry nails, center punches and cold chisels. A ball peen hammer for metal working and light shop chores. An 8 or 10 pound sledge, for breaking up concrete or driving splitting wedges into logs. A wooden mallet for chisels, gouges and wood carving knives. A tack hammer for carpeting and upholstery work.

Nails

To the person who uses nails only occasionally, the finer points of types, sizes and uses of nails may not be of much interest. Some nails are longer than others; some are skinnier than others. But a nail is a nail, right?

When it comes to buying nails, though, it's important to know the right type of nail for a specific job, the right length and approximate number of nails per pound.

Nails come in a variety of lengths that should be matched to the material so they will penetrate into the wood far enough to hold but not far enough to protrude to the other side of the work. Nail lengths are gauged not by inches, but by "d", the English symbol for "penny." According to legend, the "penny" designation originally referred to the number of pennies that 100 nails of a certain size cost.

Up to 10d, you can figure the length of a nail by dividing the "penny" size by four and adding ½ inch to get the length in inches. For example, an 8d nail is 2½ inches long (8 divided by 4 equals 2, plus ½ = 2½ inches), and is the size of common nail generally used to nail one-inch material to framing members.

Nails are sold by the pound, not by number, except for some specialized nails. Different kinds of nails have different weights: for instance, a pound of 8d common nails contains about 100 nails, and a pound of 16d common

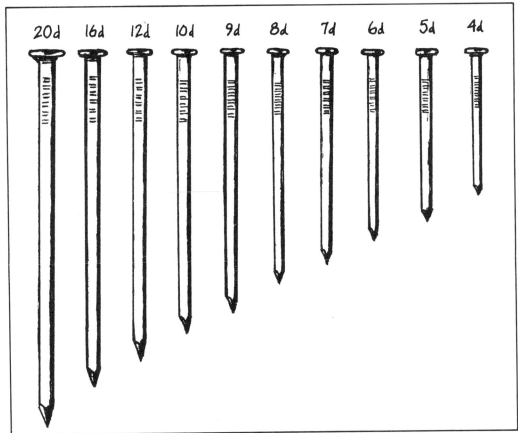

Common nails are sized by letter "d," the English symbol for "penny." Originally, this meant the number of pennies for 100 nails of a given size. Today it designates nail length.

nails contains about 50 nails. But a pound of 8d finishing nails will have closer to 200 nails; and a pound of 16d finishing nails, about 100.

For basic construction, the most frequently used nail is the common nail, a heavy duty, large headed, smooth nail. For a smoother look on trim, siding and molding, finishing or casing nails are used. Both have small heads that can be countersunk into the woodwork for concealment. Casing nails are somewhat heavier than finishing nails, and are more often used for outside work.

There are other specialized nails for particular jobs. Concrete nails, which may have smooth or spiral shanks, are hardened so they may be driven into concrete and mortar. Spiral and ring shank nails provide extra holding power, for jobs such as nailing down wood flooring. Roofing nails have large flat heads to prevent asphalt shingles and other soft materials from pulling through; some have soft lead or neoprene gaskets to help seal the hole made by the nail.

Some rules of thumb (no pun intended) for driving nails:

- Where possible, drive the nail through the thinner piece into the thicker one.

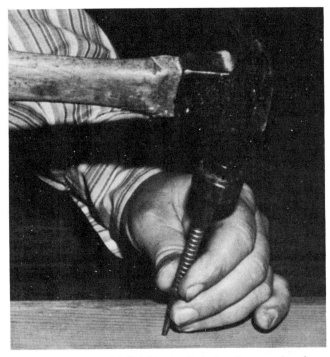

Use a nail-set to sink finishing nails below the wood surface; fill nail holes with wood putty and sand.

Interior & Other Nails

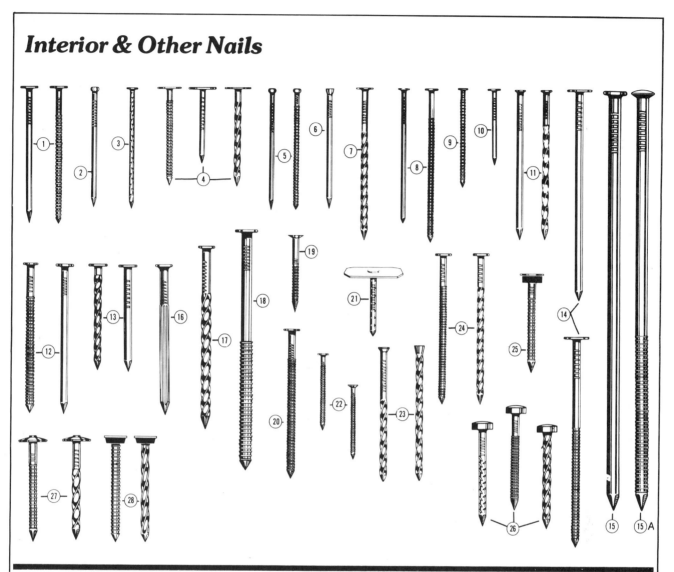

STORMGUARD® NAILS
FOR EXTERIOR APPLICATIONS
(Hot-dipped zinc-coated twice in molten zinc)

1. Wood Siding, Box (Plain & Anchor)
2. Finishing
3. Insulating, Plastic Siding
4. Asphalt Shingle (Anchor, Plain & Screw)
5. Cedar Shake (Plain & Anchor)
6. Casing
7. Cribber
8. "Split-Less" Wood Siding (Plain & Anchor)
9. Asbestos
10. Cedar Shingle
11. Hardboard Siding (Plain & Screw)
12. Common (Anchor & Plain)
13. Aluminum, Steel & Vinyl Siding (Screw & Plain)
14. Insulation Roof Deck (Plain & Anchor)
15. Gutter Spike (Plain)
15A. Gutter Spike (Anchor)

INTERIOR & OTHER NAILS

16. Masonry
17. Pole Barn, Truss Rafter (Screw)
18. Pole Barn (Anchor)
19. Drywall, GWB-54 Style
20. Underlayment, Plywood (Sub-floor, sheathing, etc.)
21. "Square-Cap" Roofing
22. Underlayment (Flat Head & Countersunk)
23. Spiral Flooring (Casing Head & Countersunk)
24. Pallet (Anchor & Screw)

Drawings: Maze Nails

METAL ROOFING NAILS

25. Rubber Washer (Stormguard, Anchor)
26. Compressed Lead Head (Barbed, Anchor & Screw)
27. Umbrella Head (Stormguard, Anchor & Screw)
28. Lead Washer (Stormguard, Anchor & Screw)

Penny-Wise Nail Lengths

2d	1″	12d	3¼″
3d	1¼″	16d	3½″
4d	1½″	20d	4″
5d	1¾″	30d	4½″
6d	2″	40d	5″
7d	2¼″	50d	5½″
8d	2½″	60d	6″
9d	2¾″	70d	7″
10d	3″	80d	8″

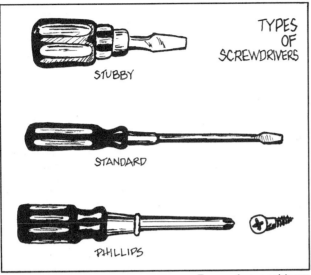

Types of screwdrivers.

- Use a nail that extends into the thick piece a distance equal to twice the thickness of the thin piece.
- Near the end of a board, where splitting may be a risk, blunting the nail point with a file or blow of the hammer reduces the chance of splitting. The blunted point cuts the wood fibers, rather than forcing them apart. Also, a hole slightly smaller than the nail diameter may be drilled to prevent splitting.
- When driving hardened concrete nails, use a sledge or hand driller's hammer, rather than a claw hammer. The hardened steel nails can damage a claw hammer face. Use safety goggles when driving concrete nails, to protect your eyes from flying bits of mortar.
- When driving nails into finished trim, where hammer marks are to be avoided, start the nail, then slip a large washer of felt or rubber over the nail as a cushion, should the hammer miss the mark.
- Copper nails should be used to install copper fittings, such as pipe straps or roof flashing.

For more information on nails and nailing refer to *"Putting it All Together,"* a Successful Book from Structures Publishing Co.

Use a screwdriver of the right length and tip to fit the screw being driven.

Screwdrivers

Nails are driven with hammers; screws are also *driven*—but with special tools designed with blades that fit into the head of the screw.

Screwdrivers commonly are described by the type of blade tip, such as "conventional" or "standard" for single slot screws; "Phillips" for screws with cross slot heads; and other, more specialized slot designs. For most general woodwork, standard and Phillips screws are used.

A screwdriver is a simple tool; used primarily for tightening and loosening screws and slot headed bolts. However, few other tools are subjected to more abuse! It is frequently used as a chisel, can opener, paint stirrer and mini crowbar—all functions for which other tools are better designed and which usually ruin the screwdriver for driving screws.

Screwdriver sizes are designated by the length of the blade or shaft. Generally, a longer screwdriver lets you apply more pressure and torque than a short one. The first step in using a screwdriver is to select a tool with the proper tip—and the proper size tip—for the screws being installed. The width of the blade tip should fit the screw slot and be no wider or narrower than the diameter of the screw head. A blade that is too wide can mar the work, and one too narrow can damage the screw or the tool. There is no all purpose screwdriver and you'll probably need several sizes.

To use a screwdriver, grasp the handle in your right hand, with the palm resting on the end of the handle and the thumb and first finger extending along the handle. With your left hand, hold the blade of the screwdriver just above the tip. Insert the blade tip into the screw head slot and turn the screw about a half turn (clockwise to tighten; counter-clockwise to loosen). While the right hand swivels for a new grip on the handle for the next turn, use the left hand to steady the screwdriver and keep the tip seated in the screw slot. Keep the screwdriver lined up with the screw, and push and turn at the same time.

Special types of screwdrivers are made for particular jobs. Some of these you may never use; some you may find indispensable. An **offset** screwdriver can be used in tight spots, where a standard screwdriver cannot be used. The offset has a short blade on each end; one on the same plane as the handle, the other at right angles to the handle. To use it, place one end in the screw slot and turn as far as possible. Then reverse the screwdriver and turn the screw as far as possible with the opposite end. Short-handled, short-bladed screwdrivers, called **stubbies**, also are made for use in cramped quarters.

Convertible screwdrivers have detachable blades, so that one handle can be used with blades of several types and sizes. This type screwdriver also comes with a reversible blade that has a standard tip on one end, a Phillips tip on the other.

For heavy duty work, square shanked **machinists'** screwdrivers are built rugged enough to be turned with a wrench applied to the blade for extra torque.

A **spiral-ratchet** screwdriver applies torque to the screw when the handle is pushed, and can be used to drive and withdraw screws. On most ratchet screwdrivers, the mechanism can be locked so that the tool can be used as an ordinary screwdriver, as well.

Screw-holding screwdrivers grip the screw head with spring steel tongs, holding it securely on the blade tip. This kind of screwdriver comes in handy to start screws where fingers cannot reach. Other screwdrivers have magnetized tips to hold the screw.

Electricians use screwdrivers with **insulated** handles. Automobile repairmen use **spark-detecting** screwdrivers with a neon tube in the handle, which lights when the screwdriver tip comes in contact with high voltage cir-

Convertible screwdriver has both conventional and Phillips in one handle.

Jeweler's screwdrivers come in handy for tightening tiny screws on eyeglass frames, cameras, etc.

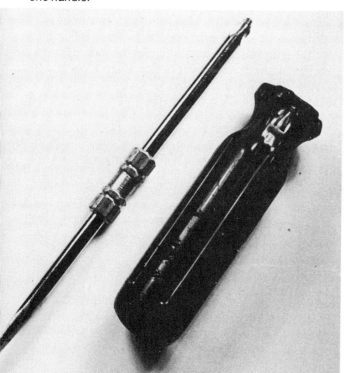

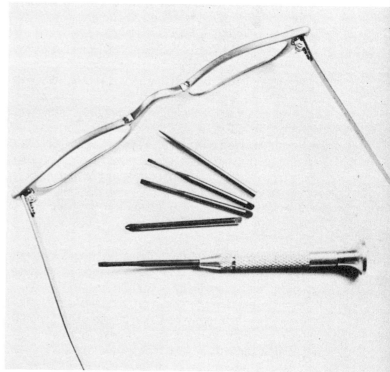

Cordless/screwdriver lets you use power without plugging in. (Courtesy of Disston)

cuits. Hobbyists and watchmakers use **jeweler**'s screwdrivers.

If you're facing a job that requires a great many screws to be driven, one of several **power screwdrivers** can save time, as well as wear and tear on muscles. Screwdriver bits can be bought in about any size and type, with shanks designed to fit into the chucks of power drivers, such as bit-braces, hand drills or electric drills.

In fact, electric screwdrivers are specially designed tools to drive screws. Some even come with rechargeable battery packs that let you use power without plugging into an electrical outlet.

If you need to drive several screws, and are in the market for—or already own—an electric drill with variable speed and reversable features, you can buy standard slotted and Phillips head driver bits to use with this tool.

Whatever route you choose to go to acquire the screwdrivers you'll need, buy quality tools. The handle, the steel in the blade and the construction of a good screwdriver are superior to the equivalent features of the less expensive, "dime-store" tool. The blade of better steel will not become burred and twisted as easily as one of softer metal. The tip of a quality screwdriver is cross ground (you often can see or feel the grinder marks running perpendicular to the blade) so that the sides are almost parallel. This lets the screwdriver tip fit more snugly into the screw slot. It also is more expensive to make tools this way.

Unless they are too badly damaged, screwdrivers that become burred or beveled can be re-shaped. We go into tool sharpening more thoroughly in Chapter 23.

Screwdrivers don't require a great deal of care, other than using them properly. Keep the tip free of grease and oil while using the tool. For safety's sake, position yourself or hold the work in such a manner that if the screwdriver should slip, it doesn't cause an injury.

Using Screws

Screws have better holding power than common nails, and permit woodwork to be taken apart with less damage. Except for some softwoods, screws fastening woodwork or metal to wood should be driven in pilot holes drilled slightly smaller than the threaded part of the screw. This allows the screw threads to take a "bite" in the wood, but makes the screw easier to drive. Hardware stores have special drill bits, called "Screwmates" that drill one size hole for threads, another size for the smooth shank and a recess for the screw head—all in one drilling operation.

The size of wood screws is designated by the gauge or diameter of wire from which they are made and by length measured in inches. The higher the gauge number, the larger the screw shank and the deeper the threads—the better the screw holds in wood. For example, a No. 2

Drill holes to receive wood screws when fastening two pieces together. Make the hole in the first piece the size of the screw shank. Make the hole in the second piece the size of the core of the screw.

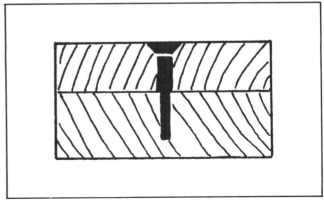

screw is made of 14 gauge wire, and measures about $^3/_{32}$ inch in diameter.

All screw gauges are made in various lengths. For fastening thin pieces of wood, which might be subject to splitting, use a thinner or lower gauge screw. For driving screws into heavier wood, where more holding power is needed, use higher gauge, "fatter" screws.

Generally, the longer the screw, the better the holding power. A screw should be long enough to penetrate a half inch or more into the bottom piece when you're joining two pieces of wood. The size of the screw and the depth it is driven depends largely on how much strain is on the screw. If you're hanging cabinets in a kitchen, screw threads should extend two inches or more into wall studs.

You can fasten small pieces of softwoods together with screws without first drilling a pilot hole. However, an awl or screw starter should be used to make a small hole, even in softwoods, to ensure that the screw is started straight. In larger pieces of wood and in all hardwoods, *always* drill pilot holes for the screws. Drill a hole through the first piece the size of the shank of the screw, or slightly larger; then drill a hole in the second piece the size of the core or threaded part of the screw, or slightly smaller. The accompanying table shows the proper size holes to drill for various sized wood screws.

Screw Size	Size of first hole (shank)	Size of second hole (threads)
2	$^3/_{32}''$	$^2/_{32}''$
3	$^4/_{32}''$	$^2/_{32}''$
4	$^4/_{32}''$	$^2/_{32}''$
6	$^5/_{32}''$	$^3/_{32}''$
8	$^6/_{32}''$	$^4/_{32}''$
12	$^7/_{32}''$	$^5/_{32}''$
14	$^8/_{32}''$	$^6/_{32}''$
16	$^9/_{32}''$	$^7/_{32}''$

Types of Common Screws

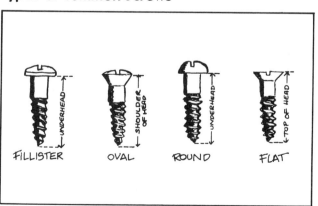

FILLISTER OVAL ROUND FLAT

When flathead screws are used, always countersink the heads to draw down flush with or slightly below the surface. Common **countersink bits** are available for both hand braces and electric drills. Countersink all screws to the same depth, and be careful not to countersink them too deeply.

The right screw to use depends on what you are doing. **Flathead** screws are most often used in woodwork, particularly where you want the head to be flush with or slightly below the wood surface. They also are used to fasten metal brackets and angle iron which have screwholes that are countersunk drilled to receive the screwheads. The screws should be selected for the suitable size and length. Diameter of the screwhead will not be a guiding consideration in most jobs, because you can bevel a countersink hole for the head. However, where metal hardware is being fastened to wood—as in the case of butt type door hinges—the screw heads should fit the pre-drilled countersink in the metal.

Roundhead screws, for practical purposes, are not countersunk below the surface. You may want to use these screws in some wood projects, for decorative purposes or so that you can remove them readily. Roundhead screws are used primarily to fasten metal, plastic and composition materials without countersinking.

Ovalhead screws are somewhat of a compromise between flatheads and roundheads. The head is tapered on the bottom so that the screws can be sunk below the surface, but the top of the head is convex and protrudes above the surface. You'll find ovalhead screws most often in the escutcheons of doorknobs, clothes hooks, window locks and other house hardware.

Fillister and **panhead** screws both have heads that are flat on the bottom, to seat tightly against the surface. The panhead also is flat on top, and is used most often on sheet metal screws. Fillister head screws resemble panheads, but have an oval top.

Lag screws are more correctly described as square headed bolts with screw threads. Lag screws are used where ordinary driven wood screws would not be strong enough to hold. They are driven with a wrench, rather than with a screwdriver.

Screws are made of a number of different metals and alloys. Steel screws are by far the most common. However, steel screws are subject to rust if installed in damp locations. Galvanized, stainless steel, brass, bronze, aluminum or chrome plated screws are a better bet for areas subject to moisture.

Brass screws often are used where the appearance of the screw lends a decorative touch. The same is true of coated or painted screws.

Screws used to attach metal to wood—or to other metal—should be of a material similar to the metal being fastened. Use brass screws with copper and brass fittings, aluminum or chrome-plated screws with aluminum hardware, etc. Using ferrous and non-ferrous metals in contact can cause corrosion.

Here are some tips for driving and removing screws:

- If you hit a piece of wood that is hard to drive a screw into, even with the proper size pilot hole drilled, remove the screw, lubricate the threads with wax or paraffin and start it again.

- Occasionally, as in re-hanging doors and re-installing door closers, you must anchor screws in worn out holes—there isn't any other choice. The best way to do this is to drill out the holes slightly oversize, then cut pieces of doweling to the proper length to fill the hole. Use a piece of dowel that is slightly larger than the drill used to make the hole. Coat the dowel plug with white glue and hammer it into the hole. When the glue has dried, drill a pilot hole in the dowel and re-set the screw.

- When a screw resists all efforts to remove it, hold a hot soldering iron tip on the screw head until the screw is hot. This expands the screw in the hole, forcing the wood fibers to compress. Once the screw cools again, it should be relatively easy to remove.

- If a screw head twists off below the surface, you'll need to use a **screw extractor** to retrieve it. These are hardened steel tools with spiral left-hand threads. To remove the screw, first drill a small hole—about half the diameter of the screw—in the screw shank. Then, tap in the extractor which is slightly larger than the drilled hole. Turn the upper end of the extractor counterclockwise with a wrench to remove the screw.

- Sort screws by length and gauge for storage. One handy method of storing screws is to tack lids of small glass jars (baby food jars are ideal sizes) to the bottom of a board or shelf; then store the screws in the jar, which can be quickly attached to the anchored lid. Or, if you store screws in boxes or cans, tape one screw on the outside of the container as a sample of what's inside. (For more information on screws see *"Putting it All Together"*)

Wrenches

There is an almost infinite variety of wrenches and their applications. Common wrenches are used to tighten and loosen bolts, nuts and headed screws. Specialized tools —also wrenches of one type or another—are made to grip round pipe, oil filters, spark plugs, set screws and car axles. Adjustable wrenches (discussed more thoroughly in Chapter 13) and locking plier wrenches have dozens of uses in nearly any household.

For your own tool kit, you'll need to evaluate your wrench purchases on the basis of need. You may get along on minor home repairs with an adjustable open end wrench and a pair of pliers or perhaps a locking plier wrench. If you do much electrical or electronics work, a set of small combination wrenches (open end on one end; boxed end on the other) and a set of nut drivers (wrenches designed with screwdriver-like handles) will come in handy. If you're a Saturday afternoon auto mechanic, you'll need a wider selection—perhaps a good socket wrench set with ratchet and high-speed drivers, and oil filter wrench, plus open end or combination wrenches for valve adjustments, battery cable clamps, etc.

Whatever wrenches you choose, buy only quality tools, made of hardened, tempered steel. Less expensive wrenches bend and break or round the corners of nuts and bolt heads.

Common wrenches (box-end, open-end and sockets) are made in two size categories: Standard (English), and metric. Standard wrenches are sized by fractions of an inch: half-inch, three-quarters, nine-sixteenths, etc. Metric wrenches are sized in millimeters.

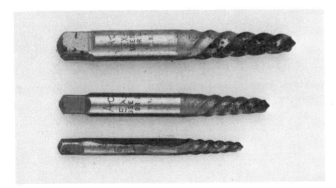

Screw extractors have left-hand spiral threads to back screws out.

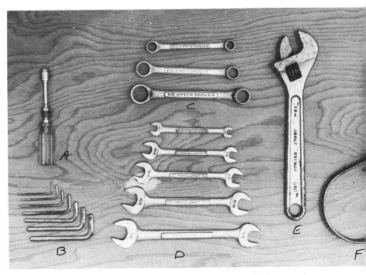

Types of wrenches: A, nut-driver; B, Allen sets; C, box end; D, open end; E, adjustable open end; and F, oil-filter wrench.

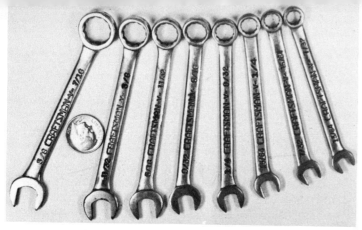

Small combination wrenches come in handy for working on automobile ignition components.

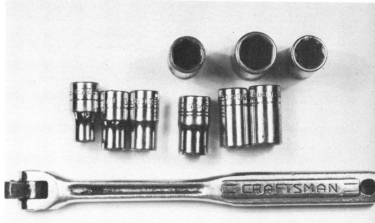

A ¼ inch drive socket set can be carried in glove compartment.

Ratchet and socket work faster than the wheel lug wrenches provided by most auto manufacturers.

There are few rules on using wrenches, other than selecting the proper size wrench to fit the nut, bolt or other fastener to be tightened or loosened. In an emergency, you may get by with a standard wrench used on a metric nut. But the wrong sized wrench rounds the corners of a nut or bolt, and puts improper pressure on the jaws on the wrench.

Don't use a section of pipe as a "cheater" to extend the length of a wrench handle and exert more torque on a nut. Get a longer wrench. Don't hammer on a wrench to loosen a rusty bolt. First use a penetrating oil or commercial solvent to loosen the rust. Wrenches should be kept clean and stored where moisture will not cause them to rust. The adjusting mechanisms of adjustable wrenches should be kept clean and free of grit, and lubricated occasionally with graphite or light oil.

Bolts, Washers and Nuts.

For heavy construction, bolts are stronger than nails or screws. **Bolts** are simply steel rods with screw threads on one end and a head on the other. They are made in sizes from ¾ inch to 20 inches long, and from ¼ inch to ¾ inch in diameter. Larger bolts with round heads are called **carriage bolts**; those with square or hexagonal heads are called **machine** bolts. Smaller bolts, with screw slots in flat or round heads, are called **stove bolts.**

In woodwork, bolts are inserted into holes drilled slightly larger than the diameter of the bolt, so that the bolt fits snugly in the hole. The work pieces are drawn together and held by a nut screwed onto the thread end of the bolt.

Washers are flat disks with holes, and are used to shield between the bolt head or the nut and the material being fastened. Often, washers also are used as spacers between different materials being bolted together. **Lock washers** of split-ring or toothed designs help prevent nuts or bolts from loosening in uses where the fasteners are subjected to vibration or rotational movement.

A nut is an internally threaded block of metal that screws onto a bolt or stud to draw together and hold two or more pieces of a work. **Square** or **hexagonal nuts** are commonly used, and are tightened with open-end, box-end, socket or adjustable wrenches. Special nuts are made for particular purposes. **Wing nuts** are used in applications where the nut needs to be removed fairly often, as on the "hold down" bolt of an air cleaner.

Wall Anchors

Anchoring devices are special purpose fasteners used to attach objects to hollow or masonry walls. Here, we will describe some anchors used with hollow walls. In Chapter 11, we'll discuss masonry fasteners more thoroughly.

A common fastener for hollow walls is the **spring toggle bolt**, a long screw headed bolt with a threaded, winged toggle attached. To use it, drill a hole large enough to allow the toggle to pass through when the wings are folded against the bolt. Remove the bolt from the winged toggle, insert the bolt through the item to be fastened to the wall (or ceiling), and screw the toggle back onto the bolt. Then, fold the toggle wings against the bolt, push it through the drilled hole and tighten with a screwdriver. The wings of the toggle spring open butterfly fashion inside the wall cavity and spread the pressure over a wider area, to hold much better than a screw or nail. Toggle bolts are particularly handy for attaching items to plasterboard or plaster walls.

Molly bolts are similar to toggle bolts in that the load on the inside surface of the wall covering is spread over a wide area. Molly bolts are available at most hardware and building supply stores, and come in sets attached to cards with complete mounting instructions included.

A variety of specialized anchoring devices are made, also; including clips, ties and tapped inserts. (See *"Putting it all Together"* a Successful Book)

Staple Guns and Staples

The number of household uses for an automatic spring-loaded staple gun is virtually unlimited for everything from repairing window shades to installing insulation. A small tool, such as the Arrow multi-purpose stapler,

Hollow Wall Fasteners

MOLLY BOLTS **SPRING TOGGLE BOLTS**

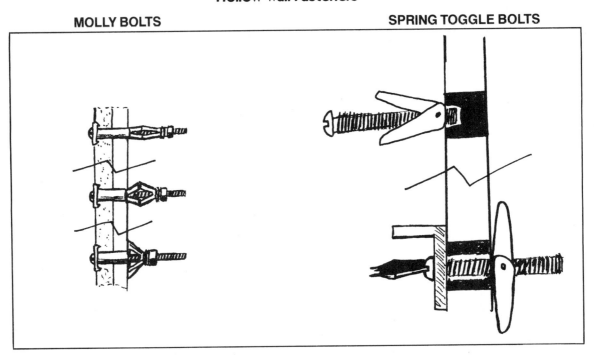

drives several lengths of staples. Here are a few of the uses for various length staples:

- Quarter-inch-long staples are handy for tacking window screening and shades, shelf paper, closet liners, drapes, etc.
- Use ⅜ inch staples for fastening light insulation, roof paper, electrical wiring, weather stripping, etc.
- Half inch staples work well for tacking carpet underlayment, porch screens, felt stripping, canvas, etc.
- Go to $9/16$ inch staples for metal lathing, wire fencing, insulation board, etc.
- Special ceiling staples are made for securing ceiling tiles in place.

Heavy duty pneumatic staplers are used more and more in building construction, especially in installing asphalt roofing. These staplers are powered by compressed air, and drive heavy wire, inch long staples.

Riveters and Rivets

Rivets are soft metal, threadless pins most often used to permanently fasten metal—but also used with fiber, wood, leather and other materials. One end of the rivet usually has a head, the other is plain.

To fasten materials by riveting, start by drilling a hole the same diameter as the rivet, through both pieces to be

For heavy-duty stapling, you may want to rent a pneumatic staple gun.

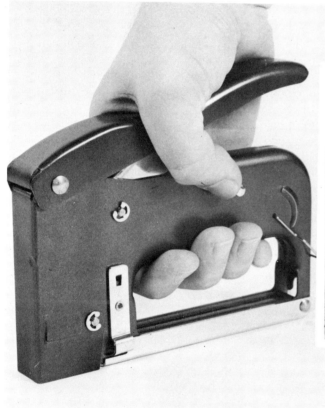

Hand staplers are useful for many light repair jobs around the house.

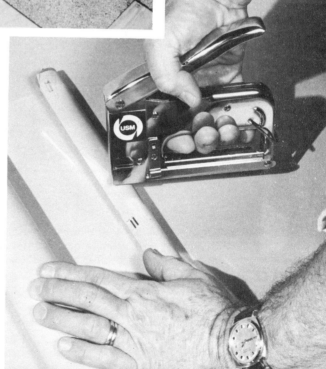

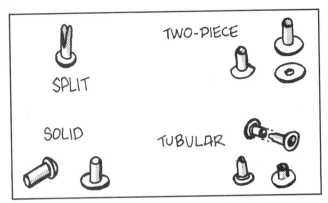

Types of rivets: Upper right, two piece hollow rivets fit together and are fastened with a hammer. Upper left, split rivet's legs are flattened on an anvil or metal block. Lower left, solid rivets are flattened with a ball peen hammer. Lower right, tubular rivets are spread and flattened with a hammer.

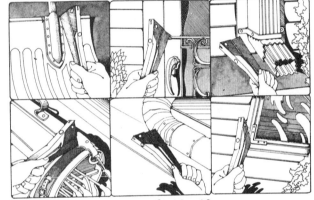

BLIND RIVETING

fastened. Use a rivet long enough to protrude through all thicknesses of the material by a distance about equal to the diameter of the rivet. Then, complete the riveting procedure as outlined in the accompanying sketch.

Automatic riveting tools operate in much the same way spring loaded staplers work, to let you "blind" rivet materials from one side only. If you have much riveting to do, one of these versatile tools is worth the money—an industrial-quality riveter costs less than $20.

Glue Guns and Glue

A thorough discussion of glues and gluing would make a good sized book in itself. It suffices to say that glue is one of the woodworker's secrets for producing smooth finished work. A good glued joint made with the right kind of glue for the application frequently is stronger than the wood itself.

Glue is made in many different types and from many different materials—from animal hair to synthetic resins. For most general woodwork, not subjected to high heat or prolonged humidity, a white glue—such as Elmer's—will hold adequately.

On small jobs, where heat and moisture resistance are critical, use a cellulose base cement, such as the household cements sold in tubes. These adhesives bond a wide range of materials and are fairly easy to use.

Riveting tool lets you install rivets from one side of the work, called "blind riveting." This is a handy tool for repairing a great many items. (Courtesy USM)

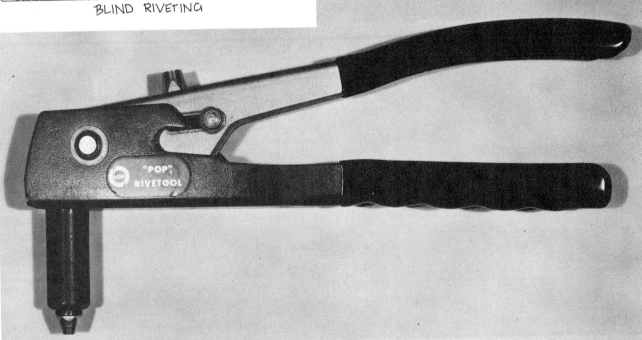

For waterproofness and high strength, use a resin type epoxy. This material comes in two separate cans; you mix the two components as needed, just before using. This type of adhesive is difficult to remove from tools, hands and brushes—be careful when applying it.

For quick, strong stick-up jobs, use fast setting, acrylic type glues. These adhesives generally are stocked by marine supply firms, and are packaged in two components which must be mixed, as are apoxies. Acrylic glues harden in just a few minutes.

For general purpose gluing, an electric glue gun comes in handy. These tools use solid sticks or pellets of all purpose adhesives that melt in the gun and are forced out through a nozzle. Since the glue gun operates at a preset thermostatic temperature, it's a good idea to use only hot-melt glue sticks made for the particular tool you're using.

The key to getting a good glue joint is to match facing surfaces carefully and clamp them tightly. A complex gluing project should be divided into as many smaller operations as possible, then glued in the final assembly. Long joints where wood grain and figure are to be matched require particular care. We'll have more on clamping in Chapter 7.

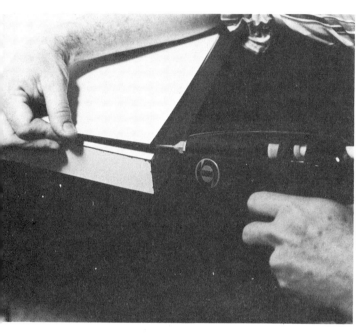

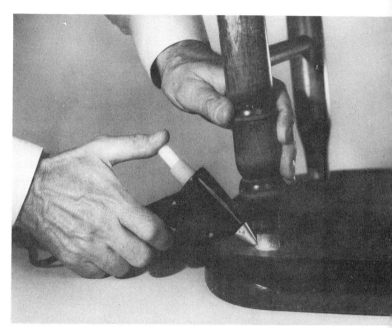

Hot-melt glue guns with interchangeable nozzles find a great many applications. (Courtesy USM)

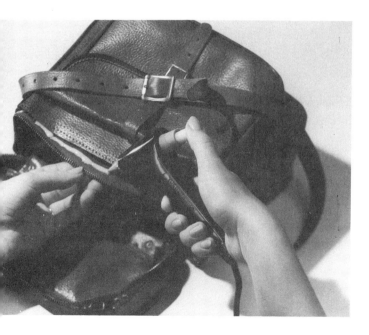

3
Can You Cut It?

The right saw for the job makes the cutting easy. With a sharp ripsaw, you can slice through a one inch thick pine board at about a foot per minute. A good crosscut saw can work nearly as fast across the grain.

With electricity providing the power, you can do the job faster and easier. In the home workshop, there are few applications of electrical power as useful as in sawing. Power saws, with their various attachments, let you cut materials with skill and precision which often would take more practice with hand saws.

Whichever you choose—hand or power—select quality, well made tools. With quality tools and a good place to work, sawing is not a burdensome chore. That is, it *shouldn't* be; if you choose and use your saws properly. A good quality hand saw cuts faster and with less effort than a less costly saw. A well built power saw is safer to use and lasts longer than an inexpensive, poorly constructed machine.

With a quality saw, each tempered steel tooth is precision ground to chisel out a small chip of wood. The teeth on a poorer quality saw do not hold set (the amount teeth are angled from the plane of the saw blade) or sharpness nearly as long, and the operation is more likely to be a tiring, arm-wrenching experience.

The saw—or saws—in a homeowner's tool kit serves many purposes. And you'll need more than one. If you perform many tasks, you'll need five or six different saws—even if you elect to have one or more of them powered electrically.

Handsaws

The precision built handsaws you'll use in your projects are in themselves examples of good worksmanship. There is more to a good saw blade than meets the casual observer's eye.

The blade is made of tempered spring steel, to hold sharpness and resist bending and buckling. If you examine the blade of a quality handsaw closely, you'll notice that it is not a flat piece of steel of even thickness. The blade tapers from the tooth edge to the back, and from the butt (end where the handle is located) to the point. The toothed edge, however, is the same thickness along its entire length.

A key feature of any saw blade is the number, shape, size, slant and direction of the teeth. Saw teeth are set or angled alternately in opposite directions to make a cut (or

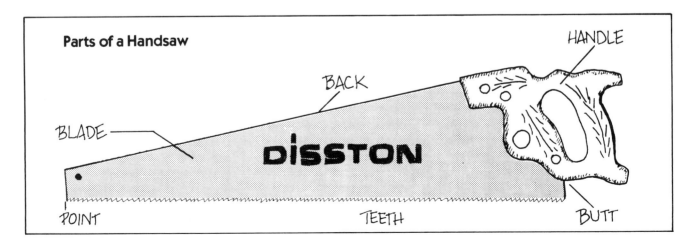

Parts of a Handsaw

HANDLE

BACK

BLADE

DISSTON

POINT

TEETH

BUTT

kerf) slightly wider than the thickness of the saw blade it-self. If the teeth has no set, the blade will bend and bind in the kerf.

Generally, the fewer the teeth per inch (called "points") the coarser and faster the cut. More teeth per inch means a slower but smoother cut surface. Ripping saws, which cut along the grain of the wood, generally have five to six points. Backsaws for cutting mitered angles in trimwork have 12 to 14 teeth per inch, for a smooth, close-fitting cut surface.

The handle of the typical handsaw is a story of evolution. Earlier handsaws often had ornamental swirls and scrolls incorporated in the wood of the handle. What has come down to us in this day and age is a comfortable, functional handhold of hardwood or plastic, with perhaps a bit of decoration carved in as a sort of salute to handle history.

Quality saw blades have highly polished surfaces. Any moisture landing here produces rust almost instantly, unless the surface of the blade is protected by a film of light oil. Rust pits and roughens the blade,which does not help the working condition of the saw. If a saw blade starts to rust, remove the rust with a fine emery cloth and apply a coat of light machine oil.

When you lay a saw down, do it gently. Never let saw teeth come in contact with stone, concrete or other metal. A dull saw makes for hard work, and filing a saw blade takes time and energy that could be spent at something else. On that subject, most workmen have their saws, sharpened by a custom sharpener. But we'll give you a few tips on sharpening and setting saws in Chapter 23. There are a variety of handsaws for different uses, below are some of the saws you may use:

Saws are called "coarse" or "fine" toothed, depending on the number of points (teeth) per inch of blade.

For crosscutting, or sawing across wood fibers, hold the saw at about a 45 degree angle to the work.

Crosscut Handsaw

The crosscut saw is designed to cut across the grain of wood, or at right angles to the way the tree grew. The teeth are like tiny knives, set at enough angle to keep the blade from binding in the kerf. Blade lengths vary from 20 inches for fine-tooth paneling saws to 28 inches. For most general uses, a 24 or 26 inch saw will be a satisfactory choice.

For thicker pieces of wood, and for softwoods, a crosscut saw with seven or eight points will do a better job than a saw with finer teeth. The teeth cut faster and are less apt to clog quickly. For finer, smoother cuts—as in hardwoods and trim—choose a saw with 10 to 12 points.

To use the crosscut saw, you'll first need to mark the cut to be made—with a square or other measuring equipment as a guide. For most construction work, a pencil mark is adequate. On pieces to be cut for a tight, precise fit, however, you may want to mark the saw line with a scribe or scratch awl.

Make sure the piece to be cut is well supported—on sawhorses, jacks or other supports. You'll want to support the "scrap" end, as well as the main part of the board, to prevent the wood from splitting as the saw kerf nears the edge. With smaller stock, you can support the scrap end of the piece with your free hand. For plywood, paneling and other wide, heavy materials, a kitchen table or other flat surface works well as a support.

Place the saw teeth on the edge of the board, just at the outside edge of the pencil or scribe mark. Use that part of the blade near the butt or handle end of the saw, as your first stroke will be pulled toward your body. Use the thumb of your left hand (or right hand, if you're sawing left handed) to support the saw truly vertical. With the saw at about a 45 degree angle to the wood, *pull* the saw to make a small groove. Then, start sawing slowly, increas-

ing the length of the stroke as the kerf deepens. Continue to saw with the blade at a 45 degree angle to the board. Don't push or "ride" the saw into the wood. Let the weight of the saw set the rate of cutting. It's easier to control the saw and less tiring that way.

Ripsaw

A ripping handsaw, as the name implies, is designed for ripping wood with the grain.

A saw cutting along the grain meets less resistance than a saw cutting across grain. Ripping teeth are larger—usually about 6 points—and are slanted or set at almost 90 degrees (or 45 degrees to either side of the plane of the blade) so that wood fibers can be ripped out of the kerf.

Mark and start a ripping cut the same way you'd start a cut across the grain. But, once you've started the kerf,

Coping saws should be used with the blade nearly vertical. Above, when sawing a curve with the work clamped in a vise, set the blade with the teeth pointing away from the handle. Below, when sawing on a saddle, point the teeth toward the handle. (Courtesy: Disston)

Ripsaws should be held at a shallower angle than crosscuts, about 60 degrees to the plane of the work. If the saw starts to veer off the cut line, twist the handle to bring it back.

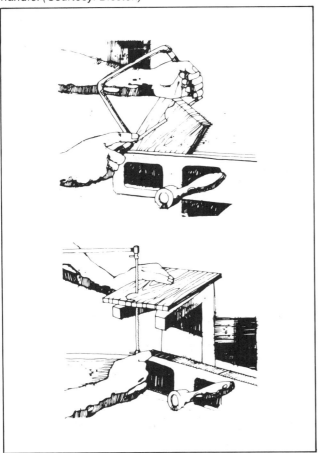

saw with the blade at a steeper angle to the wood—about 60 degrees—than you'd normally use with a crosscut. If the saw starts to wander from the line, twist the saw handle to bring the teeth back.

At times, when ripping a long board, the saw blade may bind in the kerf. You can cure this by wedging a thin piece of wood into the kerf.

Coping Saw

The coping saw (sometimes called "jigsaw") has a thin, fine toothed blade held tightly in a metal frame. It is most often used in small radius scroll work with thin materials.

A coping saw can start a cut from the edge of the wood, or from a hole drilled in the interior of the piece. To start from a hole, the blade is removed from the saw frame and inserted through the hole, then re-tightened in the frame. For work held in a vise, coping saw blades usually are clamped in the frame with the teeth pointing toward the handle, so that the cut is made on the pull stroke.

With work supported by a saw horse or bench, it usually is handier to turn the teeth points away from the handle, so that the push stroke does the cutting. Either way, when possible, it is best to position work so the coping saw blade is vertical.

Compass saw

The compass, or keyhole, saw has a narrow, tapered blade that can fit into narrow spaces. Actually, there are some differences between the compass saw and keyhole saw, although both are used for the same kind of work. A compass saw has a handsaw type of handle, whereas a keyhole saw has a handle much like that of a coping saw.

Many compass saws come with three or four interchangeable blades with different teeth points and uses. Because of its flexibility, the compass saw is especially useful for cutting curved shapes, such as circles for door locks, in heavier material than is normally handled by a coping saw.

Another popular use of the compass saw is to start a saw kerf inside a piece of wood, usually from a hole drilled in the wood. If a long cut is needed, the compass saw can be used until the kerf is long enough to admit a handsaw blade, which is used to complete the cut.

For wider uses, compass saws have generally been replaced by power saber saws, but they are still handy tools to have in the kit.

Backsaw

A backsaw (so-called because the blade has a rigid rib or brace along the back) is ordinarily used to make mitered cuts in wood. The straight blade has 12 to 14 teeth

Compass — or keyhole — saws are for inside jobs — keyholes, birdhouse holes, sharp curves. (Courtesy of Disston)

A backsaw has stiffener along the back of the blade to prevent flexing and to assure a straight cut for miter joints.

per inch, to give a smooth cut either with or across the grain. In practice, most cuts with a backsaw are made obliquely, or diagonally across the grain of the wood.

Backsaws are made in lengths from 12 to 30 inches, and are used most often with a miter box to make precise angles. Conventional hardwood miter boxes have pre-cut slots for making 45 and 90 degree angle cuts. Now available are inexpensive plastic miter boxes, also with pre-cut 45 and 90 degree slots.

If you're going into the picture framing or furniture making business in a big way, you may want to invest in a high grade, multiple angle, steel frame miter box with integral saw. These rigs cost $100 and up, but they are well built and with reasonable use, should last indefinitely. Most have roller guides that support the saw at precisely the right angle.

Many professional carpenters and woodworkers are going to the power miterbox, such as DeWalt's 10 inch, 1.5 horsepower model that makes cuts as accurate as one-quarter of a degree. But at $250 or so, this tool is a bit expensive for most homeowners to justify.

Other Handsaws

In your collection of toothed cutting tools, you may have need for some hand saws not described above. Depending on the chores you have to do, you may also have use for heavier duty saws, such as bow saws, pruning saws, buck saws. The universal hacksaw is discussed in Chapter 14. The principles for selecting, using and caring for these tools are the same—choose quality and use it properly.

Nearly every saw made is used in a slightly different manner. For infrequent uses, you can get along by substituting, say, a fine toothed crosscut saw for a backsaw. Or, you can use a ripping saw to cut a board across the grain. But for truly professional results, you will want to select the saw that does the job most effectively and with the least effort.

Power Saws

Power tools are luxuries only for people who use them too infrequently for the time and labor saved to pay back the cost of the tool and the cost of the electrical power to operate it.

This is certainly true of power saws. You can accomplish more work in the same amount of time when you let electrical power do the hard part of the job. The value of work and time saved will vary. Workshop projects may cost no more in time than an evening's TV viewing. Or, if you are a journey-person carpenter, your time may be worth several dollars per hour.

Another feature of power saws—perhaps equally as important as the savings in time and work—is their ability to turn out precision, professional quality results in the hands of a relatively inexperienced operator. In general, two classes of workers can profit by the purchase of one

A precision miter box is a worthwhile investment if you are installing a lot of interior trim; as in a house building or remodeling project.

or more power saws: those who have mastered the skillful use of hand saws; and those with little or no experience with tools of any kind.

That sounds like a contradiction, but it really is not. Homeowners and craftspersons, who have mastered the skills needed to turn out quality work with hand saws, will find that the speed and power of an electric saw saves a great deal of time and labor. They can get more out of their skills and technique by letting power do the work.

Novices will find that they can learn the rudiments of operating a power saw, and produce work of reasonable quality without going through a long apprenticeship in the operation of hand tools. A great deal of skill with a power saw is designed into the machine. Properly used, the power saw performs equally well for amateurs and skilled craftspeople.

Of course, it makes sense to buy any tool only as your needs arise. Because power tools cost more than hand tools, buying on the basis of need is doubly important. If you will be doing enough cutting to justify the purchase of a power saw—of whatever type—buy a first line saw that will perform safely for a long time. Avoid manufacturer's less expensive models—and most manufacturers build them—the inexpensive tool simply will not stand up to long, hard use.

All new saws are sold with complete operating, safety and maintenance instructions. *Read them thoroughly before* you plug in the tool.

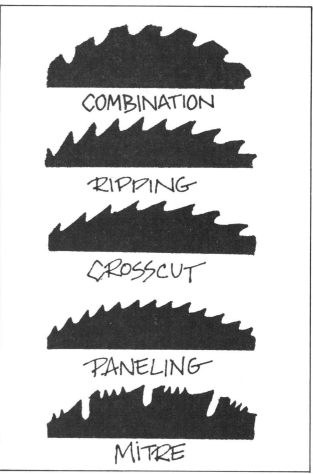

Types of power saw blades

Portable Circular Saw

The portable circular saw is the carpenter's workhorse. You may hear the portable circular saw referred to as an "electric hand saw"—something of a contradiction in terms. Or, it may be called a "skill" saw—regardless of the make of the saw. (*Skil* is but one of several manufacturers of quality portable circular saws).

Whatever it's called, this tool can cut wood and most other building materials quickly and efficiently. It can be pre-set to cut exact bevels, angles, grooves and rabbets. It can crosscut or rip thin or thick materials.

If you are planning a major construction job—adding a room, building a garage or carport—the portable circular saw is a good choice for your first power saw. It substitutes electrical power for a lot of muscle, and can save up to 80 percent in time for many operations.

Circular saws—both portable and stationary—are identified by blade size, which ranges from 6 inches to 8½ inches for portable saws. A 7 or 7¼ inch saw is a handy size for most home uses. By using different blades, it can rip boards, cut framing lumber, paneling, fiberglass, light sheet metal, slate, flagstone and most other common building materials. A 7 inch saw will cut 2¼ inches vertically and a full 2 inches at a 45 degree bevel.

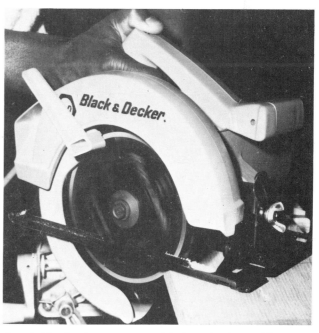

A portable circular saw sees a lot of service in most home workshops (Courtesy Black & Decker).

Whether you have ever used a handsaw or not, a power circular saw will provide more accurate cuts, once you learn to use the built-in guides and additional attachments. Accurate depth of cut is controlled by an adjustable baseplate that supports the saw on the work and limits the depth that the blade penetrates the material. On most saws, cutting depth is adjusted by loosening one wing nut, then moving the hinged baseplate to expose only the amount of saw blade needed.

A notch or groove on the front of the baseplate lines up with the saw blade, to let you saw a straight line without using a guide. Most saws also have a detachable ripping guide that lets you set the blade a measured distance from the edge of the material. The saw's base also tilts laterally (side-to-side) to allow bevel cuts of up to 45 degrees.

Most portable circular saws are turned on and off by a spring loaded switch incorporated in the saw handle. To operate the saw, you must grip the handle properly— once you release the trigger-type switch, the saw stops.

Another built-in safety feature is a retractable blade guard that automatically covers as much of the blade as possible while sawing, to lessen the chances of the operator coming in contact with the saw blade.

Keep all guards and safety devices in place and in good working order, and always use common sense when operating any power equipment. Don't wear loose clothing or dangling jewelry that might become tangled in the blade. Keep your hands away from the moving blade—don't support a piece of work with your hand on the underneath side.

Here are some more do's and don'ts for the safe, efficient operation of a portable circular saw:

1. Don't start the saw with the blade against the work. For one thing, this can cause the saw to "buck" or kick backward sharply. For another, this puts more strain on the saw's motor.
2. Do support the work securely while making a cut, to prevent the saw's shifting position or the material from binding the saw blade. If you cannot hold the work firmly with your free hand, clamp it to a bench or in a vise.
3. Don't stand directly behind or in front of the saw blade when making a cut.
4. Do wear safety goggles, (especially, when using an abrasive type saw blade to cut or score masonry materials.)

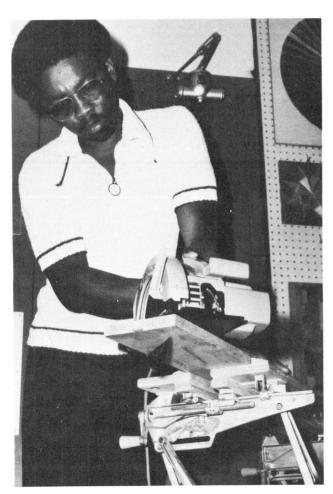

◄ *Better power saws have a notch or groove on the base plate to use as a guide when sawing. (Courtesy Black & Decker).*

Make sure the saw is unplugged from the wall outlet and the blade is wedged before loosening the lock nut to change blades.

	Blade Type	Cat. No.	Description of Blade and Use	Type of Cut	Speed of Cut	Blade Length	Teeth per Inch
	Flush Cutting	U1344	Hard or soft wood over 1/4" thick. Blade material: High carbon steel. Set teeth for fast cutting	Rough	Fast	3"	7
	Plaster Cutting	U1346	Special V-Tooth design provides constant abrading action which is most effective in cutting plaster, masonry and high density plastics. Blade material: High carbon steel.	Rough	Fast	3-5/8"	9
	Double Cutting	U1347	Most wood and fiber materials. Tooth design allows for cutting in both directions with equal speed. Blade material: High carbon steel	Rough	Fast	3"	7
	Double Cutting	U1348	Cuts most wood and fiber materials. Tooth design allows for cutting in both directions with equal speed and quality of cut. Blade material: High carbon steel	Medium	Medium	3"	10
	Skip Tooth	U1349	Cuts most plastics and plywood. Special tooth design with extra large gullets provide extra chip clearance necessary for cutting plywood and plastic. Blade material: High carbon steel	Rough	Fast	3"	5
	Wood Cutting Coarse	*U1350	Cuts soft woods 3/4" and thicker. Canted shank provides built-in blade relief, thus helping to clear the saw dust and cool the blade. Blade material: High carbon steel	Rough	Fastest	3"	7
		*75-250	Twin-Pack of two U1350 Jig Saw Blades				
	Wood Cutting Fine	*U1351	Cuts soft woods under 3/4" thick. Canted shank provides built-in blade relief, thus helping to clear the saw dust and cool blade. Blade material: High carbon steel. More teeth per inch allows for finer quality of cut	Medium	Medium	3"	10
		*75-251	Twin-Pack of two U1351 Jig Saw Blades				
		*75-256	Twin-Pack Blade Assortment (1 U1351 and 1 U1355 Jig Saw Blades)				
	Wood Cutting Hollow Ground	*U1352	Hard woods under 3/4" thick. Hollow grinding provides no tooth projection beyond body of blade, thus imparting an absolutely smooth finish. Canted shank for blade clearance. Blade material: Heat treated high carbon steel.	Smooth	Medium	3"	7
	Metal Cutting	*U1354	For cutting ferrous (iron) metals 1/4" to 3/8" thick and nonferrous (aluminum, copper, etc.) 1/8" to 1/4" thick. Blade material: M-2 high speed steel. Heat treated to spring temper hardness. Capable of cutting ferrous and nonferrous metals alike. Straight shank	Medium	Medium	3"	14
		*75-254	Twin-Pack of two U1354 Jig Saw Blades				
	Metal Cutting	75-156	For cutting ferrous (iron) metals 1/8" to 1/4" thick and nonferrous metals 1/16" to 1/8" thick. Blade material: M-2 high speed steel. Heat treated to spring temper hardness, capable of cutting ferrous and nonferrous metals. Straight shank	Smooth	Medium	3"	18
	Metal Cutting	75-157	For cutting ferrous (iron) metals 1/16" to 3/16" thick. Blade material: M-2 high speed steel. Heat treated to full hardness spring temper. Capable of cutting hard ferrous material. Straight shank	Fine	Slow	3"	24
	Metal Cutting	*U1355	For cutting hard ferrous (iron) metals 1/64" to 3/32" thick. Blade material: M-2 high speed steel. Heat treated to full hardness spring temper. Capable of cutting all hard ferrous materials. Straight shank	Very Fine	Slow	3"	32
		*75-255	Twin-Pack of two U1355 Jig Saw Blades				
	Hollow Ground	*U1359	For cutting plywoods 1/2" to 3/4" thick. For fine finish work. Hollow ground for absolutely smooth finish on all wood products. Blade material: High carbon steel. Provides the longest life woodcutting blade possible. Straight shank	Extremely Fine	Medium	4"	10
	Hollow Ground	*U1360	For cutting plywood and finish materials 3/4" and thicker where fine finish is desirable. Hollow ground for very smooth finish on all wood products. Blade material: High carbon steel. Provides the longest life woodcutting blade possible. Straight shank	Smooth	Medium	4"	6
	Hollow Ground	U1361	For cutting soft woods up to 2" thick where fine finish is desirable. Thicker blade provides less flexing when cutting 1" to 2" stock. Not recommended for scroll type cutting. Hollow ground for smooth finish. Blade material: High carbon steel. Provides the longest life woodcutting blade possible. Straight shank	Smooth	Medium	4"	6
	Hollow Ground	*U1362	For cutting plywood up to 1" thick. Hollow ground for very smooth finish. Blade material: Heat treated high carbon steel. Straight shank	Fine	Medium	3"	10
		*75-262	Twin-Pack of two U1362 Jig Saw Blades				
	Hollow Ground	*U1363	For cutting plywood 3/4" thick and under. Hollow ground for very smooth finish. Blade material: Heat treated high carbon steel. Straight shank for square cuts to work surface.	Smooth	Medium Fast	3"	7
	Hollow Ground	U1364	For plywood 1/4" to 1" thick. Hollow ground for smooth finish on cuts. Blade material: Heat treated high carbon steel. Straight shank.	Medium	Fast	3"	5
	Knife Blade	U1365	For cutting leather, rubber, composition tile, cardboard, etc. Blade material: High carbon steel. Straight shank.	Smooth	Fast	2-1/2"	Knife Edge
	Fleam Ground	U1366	For cutting green or wet woods 1/4" to 2-1/2" thick. Fleam ground provides shredding type cutting action which is most effective in sawing hard, green or wet materials. Blade material: High carbon steel. Provides longest cutting life possible. Straight shank.	Smooth	Medium	4"	10
	Fleam Ground	U1367	For cutting green or wet woods 3/8" to 2-1/2" thick. Fleam ground provides shredding type cutting action which is most effective in sawing hard, green or wet materials. Blade material: High carbon steel. Provides longest cutting life possible. Straight shank.	Coarse	Fast	4"	6
	Scroll Cut	*U1368	For cutting wood, plastic and plywood 1/4" to 1" thick. Set teeth and thin construction allows this blade to make intricate cuts and circles with radii as small as 1/8". Blade construction: High carbon steel. Straight shank	Smooth	Medium	2-1/2"	10
	Wood Cutting Coarse	75-170	Cuts most plastics and wood up to 4" thick. Special tooth design with extra large gullets provide extra chip clearance for fast cutting in thicker materials. Blade material: High carbon steel.	Rough	Fast	6"	4
	Wood Cutting Medium	75-171	Makes fairly smooth cuts in wood up to 4" thick. Extra thick back provides greater resistance to breaking during intricate scroll-type cutting. Blade material: High carbon steel.	Medium	Medium	6"	7

*Denotes most popular blades

Types of sabre saw blades (Courtesy Black & Decker).

5. Do use a grounding type electrical plug and a grounded circuit, particularly if the saw is used in damp locations or if you stand on the ground when sawing.
6. Do use the proper blade for the material to be sawed.

A portable circular saw is readily converted to a bench saw with the use of one of several tables on the market. While these tables cannot turn a portable saw into a tilting-arbor table saw, the better models allow for the saw to be mounted under the table, so that the saw is in an inverted position. This is particularly handy when you have several miters or other pre-set angles to cut.

Sabre Saw

The sabre saw, a sort of mechanized coping saw, is especially handy for homeowners, because it can make cuts no other power saw can make so easily. It's a versatile home workshop tool that often is the first (sometimes the only) power saw needed.

The sabre saw blade has a reciprocating, up and down action. The entire saw is light, weighing from 3½ to about 5 pounds, and vibration is sometimes a problem.

Some models have an on-off toggle switch; others are equipped with a spring loaded trigger switch. Most sabre saw handles are on top of the motor housing; some also have a second handle or knob toward the front of the saw for a safe two handed operation.

An almost infinite variety of blades adds versatility to the sabre saw. It cuts both ferrous and non-ferrous light metals, wood, felt, rubber, plastic, composition board, floor tiles. You can use a sabre saw to cut through a 2 x 4, but it works best with plywood, paneling and lighter woods.

Blades with more teeth per inch make smooth cuts; blades with fewer teeth per inch make coarser but faster cuts. With any kind of material, the sabre saw should not be fed through the work too fast. Let it take its time. The vibration caused by reciprocating action can affect the smoothness of the cut in many materials. Saw teeth are slanted upward, so that the blade cuts on the up stroke. Keep this in mind when you cut materials that will show —put the finished side of the work down.

Heavy-duty reciprocating saw (Courtesy Black & Decker).

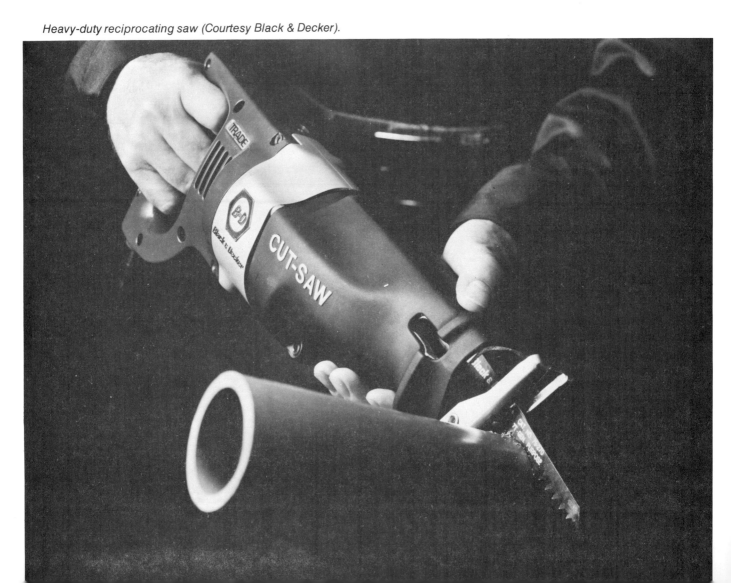

One advantage a sabre saw has over most other power saws is the ability to cut flush or nearly flush with a surface. For example, with a sabre saw, you can cut a hole in wall paneling—for an electrical outlet, perhaps—right next to a stud without cutting the stud.

You don't need a great deal of skill or experience to make straight cuts with a sabre saw. You can freehand it along a pencil line, or use a straight edged guide. Making curved cuts and inside cuts is somewhat more involved, but they can be mastered with only a few practice tries.

Most sabre saws have a circle cutting guide; an outrigger sort of arm with a pin that is positioned in the exact center of the circle. You merely set the guide to the length of the desired circle's radius, position the pin on the material and saw around it. Irregular curved shapes are more difficult to cut accurately. Until you develop a good deal of skill, you will want to position the pattern on the material so that you can make the complete cut *outside* the line. This margin allows for some error in operating the saw, and also lets you sand the work without altering the original size and shape of the piece.

You can make inside or "pocket" cuts with a sabre saw in one of two ways. First, you drill a hole in the paneling or other material to be sawed and make the cut pretty much as you would with a hand coping saw.

Or, you can make a "plunge" cut with the sabre saw, without first drilling a hole. To do this, draw lines for the opening to be cut—electrical outlet, switch, or whatever. Then, hold the saw firmly with both hands and tilt it forward so that the front edge of the base is resting on the work, but with the blade a half inch or so above the work. Start the saw motor and slowly but firmly lower the blade to make contact with the material. Lower the back end of the saw slowly until the blade has chewed its way into the work and the base of the saw is flat against the surface. Then, guide the saw along the cutting lines to complete the job. Don't try a plunge cut on material thicker than about ⅜ inch plywood. Even then, don't be surprised if you break a blade or two before you get the hang of it.

Larger reciprocating saws are often used by carpenters to cut through framing members already installed in a house under construction or being remodeled. These resemble sabre saws in that they use a similar blade, but are much heavier.

Table Saw

The table or bench saw is among the handier tools in a power-tool workshop. It can rip, crosscut, miter, bevel, cut dadoes and make moldings—not only faster than hand tools, but with more accuracy.

A good table saw is a precision piece of equipment that lets the average home handyman achieve the results of a master craftsman—at a price. Expect to spend $300 or

more for a 10 inch saw and its table—plus several more dollars for specialized blades and accessories.

Many table saws were formerly built with tilting tables. That is, the table tilted to allow angle cuts, while the saw blade and its shaft stayed put. Today, however, most table saws are of the "tilting arbor" variety; built so the blade and motor mount tilt at angles up to 45 degrees, while the table itself remains horizontal.

Reduced to its basic elements, a table saw is simply a flat metal table with a slot, through which the top of a circular saw blade protrudes. The blade rotates toward the feed end of the table—where the operator stands—so the teeth are traveling downward as they enter the wood. This helps hold the work against the table and gives better control of the cut.

Most table saws have guides to hold the work at desired angles and distances from the blade. One common guide is a "rip fence", a flat metal plate that is parallel to the saw blade. The fence can be moved in or out, to hold the work at any desired distance from the blade. On better saws, ripping cuts can be regulated in 1/16 inch increments.

Another guide generally included with a table saw is a mitering gauge. This attachment slides in or out in a groove in the saw table, and can be adjusted to let the operator cut wood at angles up to 45 degrees.

Cutting bevels is simply a matter of dialing in the desired degree of tilt and locking the blade and motor mount in that position. Most table saws make bevel cuts from 90 to 45 degrees.

Parts of a tilting-arbor table saw

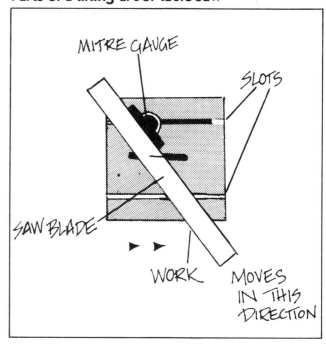

With accessories, a 10 inch table saw can cut dadoes up to 1½ inches deep and ½ inch wide; cut several different patterns of molding; cut tapers; and sand wood.

Radial-Arm Saw

Until recent years, the radial-arm saw had primarily industrial applications—and prices to match. But in recent years, several manufacturers have built high quality, scaled down models primarily for home workshops.

Briefly, the radial-arm saw is a versatile tool, able to perform most functions of a table saw—plus a few of its own—but with the cutting blade above, rather than below, the table. The motor and saw blade are mounted on an overhead track, usually on ball or roller bearings. On most models, the saw blade swivels a full 360 degrees, to let the operator make cuts from almost any position and in any angle.

A number of tool attachments let you turn the radial-arm saw into a dado cutter, molder, planer, sander, drill and jig saw. On some models, a router adapter can be mounted on the saw spindle, to turn the machine into a stationary router.

A radial-arm saw is a hard working tool for those home craftspersons who need it. Units are priced at about $400 and up. However, before you invest, you will want to investigate the features of several makes and models in detail.

A radial-arm saw is a versatile shop tool; quality saws for the homeowner are now made by major manufacturers.

Jig Saw

For craftspeople and hobbyists, a jig saw (or scroll saw) is a handy piece of equipment. The jig saw cuts straight or curved lines with a reciprocating blade action, and a good one costs considerably less than most other stationary saw types.

The range of the jig saw is rather limited, as it seems to perform best on light, thin materials. For most general projects and construction, a power circular saw or bandsaw plus a sabre saw give the operator more options than does the jig saw.

Most jig saws are capable of being operated at various blade speeds, either through gearing or different sized V-belt pulleys. This is an important feature. Harder materials are best sawed at slower speeds. However, experience is the best teacher when it comes to proper blade speed.

Band Saw

The band saw, one of the earlier power woodworking tools invented, is still around in much the same design as it was when the first one was patented in the early 19th Century.

So-called because the cutting blade is a narrow, flexible endless steel band with cutting teeth on one edge, the band saw is sized according to the diameter of the revolving pulleys that drive and support the blade. For most practical purposes, the band saw will do the fine curved scroll cutting of a jig saw, and has the added advantage that the cutting is all done in one direction—rather than vibrating up and down, as with a jig saw or sabre saw.

Blade sizes and tooth sizes let the band saw cut a variety of materials and thicknesses. Generally, the widest blade that will do the job should be used. Woodcutting bands for smaller saws range from ⅛ to ¾ inch wide, and have 3 to 7 teeth per inch of blade. Some band saws are equipped with miter gauges and rip fences, to allow accuracy in cutting joints and angles—although these operations probably can be done more precisely on a circular saw. On some models, the saw table tilts for making angle cuts; on others, the saw head tilts and the table remains horizontal.

Circular Saw Blades

Blades for portable or stationary portable saws vary according to purpose and on most saws can be changed in a few minutes. So-called combination blades will suffice for several uses, and cut either across or with the wood grain. But for best results, the saw blade should be selected for the kind of material being cut.

A **ripping blade** has coarser teeth and cuts faster with the grain than does a combination type. However, a rip blade makes a coarser cut, and should be used only for ripping along the grain. A **crosscut blade** makes a smoother cut across the grain, but is finer toothed and cuts more slowly than a rip blade. Plywood paneling blades have fine teeth and usually are hollow ground to make a smooth cut.

All saw blades can be re-sharpened, and we go into that subject in Chapter 23. Sharpening takes time if you do it yourself, or dollars if you hire it done. **Carbide tipped** blades stay sharp up to 10 times longer than regular steel blades—but they cost up to 10 times as much. Generally, carbide tipped blades are available in sizes from 6½ to 10 inches, and fit either portable or table saws. However, because of the cost of these high performance blades, you may want to limit your purchases of carbide tipped blades to those you use most often.

Carbide tips come in various teeth sizes, for different cutting applications, with 8 to 72 teeth per blade. As with other saw blades, the number of teeth affects both the smoothness and speed of the cut. With carbide tipped blades, the number of teeth also affects the price. An 8 tooth, 7 inch blade will cost about $12. A 60 tooth, 10 inch blade will cost $40 or more, and a carbide tipped blade with 72 teeth will run on the high side of $50.

Some people prefer to buy carbide tipped blades for general use, but use regular steel blades for cutting paneling and plywood. The reason: paneling blades have a lot more teeth than, say, a general crosscut blade. A carbide tipped paneling blade will therefore cost a great deal more than a similar blade with fewer teeth. So, the conventional steel paneling blade is used. When it gets dull, it may be more economical to discard it and buy a new one than to sharpen all those little teeth.

Your own choice of saw blades will depend on what kind of materials you need to cut most often. If you saw lumber that has been used in concrete forms, you may want to buy a cheap blade, rather than risk a better quality blade. It doesn't hurt nearly as much to toss out a $4 blade, rather than one costing $15.

4
Smoothing the Way

Fairly inexpensive electric tools have replaced the hand smoothing and shaping tools in many homeowners' kits. It's understandable in a way: a beginner (or veteran) woodworker can turn out a lot more work in the same amount of time with power tools. An electric router can do in minutes what chisels, planes and gouges require hours to do. A power tool performs pretty much the same way for each operator; given a certain amount of skill in its operation.

In another way, though, it's unfortunate that many basic hand shaping and smoothing tools have lost ground to power equipment. A person who understands his tools and the materials he works with can produce finished results that approach fine art.

Planes

Take the woodworking plane. It's a basic, versatile tool that has been pushed to the back of the workbench by many people. One reason, as mentioned, is that modern electric tools can do a good many of the plane's jobs.

But another reason may be that some handymen have not kept their planes *sharp*. It's vital to a plane's operation that it be sharp and properly adjusted. If you've ever tried to use a dull plane, you can understand why some people may have put theirs on the shelf.

The woodworking plane—or planes, rather—is a versatile tool that can perform many functions. Woodworkers of days gone by often owned dozens of different planes; each with a specific application to the work at hand.

It's still a handy tool to keep around—and keep in good working condition. Reduced to its basic elements, a plane is a chisel blade held in a frame, with the depth of cut regulated by a guide. The plane is used primarily to bring woodwork down to finished size or to smooth off rough surfaces.

Planes differ in size, length, weight, width and type of blade, depending on the work they are designed to do. Small block planes and smoothing planes are 4 to 10 inches long, with a blade that is 1½ to 2 inches wide.

The block plane is a good all around tool for a home handyperson. It's relatively inexpensive, and easy to ad-

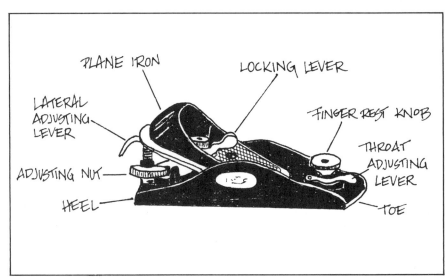

This is a small block plane, also called "model-maker's" plane, and is held with the hand cupped over the tool, the heel of the hand pushing on the frame behind the locking lever.

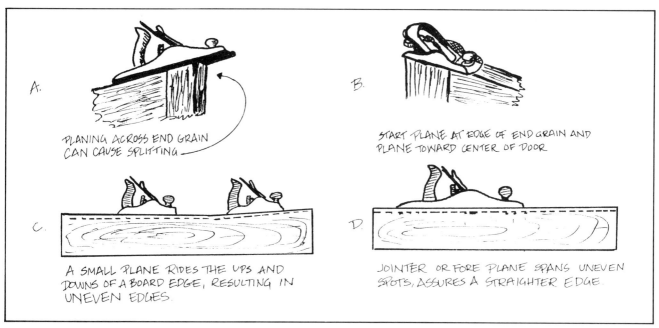

A. PLANING ACROSS END GRAIN CAN CAUSE SPLITTING

B. START PLANE AT EDGE OF END GRAIN AND PLANE TOWARD CENTER OF DOOR

C. A SMALL PLANE RIDES THE UPS AND DOWNS OF A BOARD EDGE, RESULTING IN UNEVEN EDGES.

D. JOINTER OR FORE PLANE SPANS UNEVEN SPOTS, ASSURES A STRAIGHTER EDGE.

Do's and don'ts of planing wood. A, planing across end grain can cause splitting. The proper way to do it is B, start plane at edge of end grain and plane toward the center of the door. C, a small plane rides ups and downs of a board edge, resulting in uneven edges. Better to use a jointer or fore plane, as at D, to span uneven spots and assure a straighter edge.

Plane in the "uphill" direction of wood grain when possible.

just and maintain. You can do a number of simple jobs with it: smooth rough edges; trim doors to fit; bevel the edges of a shelf or bring smaller pieces of stock down to fitting size.

To plane the edge of a board, you need to brace the work firmly so that it doesn't move. You can clamp the piece in a wood vise, or make a bench stop from a piece of scrap lumber. (A bench stop is simply a board with a V-shaped groove cut in it to hold the work being planed. Nail or clamp the bench stop to a workbench or other handy working surface).

Always plane in the "uphill" direction of the wood's grain, to avoid splitting and splintering. If you must plane against the grain, adjust the blade for the thinnest shaving possible. When planing across end grain, plane from each edge toward the center of the board.

A plane works best when the blade is adjusted to remove only a thin shaving of wood on each stroke. Adjust the blade depth by turning the adjusting screw. If the wood shaving is thicker at one side, loosen the blade and align it parallel with the plane's bottom edge. When the plane is easy to push and a thin, uniform shaving curls away from the blade, you've adjusted it properly.

For smoothing or sizing longer boards, use a longer plane, such as a jack or fore plane—from 14 to 20 inches long. A longer plane keeps the cut true, rather than riding up and down with the shape of the board.

It's essential that a plane blade be kept razor sharp and free of rust. A plane will not perform if the blade is dull or rusty.

To keep a plane blade sharp during normal use, hone or whet it on a carborundum oil stone to keep a fine cutting edge. Use a fine grit oil stone, and slide the blade (removed from the plane body, of course) bevel side down back and forth on the stone. Don't use too much pressure, and keep the bevel flat against the stone. Then, turn the blade over and slide it across the stone with the bevel up, to remove the burr or "wire edge" produced by whetting. A special plane blade clamp helps hold the blade at exactly the proper bevel.

Store the plane in a dry place, where the blade will not come in contact with other tools or metal. If humidity is a problem that might cause the blade to rust, put a film of light oil on the tool before storing it.

Chisels

Wood chisels are more versatile today than ever, thanks to improved designs and modern alloy blades. Blades do not have to be thick to be strong enough for heavy duty work; plastic handles have replaced wood on tang chisels and will stand a moderate amount of pounding with a mallet.

A chisel is not just a chisel. There is an amazing choice in types and construction. Size is the principal factor in selecting the chisels you will need. **Butt chisels,** with blades about three inches long, come in widths from ⅛

To adjust a plane, turn the depth adjusting nut until the blade barely projects through the slot. Turn the plane upside down and sight along the bottom. Move the adjusting lever until the plane blade is even all the way across.

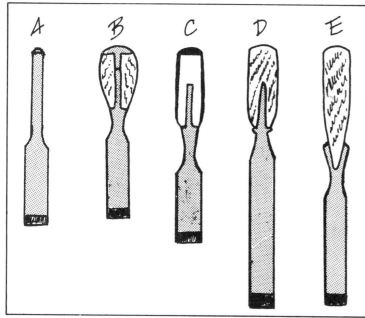

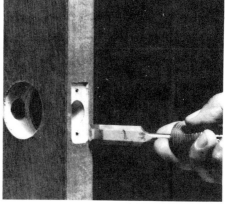

Wood chisels are often used to make recesses for strike plates and door hinges.

Basic chisel types: A, All metal chisel for striking with mallet; B, metal cored, wood handled chisel, also for striking; C, plastic handled tang chisel; D, wood handled tang chisel; and E, socket chisel with wooden handle.

inch to 2 inches, and are designed to be used in tight spaces. The **pocket chisel** is somewhat longer, with a 4 or 5 inch blade, and is probably the handiest for general use. **Mill chisels,** the largest, have heavy blades of 8 or 10 inches, with widths of 2 inches or more. You aren't likely to need mill chisels for average work.

Chisels are further classified by the method of use. **Paring** chisels have thin blades ground to about a 20 degree bevel on the cutting edge, and are designed to be driven by hand, to make light shave cuts. **Firmer** chisels are heavier, with a thicker blade and a metal cored handle that can be driven either by hand or with a mallet. **Gouges** are chisels with curved blades, for cutting rounded grooves.

As a practical rule, don't use a chisel for a job another tool could do better or faster. You can shave the edge of a board with a chisel, but a plane does it better. A chisel can be used as the only tool to make a deep recess or mortise, but it works best to clean out and shape the recess after most of the wood has been bored out with a drill or auger bit.

A common use of a chisel is to make a recess for butt type hinges. Use the hinge as a template to draw the outline of the recess on the door or frame. With a utility knife, score the outline to prevent wood fibers from splitting out. Then, set the chisel at one end of the outline, with its edge on the cross grain line and the bevel facing the recess to be made. Strike the chisel head lightly with a mallet. Don't

use too much force, as you will want the scoring cut to be only as deep as the hinge thickness.

Repeat the scoring process at the other end of the outline, again with the bevel of the chisel blade toward the recess. Then make a series of cuts about ¼ inch apart from one end of the recess to the other. The notched wood is easily pared away with the chisel held bevel up to slice away from the edge of the wood inward.

Chisels are sharpened in much the same way as are plane blades. Most chisels made today are factory ground to about a 25 degree bevel. For general work, you can maintain this angle when honing or grinding the blade. However, if you use a chisel for fine work, you may want to re-bevel the blade to about 15 degrees. This shallower angle lets you shave off smaller slices of wood, but the thinner blade is subject to more nicks and chips in heavy work.

Scrapers

Scrapers come in a variety of types and sizes, and are usually "in-between" tools that prepare a planed surface for sanding.

One such scraper—actually a specialized plane—is the **spokeshave,** a two-handled tool with either a straight or convex adjustable blade. This tool is particularly handy for smoothing curved shapes. Its name comes from the former major function of smoothing round wooden

Top: chisel is used to make shallow cuts for door lock strike plate. Score the outline of the cut first with a knife, then make a series of cuts with chisel. Center: chiseled sections of wood are removed with chisel in prying sort of movement. Below: when making mortises, it's faster to bore out most of the wood with a drill or auger bit, then trim up the mortise with the chisel.

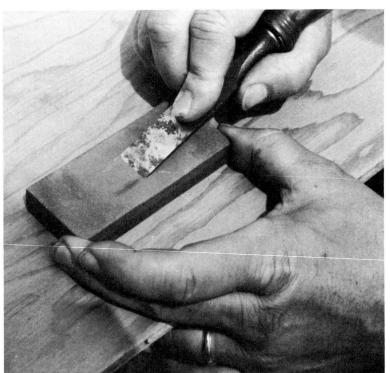

Cutting edges can be kept keen by drawing the chisel across a flat oilstone. Whet the beveled side of the blade, then lightly whet off the wire edge that is produced on the flat side of the chisel.

spokes for wagon and buggy wheels. The spokeshave is pushed, as a plane, with the grain of the wood. It can also be used to chamfer or round the edges of a curved piece.

A smaller version of the spokeshave is the **cabinet scraper,** which also has an adjustable blade. This tool commonly is used to smooth small ridges left by a plane or to remove the last vestiges of old paint or varnish in a refinishing project, before the work is sanded.

Hand scrapers are thin steel blades used in tight places or on small areas to shave away a minute amount of wood. With the advent of power sanders, abraders and other wood smoothing tools, hand scrapers are being used less frequently by most handypersons.

A fairly recent development is the **abrader,** a hand tool that can do many of the jobs of both scrapers and sandpaper. The working surface of abraders generally is chrome plated stainless steel, etched with sharp cutting pillars that are coarse or fine cut abrading surfaces. These tools are made in a variety of shapes and sizes, to finish flat, round or angled work.

Rasps and files

Wood rasps are coarse, fast cutting tools used to remove material quickly from wood and other non-metallic materials. Wood rasps are from 6 to 16 inches in length, and are flat, half-round or round in shape. The rough surface left by a rasp can be smoothed with a wood file, a tool similar to a rasp, but with finer cutting teeth.

Sanders and Sandpapers

Most sandpaper is made of tough, heavy paper coated with glue, onto which are sprinkled small particles of an abrasive compound. Most abrasives used today are manmade materials nearly as hard as diamonds.

Sandpaper ranges from very fine to coarse grades. A No. 1 sandpaper (coarse) generally is used for initial sanding, to remove a lot of material quickly. Then, successively finer papers are used, until the final sanding is made with a fine-grit paper (6/0 is the finest grade) to smooth out marks left by the coarser sandpaper.

It's important to sand surfaces so as to retain the desired shape. Square edges should still be square after sanding, not rounded. A square block of wood with sandpaper wrapped around it helps keep flat surfaces flat and square edges square.

An inexpensive but handy tool that saves fingernails and knuckles when you have a good deal of hand sanding is a padded sandpaper holder. These tools, usually made of metal or plastic or parts of both, clamp the

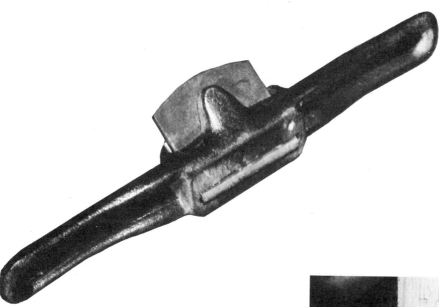

A spokeshave, a sort of short-bodied plane, can be used to smooth round and irregular surfaces. (Courtesy Bill Mason)

Scrapers are handy for removing paint and varnish, and for trimming high spots on work prior to sanding.

Intermediate finishing tools, such as Disston's Abraders and Stanley Surform, are used after planing or drilling to produce a smooth surface. Often, no additional sanding is needed (Courtesy of Disston & Stanley)

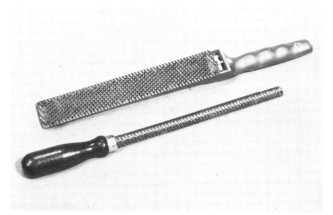

A flat and a round rasp

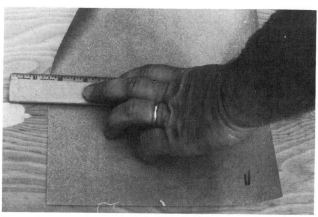

For economy, tear sheets of sandpaper into halves or quarters.

To sand flat pieces but maintain square edges, use a sanding block. Wrap sandpaper part way around a flat wood block and sand back and forth with the grain—never across it.

Plastic padded sandpaper holder.

sandpaper over a rubber pad. Most have a handle at the top. The plastic sandpaper holders go for about $2 at discount hardwares, but a good quality metal holder costs less than $5—and, again, you're money ahead in the long run to buy quality.

If you have much sanding to do, a power sander is worth considering, from a time and energy saving standpoint. **Flexible Disk** sanding wheels let you turn your electric drill into a power sander. The kind of sanding disks fitted on a swiveling ball joint are better than the fixed kind. And if your only need is to remove old built-up paint or to do rough shaping work, this may be the most economical way to go. However, drill mounted sanders are not suited to fine finish work.

For sanding smooth surfaces on woodwork and other materials, a **finishing sander** is the better choice of power tool. Finishing sanders are made in three basic types: orbital, reciprocal and belt sanders. Which type you choose depends partly on how much money you want to spend and how much sanding you have to do. With coarser abrasive papers, for rough work and, with fine paper for most finish work, either type of power sander will do very well. However, there are some limitations you may consider.

The **orbital** or pad sander is an economical, popular choice for most finish sanding. Its abrasive surface "shimmies" in small circles, which is fine for sanding joints like miters, where wood grain meets from different

53

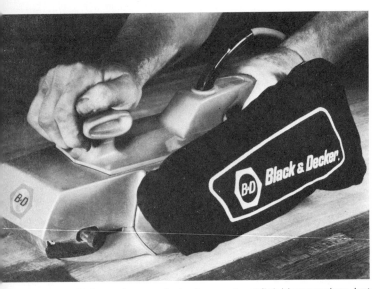

Belt sanders are fastest, smoothest finishing sanders, but don't let them stop in one place–the sander can quickly cut the wood down below the surrounding surface. (Courtesy of Black & Decker)

directions. The sanding pad extends slightly beyond the machine's frame, which lets the workman sand flush against square corners.

Most orbital sanders are made in sizes that let you use a standard sheet of sandpaper—or fractions of a standard 9 x 11 inch sheet, so there is no wasted paper. Clamps or locking levers hold the paper in place.

Always be sure the abrasive paper is stretched tightly across the pad. Otherwise, the paper can crinkle and mar the work surface. For final sanding, you may want to use tougher (but more expensive) abrasive cloth, to prevent this.

Orbital sanders are lightweight—typically 5 to 8 pounds. However, the circular sanding action is not ideal for final finishing on some surfaces.

The **reciprocating** sander resembles the orbital sander, in that it uses sandpaper clamped to a felt pad or foot. However, the sanding action is a back and forth motion, rather than in small circles. This straight sanding action is better for fine woodwork.

Most major manufacturers now make "dual-action" pad sanders, with orbital action for rough sanding and reciprocal straight line action for finishing work. You merely flick a lever to select the sanding action you need.

Belt sanders are well suited both to fast removal of materials and to finish sanding. The continuous abrasive belt moves in one direction. To remove material fast, the belt should travel across the grain. For finishing, a fine abrasive belt should move parallel to the grain.

Orbital sander can be used for finishing and it fits into corners. (Courtesy of Black & Decker)

Accessories turn orbital sanders into buffers and polishers. (Courtesy of Black & Decker)

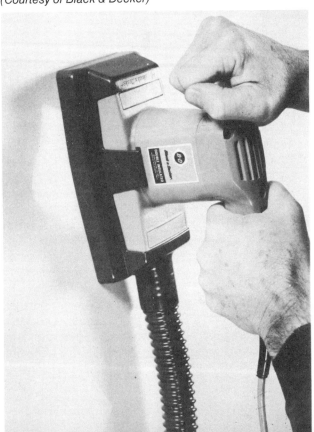

Belt sanders typically cost more than orbital or reciprocal sanders—or even "dual-action" models. But a belt sander can save a lot of work when you have to sand a large, relatively flat surface, such as a door, a table top or boat hull.

When a lot of material must be removed from a rough surface, hold the sander diagonally across the grain, *but* move the machine in the same direction as the grain of the wood.

With any electric sander, turn on the sander switch before the abrasive is applied to the wood surface. This lets the motor reach operating speed before it touches the material. It's a good habit with most portable power tools to pick up the tool (by the handle, of course) *before* the cord is plugged into the outlet.

Also, whatever type of sander you're using, always keep it moving over the work. If the sander stops in one place, even for a moment, it can quickly gouge an area deeper than the surrounding surface.

Some woodworkers like to use "wet" sanding to get a super smooth finish on wood. In this technique, the wood is wiped with a wet sponge, then allowed to dry. When the wood has dried, the grain will be raised or "lifted" and can be sanded more smoothly. You may want to try this, but practice first on a scrap piece of the material to

Beading cutters let you use an electric drill to make decorative moldings. (Courtesy of Black & Decker)

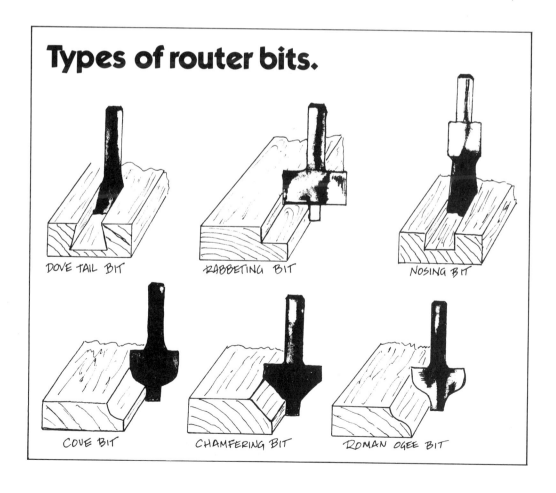

Types of router bits.

DOVE TAIL BIT

RABBETING BIT

NOSING BIT

COVE BIT

CHAMFERING BIT

ROMAN OGEE BIT

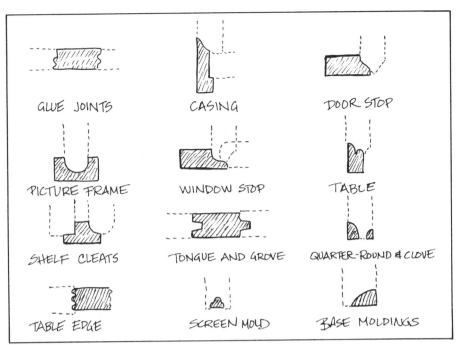

Cross-sections of typical moldings.

GLUE JOINTS · CASING · DOOR STOP
PICTURE FRAME · WINDOW STOP · TABLE
SHELF CLEATS · TONGUE AND GROVE · QUARTER-ROUND & COVE
TABLE EDGE · SCREEN MOLD · BASE MOLDINGS

be sanded. Not all woods behave the same way when dampened.

Router

An electric router is a useful power tool, particularly in woodworking and cabinet making. Basically, it's a high speed electric motor mounted vertically on a flat base. A chuck on the operating end of the motor shaft lets the operator attach router bits with an almost infinite variety of shapes.

Guides regulate the distance below the base of the machine the router bit extends, and thus the depth of the cut. With the proper cutter or bit, you can cut about any shaped groove or edge in wood.

You can chamfer (bevel) the edge of a board, cut grooves and recesses for door hinges and locks, cut dadoes and rabbet joints, make simple and compound dovetail joints, cut square, round or V-shaped grooves and do any number of other jobs. You can even write or print words, etched into wood or plywood.

However, a router is seldom used "freehand." Better quality routers come with guides for straight and circular cutting. For other, non-standard router work, a template guide lets you use pre-cut outlines to route about any shape you wish. With a table built for the purpose, you can even mount a router upside down and use it as a stationary shaper.

A router operates at high speeds—some as fast as 30,000 revolutions per minute. As the router bit enters the work, the motor will slow somewhat. Also, the torque generated by the whirling bit making contact with the wood will tend to twist the router. With experience, the operator acquires an "ear" as well as a "feel" for the speed and handling of the tool, so that the work can be fed quickly without causing the motor to labor.

As with any power tool, it's a good idea to practice with a router on some scrap material before undertaking a project. Hold the router firmly and keep fingers away from the revolving bit. *Always* disconnect the machine before changing cutters or bits.

Stationary

If you're very involved in woodworking, you'll likely need the use of one or more stationary smoothing and shaping tools: wood-turning lathe, planer, molder, high speed shaper or bench sander.

We're talking about fairly expensive, specialized tools here, for the most part. If you have already acquired the skill needed to graduate to these machines, you know that your buying decision demands considerable investigation of brands, models and features of different tools before you make the investment. You need more information than we could possibly include in these pages.

Several manufacturers build quality power tools that perform a variety of functions, and one of these may very well suit your purposes—and your pocketbook—better than a collection of individual machines.

For example, there is a combination planer-molder-ripsaw machine that is suited both for homeworkshop and industrial duty. Perhaps the best known of these power tools is a multi-purpose machine built with a combination circular saw, drill press, disk sander, horizontal drill and wood turning lathe.

However, if you have the volume of work that justifies a major investment in stationary shop tools, you'll likely want to buy individual tools for most of the functions you need.

5
Measuring and Marking Tools

By some rights, this discussion of tools used to measure and mark work might be the first chapter in the book. Measuring is basic to most other functions—sawing, drilling, fastening—and it's the first requirement for success in a good many jobs around the home and workshop.

The tools you select to measure, gauge and mark your work should be, first of all, accurate. Secondly, they should be durable. It doesn't matter a great deal whether you use a retractable steel tape, a folding rule or some other measuring device—so long as the tool tells you the truth about lengths, widths and dimensions. Beyond this basic accuracy, other features of measuring tools deal mainly with convenience and cost.

Tapes and Rules

Perhaps the most useful measuring tool for most people is the **flexible steel tape.** These are made in 6, 8, 10, 12 and 20 foot lengths, and in ½ inch and ¾ inch blade widths. A 10 or 12 foot tape with a half-inch blade is a handy choice if you own just one steel tape.

On most **steel tapes,** measurements are graduated in inches and common fractions to 16ths or 32nds of an inch. Many also have a colored mark at multiples of 16 inch spacings, for quickly marking off standard stud and rafter intervals.

Most carpenters own several steel tapes of different lengths. Whether you will buy one tape or many, look for wearing ability, legibility of markings and convenience of use. The tape should have a sturdy, "true zero" hook at the end to hold at the edge of the piece being measured. Look for ease of reading, also. Black numerals on yellow or off-white backgrounds are easiest to read.

Better quality tapes have a polyester film bonded to the steel blade. This finish guards against wear and acids. The tape should have a lock that holds the blade in open position, and a rewind spring that returns the blade to the case.

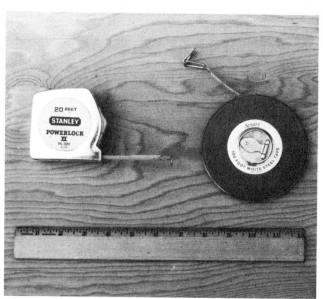

Measuring tools should be convenient to use and tell the truth about lengths.

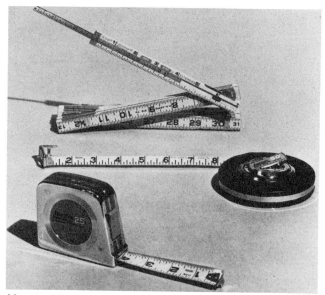

Most handymen need more than one kind of rule or tape. Folding wood rule, 100 foot steel tape and retractable tape shown here are made by Lufkin.

For longer measurements, you may need a 50 or 100 foot steel tape. Most of these are ⅜ or ½ inch wide, and are manually retractable. That is, the tape is wound back into the case with a hand crank, rather than automatically by a spring.

When using a steel tape, be sure it is not kinked or twisted. It's not a good idea to measure around corners with a steel tape; although better quality ones are flexible enough to allow this. Keep the tape dry and clean, and wound within its case when it is not in use.

For some measuring jobs, and general all purpose work, you may prefer a **zig-zag folding rule**. These are

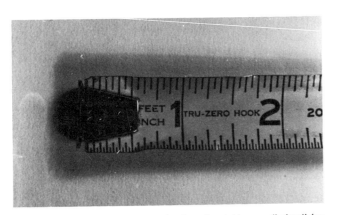

Measuring tapes and rules should be easily legible; black figures on off white or yellow background are used most often.

available in various lengths, and are more useful than steel tapes for one person use in making shorter measurements. Better zig-zag rules are rigid enough to measure across horizontal openings, and some of them have an extension feature that lets you take inside measurements accurately.

A **carpenter's measuring stick** also can be used for taking inside measurements. This rule consists of two overlapping rules held together with brass clamps. The two sections of the rule can be extended and fastened at the correct length—say the width of a door frame. Or, lacking such a measuring device, you can use two small boards or sticks to measure an opening, then use a tape or rule to take the measurements from the sticks.

Except for rough measurements, do not use fabric or paper tapes, such as garment makers' tapes. These can stretch enough to give an inaccurate reading where precise measurements are necessary.

A **caliper rule,** a tool that comes in several sizes, can make accurate inside and outside measurements of small items and openings. It is especially useful in measuring diameters of pipe, dowels, rods and other round stock.

Most tapes and rules have graduation lines that are varied in length for quick reading. The even inches are marked with the longest line, half-inch lines are some-

Better steel tapes have end hooks mounted that are adjustable to give a true reading for both inside and outside measurements.

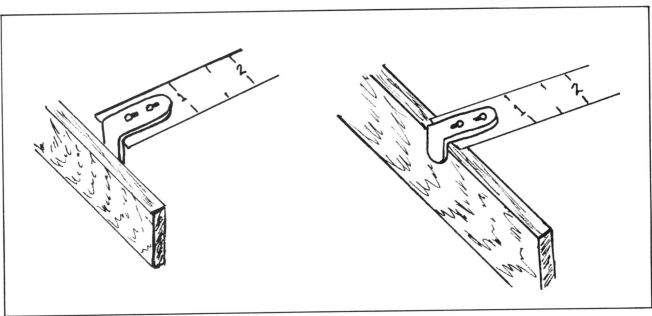

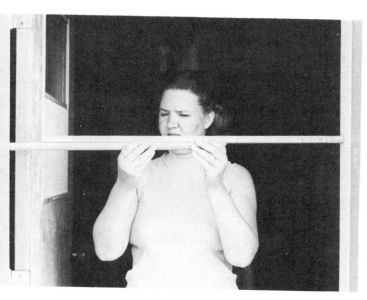

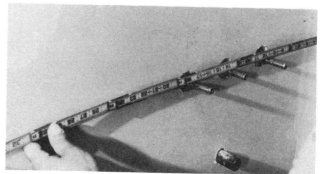

Semi-rigid folding rules are handier for some measuring jobs than steel tapes.

◄ *Widths of openings can be measured with two pieces of scrap lumber held to just span the opening, then measured with a tape or rule.*

what shorter, quarter-inch marks are shorter still, etc. Tape and rule measurements usually are in inches and fractions; however, some are graduated in inches and tenths. Be sure you know which scale you're using.

When using measuring tools, develop techniques that help insure accuracy. Suppose you need to lay out holes to be drilled at 6 inch intervals along a board. Place the end, or "zero" mark, of the tape or rule at one end of the board and mark at the 6, 12, 18 and 24 inch marks; rather than mark the first hole, then move the rule to mark the second hole 6 inches from that, and so on. There are several reasons for doing it this way. For one, each time you move the tape or rule, you have increased your opportunity for measuring error. Also, if you measure from the end of the board and make a mark, then measure from that mark, the width of the pencil marks can throw your measurements off—especially if you are measuring a long series.

Marking Equipment

Most carpenters and woodworkers use several types of pencils and scribes to mark measurements in wood. For most measurements, a common No. 2 lead pencil or the **carpenter's pencil** with a flat, hard lead will do an adequate job.

For greater accuracy, use a sharp pointed knife or **scratch awl** to make the mark. Be careful if you're marking finish work this way. Do not mark work if the scribed line will show in the finished surface. Also, for very accurate measuring, lay the rule on edge, so that the gradua-

tions touch the work being marked.

Remember that marks for saw cuts should take into account the kerf, or thickness of the saw blade as it cuts through the wood. Always saw on the "waste" side of the mark.

A **marking gauge** comes in handy for measuring and marking lines parallel to the planed edge of a workpiece. Made of hardwood or metal, the marking gauge has a beam graduated in inches and fractions of an inch, and a marking head that slides back and forth on the beam. A sharp scribing spur or pin is located at one end of the beam, to scratch a line parallel to the edge of a board when the marking head is clamped at the desired distance.

The marking gauge is used most often to scribe a line for ripping a board. A larger version of the gauge is made for marking plywood and paneling.

Try Square

Actually, any square that is *square* can be a *try* square, for checking angles on work. The term usually refers to an L-shaped tool with a steel blade 6 or 8 inches long and a wooden or metal handle 4 to 5 inches long.

The try square commonly is used for testing and marking boards for cutting, planning and fitting; functions that demand accuracy. To keep a try square accurate and true, don't drop it, don't use it for prying or hammering. Its usefulness depends on the tool forming a perfect 90 degree angle. Some try squares also have a 45 degree bevel on one side of the handle, for laying out and checking miter joints.

Combination Square

There are any number of special purpose squares available, but the handiest for home workshop use is the versatile combination square. With it, you can test work for squareness, mark 90 and 45 degree angles, level and plumb surfaces, find the depth of holes and recesses, and measure lengths and widths. The combination square also functions as a straightedge and marking gauge.

Buy a good one. Prices range from about $4 to over $10. You don't have to buy the most expensive, but you should look for a tool with: all metal parts; a blade that slides freely but which can be clamped securely in position; a glass tube spirit level that is truly level and tightly fastened. Better combination squares have two bubble vials—at 90 degree angles to each other—to let you check level and plumb at the same time.

A combination square needs little maintenance, other than reasonably careful use. A light coating of oil on the blade, and occasional cleaning of the blades groove, and your combination square should last a lifetime.

When marking a line with a try square, hold the square against the board edge and use a pencil or scribe to mark along the blade.

Parts of a combination square.

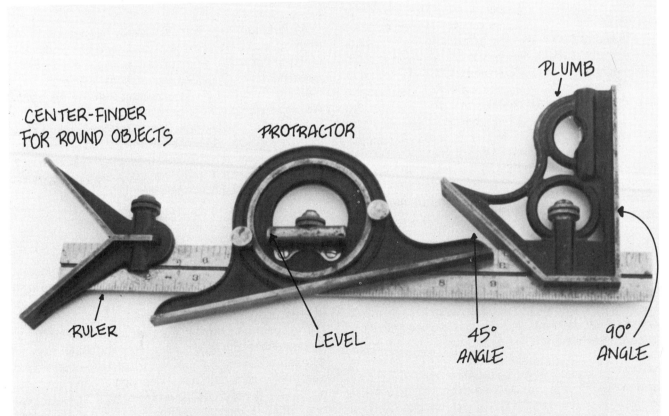

CENTER-FINDER FOR ROUND OBJECTS

PROTRACTOR

PLUMB

RULER

LEVEL

45° ANGLE

90° ANGLE

Bevel

The bevel is an adjustable tool for laying out and checking angles and bevels. The blade is adjustable and is locked in place with a thumb screw. After the bevel blade is locked at the desired angle, it is used in much the same way as a try square.

Steel Square

The steel, or **framing square,** is a right angle of steel, about ⅛ inch in thickness and marked with measurement graduations and special tables for computing angles and lengths of various framing members. Most steel squares have a 24 inch long body that is 2 inches wide, and a 16 inch long tongue that is 1½ inches wide.

The steel square in the hands of a skilled carpenter is virtually a right angle computer, with an amazing range of applications. It can square lines for layout work, determine and mark off angles, lay out basic cuts involved in the most complicated roof framing problems—even lay out perfect circles. A full discussion of all the jobs a square can do would require a book in itself. Here, we will touch on the essentials.

The basic function of the steel square is to make an angle; and with practice, a handyman can learn to use the square to make about any angle from 0 to 90 degrees. Better squares also have rafter tables stamped in the metal of the body, and many contain tables for converting common board dimensions to board feet, for determining the length of common braces and for laying out figures with 6 or 8 equal sides.

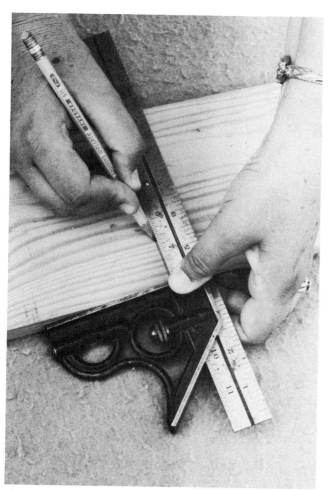

A more common use of the combination square is for marking 90 degree angles on materials, or using for a try square.

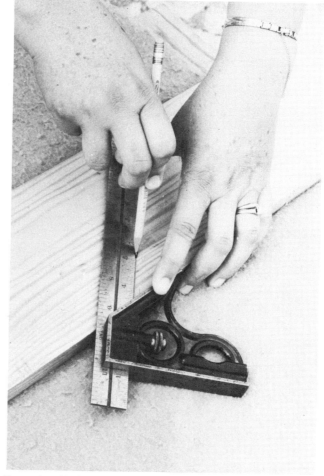

To mark a 45 degree angle, place the angled handle against the edge of the board, and make sure the blade is flat against the work.

You can use the combination square as a marking gauge. Tighten the blade to the length needed, then hold a pencil or scribe on the end of the blade and slide the tool along the material.

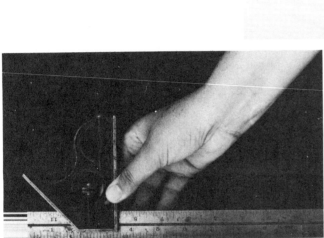

The spirit level on a combination square can be used to test surfaces for level and plumb.

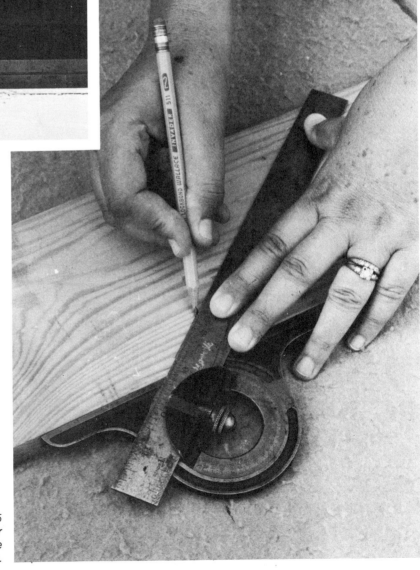

For marking angles other than 45 and 90 degrees, slide the protractor onto the combination square's blade and dial in the desired angle.

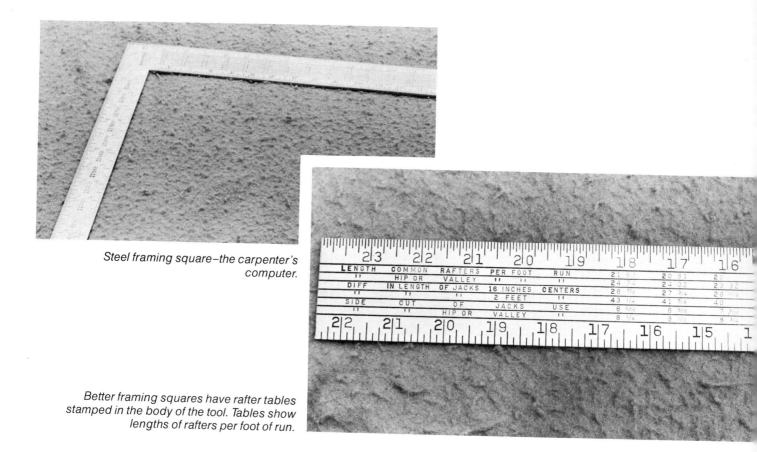

Steel framing square–the carpenter's computer.

Better framing squares have rafter tables stamped in the body of the tool. Tables show lengths of rafters per foot of run.

Suppose you want to lay out a straight stair—maybe from the basement to the first floor of your house. The place to start is to measure the height (called "rise") from the top of the floor where the stairs begin, to the top of the floor on which they are to end. Next, determine the horizontal distance (called "run") the stair will extend. For comfortable climbing, a stair should have risers, or vertical steps, of 7 to 8 inches, and treads, or horizontal steps, of 9 to 10 inches.

The next step—no pun intended—is to divide the rise, or height, by the number of stair risers desired. Let's say the rise of the total stair is 8 feet, 2 inches—98 inches—and you want to divide it into 14 equal steps, including the first and last step (Remember: there is always one more riser than the number of treads, because the last step is onto the upper floor.) The total height, 98 inches, divided by 14 risers comes out to 7 inches per riser, or vertical distance per step.

For easy figuring, let's say the run, or horizontal distance, of the entire stair will be 130 inches. Divide that by the number of "treads", or horizontal steps. In this example, there are 13 treads (one less than the number of risers, you'll recall) in the stair, which makes each tread 10 inches in width.

Now you're ready to cut the stair stringer, or carrier—the member that will support the individual steps. Place the square as shown in the illustration, so that 10 inches on the square's body touches the edge of the stringer, while the 7 inch mark on the square's tongue touches the same edge to form a 90-degree notch that is 10 by 7 inches. Repeat this procedure along the stringer for all 13 treads and 14 risers.

The bottom of the stringer should be cut to sit flat on the lower floor, and the thickness of the tread material should be deducted from the first riser, so this first step will be of the same height as all the others. At the top of the stringer, a vertical (plumb) cut should be made to fit flush with the joist of the upper floor.

The procedure for laying out common gable rafters with a steel square is much the same as for layout of a stair. Jack, hip and compound rafters require more complicated square work, and will not be covered here.

Levels

A **spirit level** is a simple tool that can tell if a surface is perfectly horizontal (level) or exactly vertical (plumb); important things to know whether you are leveling a refrigerator or plumbing a house wall.

Levels of about the same design have been around since the time ancient Eqyptians built the pyramids.

Steel square used as a try square.

A steel square can be used to mark any of 360 degrees of angle.

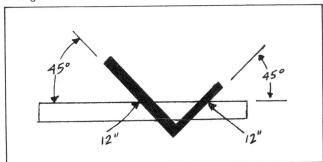

Measure the total height (rise) and length (run) of a stair to determine the height and width of each individual step.

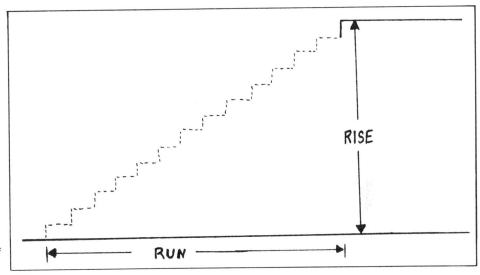

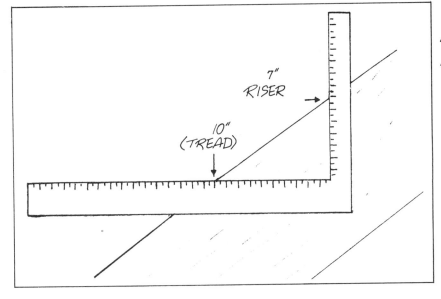

An Application of the Steel Square

Position the square so that the figure for the tread width is at one point on the stair carriage, and the figure for the riser height is on the same edge of the carriage.

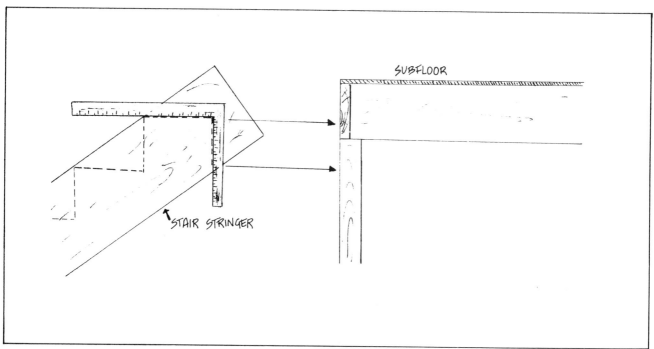

Mark a plumb cut where the stair carriage abuts the floor joist of the upper floor.

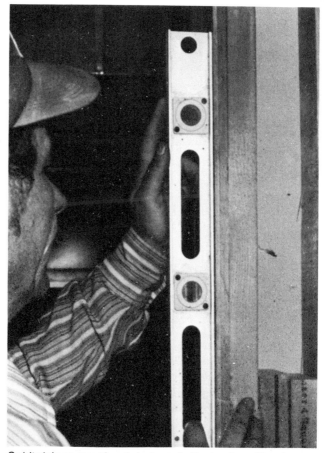

Today, however, better levels are built of hardwood, aluminum or magnesium I-beam construction. They contain sealed vials or tubes, slightly crowned and partially filled with a colored liquid (usually alcohol), with an air bubble that comes to the top when the level is held horizontally (or vertically, in the case of vials indicating plumb).

The vials are mounted so that the bubble centers on a mark, or between marks, when horizontally level or vertically plumb. Some levels have vials housed in pairs, so the tool can be used either side down for horizontal readings, or either end down for vertical readings.

Key points about a quality level are that the top and bottom surfaces be ground perfectly parallel, the vials or tubes should be easy to see, and—of course—the tool should accurately demonstrate level and plumb positions.

For a general purpose level, consider a triple vial aluminum or magnesium tool from 22 to 28 inches long. For handier use in leveling and plumbing shorter pieces of work, you may also want to own a small "torpedo" level with vials that read level, plumb and 45 degrees. If you are laying brick or concrete block, you may need a mason's level—up to 48 inches long, and usually made of brass bound hardwood.

For finding nearly horizontal planes in terracing and landscape work, a **string level** can be attached to a long cord. However, these are not accurate enough for more critical work, because the string can sag out of truly horizontal position even though the vial indicates level.

Spirit vials on most levels indicate both plumb and level; some also have a vial to indicate 45 degrees.

A chalk line is used to strike a straight line between two points.

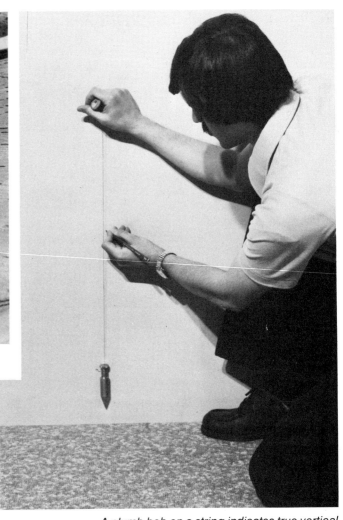

A plumb bob on a string indicates true vertical.

Other Measuring Tools

Depending on the jobs you will undertake, you may need one or more specialized measuring tools. More than 2,000 measuring tools are manufactured today—we will make mention of only the more commonly used ones.

A **plumb bob** is simply a heavy metal weight, with one end pointed, the other with a fixture to which a string can be attached. It is used to locate a point exactly below an overhead point, or to mark a vertical reference line. Suppose you want to install a post under a beam. A plumb bob can indicate the point on the floor that is directly under the section of the beam you need to support.

A **chalk line** is a piece of string or cord that has been coated with chalk. The line is stretched tightly between two points that are to be joined by a horizontal mark, then "snapped" to transfer a chalky line to the surface. You can use a piece of string rubbed with chalk, if you only need to snap a couple of lines. But for steady use, a mechanical self-chalking line is much handier. These metal boxes have a line on a reel and are filled with colored chalk powder. The line is automatically chalked each time it is withdrawn from the box. Some models have a point on the end of the box that can double as a plumb bob.

For drawing small circles and arcs, a **divider** comes in handy. Dividers have adjustable legs, usually one leg with a point and the other with an attachment to hold a pencil or scribe. To make a circle, set the divider's legs to the distance equal to the radius of the circle needed, then hold the point leg fixed and scribe the circle with the other leg. For marking and checking larger circles, use **trammel**

points, metal pins clamped to a piece of wood or metal.

To measure the depth of holes or recesses, a **depth gauge** is the tool to use. Several types are made, but the model that resembles a thin ruler with a moveable clamp to mark the distance on the gauge is accurate and economical. Even more economical is a piece of dowel, with the depth measured off on a tape or rule. **Calipers,** used to measure inside and outside diameters, resemble dividers. The simplest calipers are hinged to open and close, and can be locked in position. After the tool is adjusted to fit the object or opening being measured, the legs are locked in position, then measurements are taken off with a rule. The most precise caliper is the **micrometer caliper**—both inside and outside measuring—that can make measurements accurately to ten thousandths (0.0001) of an inch. These tools are used primarily by machinists, tool and die makers and other workmen who need extremely accurate measurements.

Precision measuring equipment is seldom needed for most home repair and maintenance chores. Shown here are, A. Thread gauge; B. Depth micrometer gauge, for finding depth of recesses; C. Inside and outside calipers; and D. micrometer calipers.

A compass can be used to scribe wall coverings and trim for a tight fit around irregular objects and surfaces.

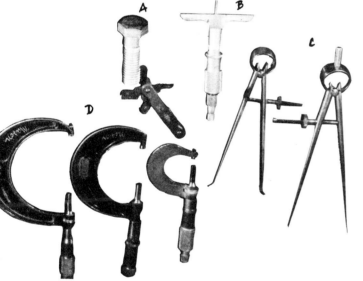

Micrometer calipers can be used to measure thicknesses to 0.0001 of an inch.

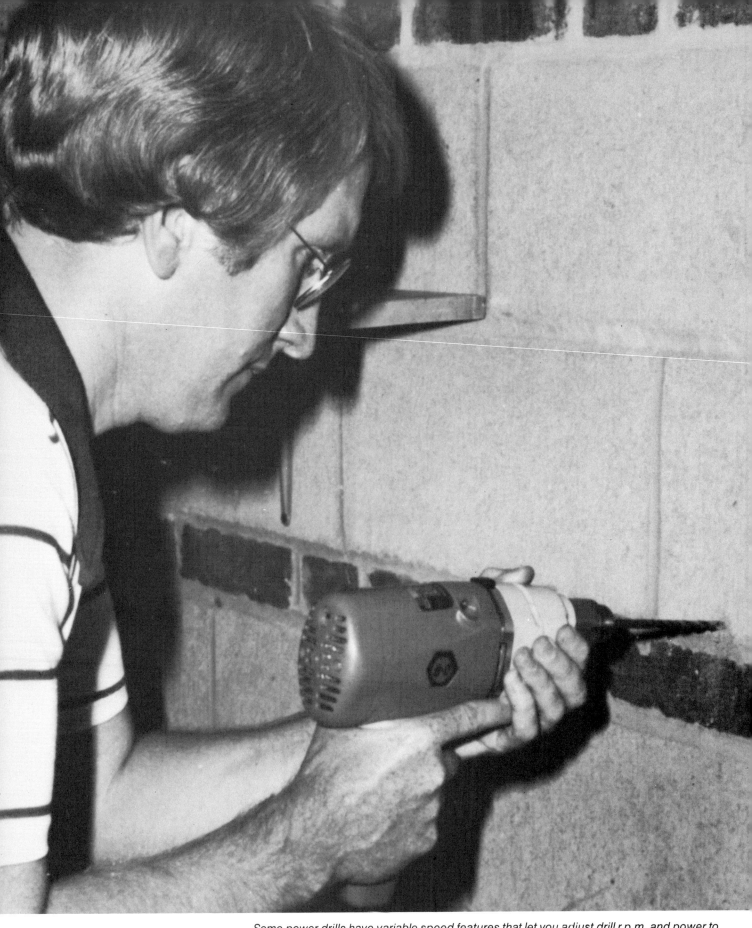

Some power drills have variable speed features that let you adjust drill r.p.m. and power to suit the material being drilled (Courtesy of Black & Decker)

6
Making a Hole in One

Few homes and workshops are without some sort of tool for drilling or boring holes in wood and other materials. While many handymen get along very well with a brace-and-bit, or perhaps a small hand push drill, an electric drill is usually among the first power tools purchased.

In fact, the ratchet action brace has been replaced in many home workshops by the power drill. But few carpenters and woodworkers rely on power hole making equipment entirely. For some applications, a bit brace or hand drill can do a more careful hole making job than an electric drill. It's handy—and extra insurance—to possess both hand and power drilling tools.

Hand Hole-Boring Tools

There are several hand tools designed for making holes in materials. But the three most popular tools for boring and drilling in wood are the bit brace, the push drill and the hand drill.

You might very well include an **awl** in this category, as it's useful for making small holes in light materials, as well as for making guide holes for larger drills or bits.

The **bit-brace** is an old, but still useful boring tool. The brace is a crank that has a chuck to hold a bit. For most wood boring, auger bits are used in a brace. The large "crank sweep" of a brace provides a great deal of torque leverage. The throw, or circle in which the crank handle turns, is about 10 inches on standard model braces, up to 14 inches in heavy duty tools.

Better quality braces have built in ratchet mechanisms that let you turn the bit in a single direction with a short back and forth motion of the crank. This is a useful feature when you're boring in cramped quarters and a full crank sweep cannot be made.

To place a bit in the brace's chuck, hold the knurled (or checked) shell of the chuck and turn the brace handle counter-clockwise to open the chuck jaws. Insert the tapered, squared tang of the bit into the chuck, and turn clockwise to tighten the jaw firmly on the bit. Make sure the

chuck jaw tightens squarely on the bit, a loose bit can damage the chuck.

A variety of bits can be used with the brace, including countersinks and reamers, expansive bits (which bore holes of several sizes), screwdrivers, nut drivers and other specialized tools, as well as auger and twist drill bits. We'll have more to say about bits and drills later.

A hand drill is useful for drilling small holes in both wood and metal. (Courtesy of Bill Mason)

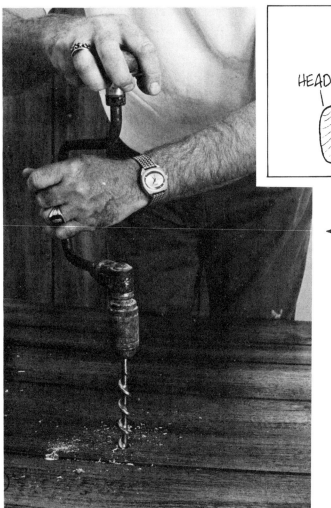

Parts of a bit-brace.

◄Hold the brace steady, to drill perpendicular to the wood surface.

A bored hole should be something more precise than a cavity in a piece of wood. It's fairly simple to bore a hole perpendicular to the work surface, once you get the knack. It's a good idea for the beginner to use a try square or other guide to make sure the bit is going straight, until you get the hang of sighting from right angles to line up the tool.

Once started in wood, the lead screw on an auger bit provides the digging in power—you just turn the crank. For vertical boring, cup the head of the brace in your left hand and turn the crank handle with your right hand. For horizontal boring, cup the head in your left hand and support the brace in a steady horizontal position with your chest or stomach.

Boring entirely through a board from one side can split and splinter the wood when the bit emerges. To avoid this problem, bore from one side only until the tip of the screw appears on the opposite side, then reverse the bit out of the wood. Turn the board over and complete the hole from the other side. This gives a clean, smooth edged hole.

Another way to prevent splintering is to clamp a piece of waste stock to the work directly over the area where the bit will exit.

Bit-braces need little care, other than keeping them dry, clean and free of rust. A few drops of light oil on moving parts and the working mechanism of the chuck should keep the tool in good condition indefinitely.

Specialized braces are made for boring holes in hard to reach places. The corner brace is a bevel geared tool with the crank sweep at about a 45 degree angle to the line of the chuck. The short brace has a short, straight handle, rather than a crank, and works with a back and forth ratchet action.

The **hand drill,** or crank drill, is operated by turning a geared crank which turns a chuck similar to that in a bit-brace. The action is similar to that of a hand operated egg beater.

The hand drill is not designed for heavy duty work. Twist drills from 1/16 inch to 1/4 inch can be used in most hand drills. Larger bits and drills, which require more torque, ordinarily are used either in a bit-brace or power drill. Since most hand drills are geared to turn the bit 2½ or 3 revolutions for each turn of the crank handle, the gear ratio gives more speed than power.

To use a hand drill, hold the vertical handle in your left hand and crank the "egg beater" handle with your right hand. Use a moderate downward pressure and hold the tool straight and steady to avoid breaking the bit.

With practice, you'll learn to coordinate the pushing pressure with the up and down movements of the crank to help hold the drill perpendicular to the drilling surface.

A larger form of the hand drill is the **breast drill,** with a breast plate at the top of the handle, against which the

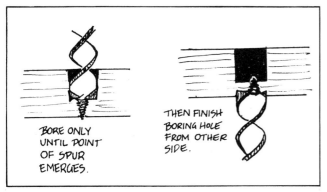

To prevent splitting and splintering the wood where an auger bit is used to bore completely through a board, bore from one side only until the tip of the lead screw appears, then turn the piece over and finish boring the hole from the other side.

operator braces his chest or shoulder. Most breast drills take twist drills up to ½ inch, and also use auger bits. Better quality breast drills have a "gear shift" sort of selector that changes the gear ratio from 3:1 to 1:1, depending on the size of bit used and the material being drilled.

The **push drill** spins its fluted bit as you push downward on the handle. A spirally threaded shaft spins each time the handle is pushed. When the pressure is released, a spring returns the handle for the next drilling stroke.

A push drill ordinarily is used with light, easily drilled materials. Bits and drills used with a push drill are typically ¼ inch and smaller. The drill can be operated with one hand, while you hold the work with the other hand.

The push drill has rather limited application for most householders and wood workers, but comes in handy for drilling sheet rock, plaster or other materials that would dull more expensive types of drills.

Power Drills

The electric drill often is the first power tool purchased for household use. It's one of the more versatile power tools, and is a good choice for the first in your kit.

The most common use of the electric drill is to make holes in materials, by driving drilling bits into wood, metal, plastic and other materials. However, with a variety of attachments and accessories, the power drill can also serve as a sander, polisher, grinder—even as a saw.

Electric drills are sized by the maximum diameter of the drill bit shank that can be clamped in the chuck. The ¼ inch drill is a popular size for most household and home workshop use, for drilling as well as light sanding and polishing. The ¼ inch drill's chuck has little bearing on the size hole the tool can drill, as drill bits of various sizes are made with ¼ inch shanks.

Power drills with ⅜ inch chucks are somewhat heavier duty, although many of them have the same size motor as a corresponding ¼ inch drill. For heavier work, a ½ inch drill delivers up to ¾ horsepower and accommodates several attachments for operations other than drilling. Three-quarter inch drills are commonly used for industrial and construction applications.

In general, the larger the drill, the slower the drilling speed in revolutions per minute (r.p.m.). Larger drills are designed to run at slower speeds because more torque is needed. A ¼ inch drill may run at 2,000 to 2,250 r.p.m. at full "no-load" speed, while a ½ inch drill turns at about 600 r.p.m.

Some drills have a fixed single speed of rotation. Others have a "high and low" two-speed setting. Better quality drills often have variable speeds from zero to maximum r.p.m., to accommodate the type of drilling or other operation. Some have a combination drilling and hammering

This drill features both drilling action and a jack-hammer sort of reciprocating action. (Courtesy of Black & Decker)

action, to provide a "jack-hammer" sort of driving when drilling masonry and other hard substances.

The work you need to do will guide your selection. However, if you will use the drill extensively for heavy-duty drilling and other drill adapted functions, a top grade variable speed drill is a good investment. Avoid buying inexpensive drills; even those made by major tool manufacturers. It may have the motor and gear case enclosed in a single housing that is divided in halves longitudinally, whereas a better quality drill will have separate housings for motor and gear box, with the two housings bolted together.

Also, be sure the tool is double insulated, to help insure against short circuits and electric shock.

Most smaller drills (½ inch and under) have a pistol grip type handle, with perhaps an auxiliary handle at right angles to the drill chuck, toward the font of the gear case housing. On larger drills, the rear handle may be a combination handhold and breastplate sort of fixture.

Electric drills are controlled by a trigger switch. Variable speed models increase in r.p.m. as the trigger is squeezed. On some variable speed models, a trigger lock sets the r.p.m. at any desired speed. Some drills also have a reversing switch feature, for backing out auger bits and removing screws (with a screwdriver bit in the chuck).

Power drills feature two types of chucks. Smaller drills occasionally are equipped with a threaded, cam-type chuck, similar to that on a bit-brace, that is tightened by hand. Larger drills have a geared chuck that is tightened by a bevel geared chuck key.

To load a bit in the drill, open the chuck, (by turning its outer barrel counter-clockwise) until the bit shank can be inserted. Then, tighten the chuck by hand until the jaws grip the bit. Check to make sure the jaws are well seated on the bit shank, then insert the key in one of the holes in the chuck so that the key's gear meshes with the geared end of the chuck. Turn the key clockwise for a firm tightening, then remove the key from the chuck.

Caution: Don't forget to remove the key. If the drill is started with the key left in the chuck, the key can fly out and cause injury.

To drill a hole, first make a starting hole precisely where you want it. In wood, use an awl or small punch to make an indentation. In metal, use a center punch. If you are drilling a large hole in metal, you may need to enlarge the punched indentation with a small twist drill, then use a larger twist drill to bore the size hole you need.

Always firmly clamp or support the work being drilled, especially when drilling smaller pieces of work. A bit can "grab" the piece and spin it before you can remove your finger from the trigger switch.

Apply only moderate pressure when drilling. The drill motor should operate at close to full r.p.m. Relax the pres-

Change drills in geared chucks by loosening the chuck with a special key. To keep from losing the chuck key, tape it to the cord. Be sure to remove the key from the chuck before starting the drill.

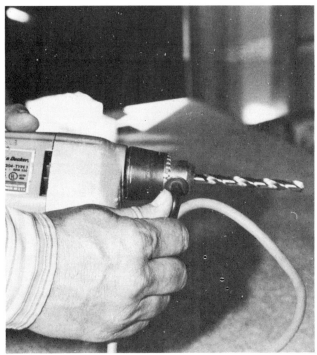

sure when the bit is about to emerge from the opposite side of the work, particularly when drilling metal. If the bit is turning too slowly, it can catch on the metal and jam or break. So back off on the pushing pressure, so the drill motor is running at close to full speed when the bit emerges.

When drilling metal, lubricate the bit to help cool the cutting edges and produce a smoother finished hole. A small amount of kerosene and light machine oil mixed together makes a good lubricant for drilling softer metals. Drilling in wood requires no lubrication.

Drill guides of several different designs are available from hardware stores. These can be used with twist drills to help you drill a hole that is precisely perpendicular to the work surface. You can even buy an attachment that turns your portable electric drill into a drill press.

For making large holes in wood, a variety of expansive bits, wood boring bits and hole saws let you make holes up to three inches in diameter; all with your power drill. For specialized work, such as drilling for doorknob-and-lock sets, guides and templates are available both from drill manufacturers and from makers of door hardware. Be sure you choose the correct guide or template for the type of door lock you are installing, of course.

Accessories available for most drill models can convert the tool to a circular saw, saber saw, hacksaw or router; to a sander, polisher, grinder or paint mixer. While these seldom work as efficiently as a tool designed specifically for these functions, you may want to consider them if you have only a limited amount of work to do.

You can also buy attachments for your drill to let you drill holes at right angles to the drill; extensions and "step-down" gearing accessories also add to the tool's versatility.

When using an electric drill with sawing, sanding, polishing or grinding accessories, use enough pressure to make the tool work, but not enough to slow the motor r.p.m. appreciably. Because these attachments are larger in diameter than most drilling bits, they can put more "drag" on the drill motor. When using a power drill for any of these functions, check to make sure the motor does not overheat. If you smell the acrid odor of scorched insulation, some damage probably has already been done. It's better to test the motor housing with your hand at frequent intervals. If the housing heats to where it is uncomfortably warm, stop the drill and let it cool.

Drill Press

While special stands can convert your portable power drill to a fairly efficient bench drill press, you may have need for a stationary drill press in your workshop; particularly if you will be drilling heavier metals.

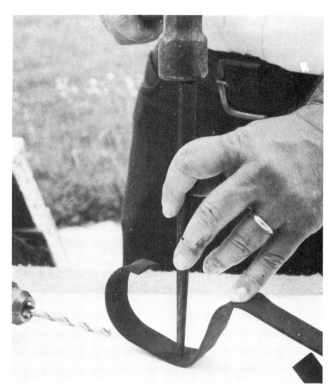

Make starter holes in metal with a center punch; in wood with an awl. This lets you start the drill in exactly the right spot.

Accessories turn your electric drill into a sander, wire brush, buffer, polisher—even a sabre saw.

The drill press has a great many other applications, too—with a variety of accessories. It's a versatile power tool for working with all kinds of materials, including wood.

A drill press has four basic parts. A base, usually of cast metal, supports the machine. A polished steel column is fitted with an adjustable table (where the work is held) and a movable motor driven drilling head. Most drill presses are belt driven, with multiple V-belt pulleys for varying the drill r.p.m.

With a host of accessories, a drill press can plane, mortise, rout, shape and sand wood. It can accurately drill holes in pipe and other metal shapes.

Be prepared to spend $350 or more for a drill press, with electric motor. If you're planning that kind of investment, you'll no doubt want to do some scouting for the machine that suits your purposes.

Bits and Drills

Auger bits can be used in both hand and power tools to bore holes in wood from ¼ inch to 2 inches in diameter. The threaded feed screw at the end of the bit controls the rate of advance into the wood. Raised spurs on opposite sides of the screw score the wood fibers and outline the hole. The chisel shaped cutters actually pare away the wood, which is carried out of the hole by the bit's twist.

In a well designed bit, the different parts are not performing one at a time, but in unison. Each part—screw, spurs, cutters and twist (or throat)—must be sized and shaped correctly in relation to the others.

For this reason, an auger bit is something more than a tool that makes a hole in wood. The bit should carry itself into the hole, cut a clean hole, remove the chips and turn easily without undue pressure on the brace or drill.

Twist Drills

Much the same is true of twist drills; used for drilling metal, wood and other materials. For metal, the cutting edges at the business end of the drill are ground at about a 60 degree angle on either side, to form about a 120 degree point for most metal drilling work. Wood drilling bits usually are ground to a sharper point, perhaps 60 to 80 degrees.

The chisel shaped cutting edge is sloped about 12 to 14 degrees back toward the trailing edge of the drill tip. The idea is that only the cutting edge, or "lip," makes contact with the material being drilled.

Power Boring Bits

Flat boring bits are made for use in power drills and drill presses, to bore into wood. These spade type bits are made in sizes from ¼ inch to 1½ inches. a similar, but

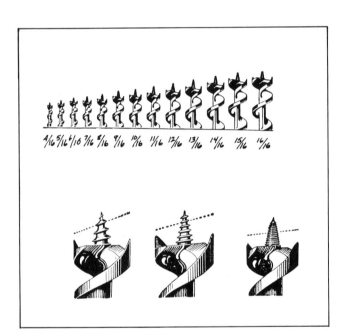

Wood-boring auger bits.

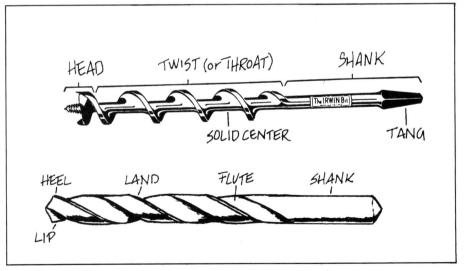

Parts of an auger bit (above) and twist drill.

larger bit with cutting spurs is used to bore doors for lock sets.

Expansive Bits

Expansive bits are adjustable wood boring bits with a single spur cutter that an be extended various distances from the lead screw, to bore holes of several different sizes with the same bit. In this way, one expansive bit can take the place of several large bits.

Most adjustable size bits are made to be used in bitbraces and drill presses. Hand held electric drills should be used with power boring bits or hole saws to make larger holes in wood. If you own a variable speed electric drill, you may use an expansive bit at low r.p.m., but the bit is by design unbalanced in weight, and should not be used at high r.p.m.

To set the expansive bit, a screwdriver is used to loosen a set screw, which allows the cutter to be adjusted to the desired setting. Then, the set-screw is tightened and the bit chucked in a brace or drill press and used as any other bor-

High-speed twist drills are made in various sizes and lengths; often, it's cheaper to buy a set of drills —perhaps in a storage case—than one at a time.

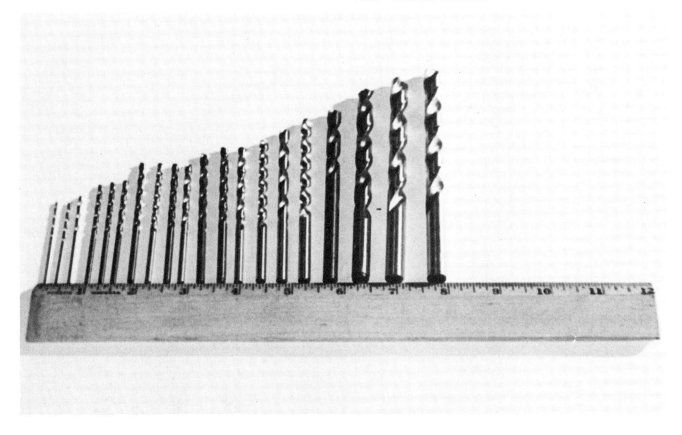

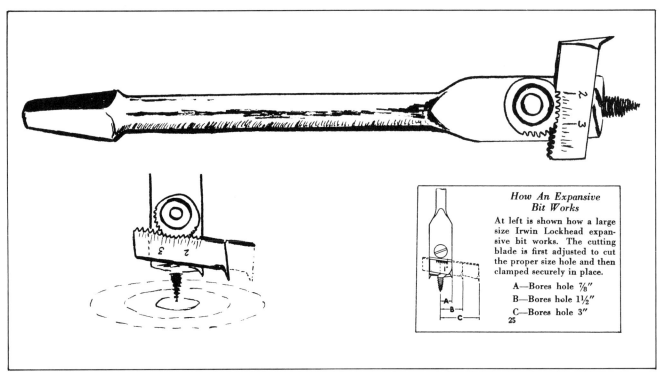

An expansive bit adjusts to cut holes of several sizes with one tool.

ing bit. Some expansive bits have a dial, rather than a set screw, for adjustment.

Better quality expansive bits can be accurately adjusted and locked in place. Still, it's a good idea to test the setting by boring a hole in a piece of scrap wood. Remember: moving the cutter by 1/32 inch actually changes the diameter of the hole bored by 1/16 inch...or 1/32 inch on both sides.

Specialized Bits

A number of special purpose bits are made for use in both hand and power drills. Among these are **hole saws,** with saw teeth on a circular band of steel, guided by a twist drill in the center.

Countersinks widen screw holes so that flat-head screws may be driven flush with the work surface. **Reamer** bits are for trimming off the burrs left by a pipe cutter on metal pipe and electrical conduit. **Plug-cutters** remove round sections of wood that can be used as short dowel pieces in furniture construction and other woodwork.

Screwdriver bits, in standard and Phillips types and several sizes, convert both hand and power drills to power screwdrivers.

Auger bits and twist drills require little care, with proper use. Moisture from hands, or sap from green wood, can

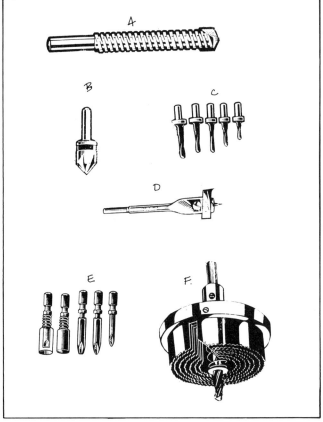

Specialized bits: A. Carbide tipped masonry drill; B. High speed countersink; C. Stanley "Screwmate" to drill pilot holes for screws; D. Expandable bits let you dial any size hole from 5/8 inch to 1½ inches; E. Screwdriver bits; and F. Hole saw chucks into drill to cut holes from an inch to 2½ inches.

cause rust spots on bits and drills. To prevent this, wipe the tools now and then with a lightly oiled rag.

One of the more practical features in the care of bits—as with any cutting tool—is to have a good place to store them. Don't keep bits and drills loose in a tool box or drawer.

In Chapter 23, we talk about filing and grinding auger bits and twist drills. For right now, all we will say on the subject is: don't over do it. Removing too much material or removing material from the wrong place will affect a bit's boring ability.

We also make one departure from our counsel to always buy quality tools. If you have rough material to drill, that would likely dull or damage bits or twist drills, buy a "cheapie" for the job, then discard it when the job is finished.

The workbench, with vises and bench stops, is the principal "holding" tool for most home-owners. (Courtesy of Belsaw)

7
Holding It

Like measuring and marking, holding and supporting the work is basic to most other functions: sawing, planing drilling, fastening, gluing, soldering, etc. In fact, this section might well have been included with Chapter 5, on measuring and marking tools, as many "holding" tools also double as jigs and guides.

Generally, holding, clamping and supporting tools can be classified into "fixed" and "portable" devices. A vise, for example, is usually mounted on a bench in a fixed position. A C-clamp, on the other hand, is easily portable to bind or press parts together in about any location.

Some holding and supporting tools, such as saw-horses, jacks, bench stops and saddles are fairly portable, but are generally used in a fixed position.

Fixed Holding Tools

The workbench, in all its variations, is probably the principal stationary supporting equipment for most wood and metal working jobs. We'll talk more about workbenches in Chapter 20.

However, a major feature of most workbenches is a **vise**—either a wood vise, machinist's vise, pipe vise or

Wood vises are made with replaceable wooden inserts; many have quick release features.

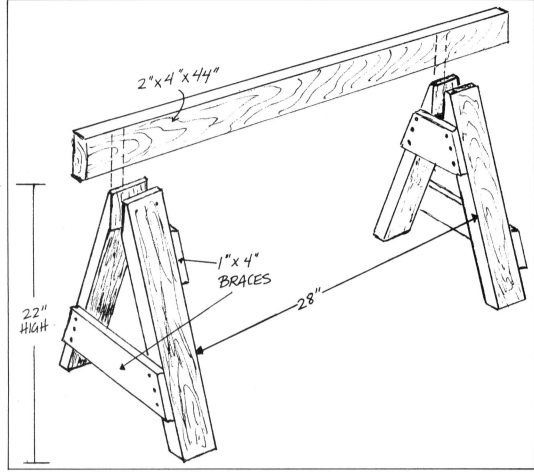

2"x 4"x 44"

1"x 4"
BRACES

22"
HIGH

28"

You can build saw-horses to suit your particular needs, and it's a good practice for novice woodworkers.

some other variety of this jawed holding tool. A wood vise usually is mounted at one corner of the workbench, with the top jaws of the vise flush with the top of the bench. Better made wood vises have a "dog" that can be extended above the level of the bench, to hold work that is too wide to be clamped in the vise itself.

A machinist's vise commonly is mounted at a front corner of the workbench, and is bolted to the top of the bench. The location of the vise should allow ample room for holding long work pieces.

Most vises are opened and closed by a heavy bolt with screw threads. Wood vises have replaceable wood jaws that open from 6 to 12 inches to hold most work pieces for sawing, sanding, planing and other operations. Some have quick disconnect features for rapid opening and closing.

The machinist's vise has two parallel iron jaws—coated with nylon on some models—with a wide throat opening to allow as much working room as possible. Most machinist's vise jaws have patterned inner edges that should be covered when clamping wood and soft metals, to prevent marring the work.

What kind of vise should you buy? For general work, a 3½ or 4 inch machinist's vise of good quality is a wise first choice. It can do most holding jobs of other, more specialized vises, and is rugged enough for metal work as well. Choose a vise with a tight screw action that is free of "wobble" but still easy to turn. On better quality vises, most of the working parts are replaceable.

Later, if you're doing a lot of woodwork, you may want to buy or build a wood vise to mount on the opposite corner of your workbench. These usually come without the hardwood jaws that actually hold the work, but are drilled and tapped to receive the wooden jaw inserts.

Clamp-on or bolt-on vises are available for mounting on saw-horses or other temporary supports.

Semi-Portable Holders

The **saw-horse** (saw-horses, actually—you'll need two) is a handy piece of equipment that often can double as a workbench. You can build your saw-horses out and

DOG

WOODVISE

Top view of work-bench shows how to locate holes for bench stop.

out, as in the accompanying sketch, or you can buy saw-horse brackets, metal supports that accept 2-by-4 boards to form the legs and top.

Whichever route you choose, make your saw-horses sturdy and wide enough to adequately support 4-by-8 sheets of plywood and paneling. When cutting lightweight plywood and other 4-by-8 foot sheets, lay several two inch thick boards across the saw-horses to give more support to the material.

The **bench stop** is a handy fixture if you're doing much bench work, especially planing. It generally is used in conjunction with a wood vise to hold work securely to the workbench. The "dog" at the top of the movable vise jaw is raised to hold one edge of the work, while the bench stop is located to hold the other edge. See the accompanying sketch for details of how to align bench-stop holes with the wood vise.

A similar tool is a **bench hook,** which is merely a two-inch board with a V-groove cut into one end. The bench hook is nailed or screwed to the workbench to hold the end of a board for edge planing, sanding, etc.

Other semi-portable holding tools include the **miter vise,** such as those for cutting 45 degree angles in molding and picture framing materials; **bar clamps,** which screw onto threaded steel pipe to make a clamp of almost unlimited length. Other specialized holding tools are used with drill presses, table saws and similar power workshop equipment.

Portable Clamping and Holding Tools

Many different types of clamps are manufactured, each designed to solve a different holding problem. Which you choose will be dictated by the kind of clamping you need.

Start off by purchasing only those types of clamps that will have wide application in your work. Two pairs of C-clamps, in different sizes, will see a lot of work in any household or home workshop; as will a pair of spring clamps. Beyond that, acquire clamps only as you need them for special purposes.

Carriage makers' **C-clamps** are probably the most widely used. Named for the shape of the clamp frame, C-clamps are made in various sizes and come in handy for

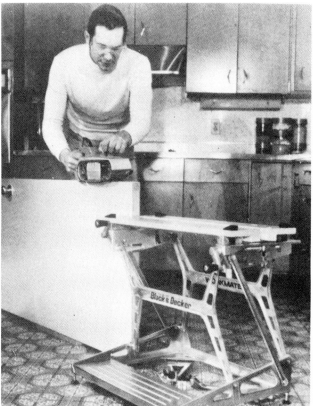

Portable "workmate" doubles as bench, vise and clamps.
(Courtesy of Black & Decker)

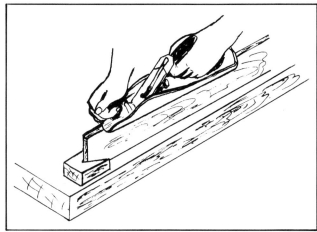

A block with a V-shaped notch in one end makes a good way to hold a board for edge planing.

woodworkers, hobbyists, model makers and handymen in general.

The C-clamp has one fixed jaw and one adjustable jaw, moved by a threaded screw. The moveable jaw has an anvil on a ball joint swivel, which makes the clamp self-aligning to most work surfaces.

C-clamps are sized by the maximum opening of the jaws, and are made in sizes from one inch to 24 inches. The depth, or throat, of the clamp is also important, as it determines how far from the edge of the work the clamp can be attached. Regular C-clamps have throat depths from 1 to 16 inches.

For wood and other soft materials being clamped, place thin blocks of wood between the work piece and the clamp anvils to protect the work. Then, tighten the clamp's T-bar handle only hand tight. Don't use a pliers or section of pipe on the handle. If you're clamping work that has been glued, be certain not to tighten the clamp so much that all the glue is squeezed out of the joint.

Wood **handscrew** clamps are made of two heavy pieces of hardwood connected by parallel threaded bolts. These are used principally to clamp pieces of wood together for gluing.

Handscrews vary in opening widths from 2 to 14 inches. The handles of the screw spindles or bolts are located on opposite jaws, so that the clamp can be opened and closed quickly with a "pedaling" sort of motion. To be effective, the jaws of a handscrew should be maintained parallel or flush against the work while clamping.

Among the more useful clamps you'll need is the simple **spring clamp.** Designed on the lines of the spring clothespin, spring clamps come in lengths of four, six and eight inches. They are particularly handy for clamping round or odd-shaped pieces, and as a "third hand" to hold work for soldering, welding, etc.

A **band clamp** consists of a canvas band that is tightened by a hand screw. It is used primarily for clamping round or odd-shaped work. A variation is the **column clamp,** which encloses circular and irregular shaped work with a chain that is tightened at one end. For much the same kind of clamping job, a **strap clamp** (also called a "web" clamp) employs a strip of nylon webbing and a ratchet and pawl tightening mechanism.

Care and Maintenance

Vises and clamps that employ screw tightening mechanisms should have the screw and other moving parts cleaned and lubricated with oil occasionally. Jaws of clamps and machinist's vises should be cleaned with steel wool or a wire brush now and then, to remove dirt and chips.

When using clamps to hold work being glued, a light coating of wax on screws and jaws will keep glue from sticking to the tools. Don't store wooden jawed clamps and vises with the jaws tightly closed; wood can expand with

Handscrew clamps find many uses around the home and shop.

Small metal handscrews, midget versions of wood handscrews, are useful for holding metal parts for assembling, soldering and welding. (Courtesy of Bill Mason)

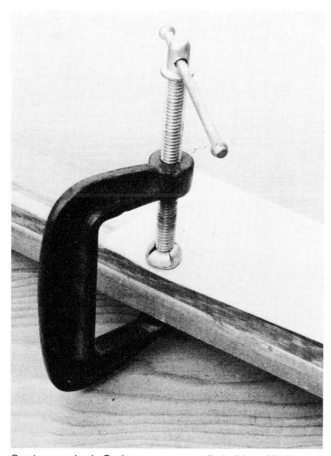

Carriage maker's C-clamps are versatile holders. You'll want to protect finish work from being marred by the clamp.

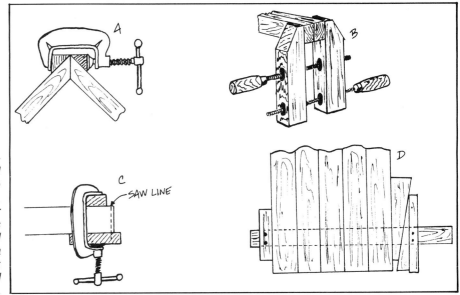

For some jobs, you may need to improvise clamps: A. C-clamp and blocks cut to 45 degree angles make a pinch-hitting miter clamp; B. Handscrews can be used with other pieces of wood to make various clamping jigs; C. Scrap wood held by a C-clamp lets you make a smooth cut when shortening a door; D. Braces and wedges can hold flatwork for glueing.

Spring clamps hold a straight edge as a sawing guide for this builder.

changes in temperature and humidity. When the wooden jaw inserts of a wood vise become scratched and scarred, you can remove them, plane them smooth and re-install them on the vise.

Make-Your-Own Clamps

Even with the wide variety of clamps at the hardware store, it would be surprising if you found exactly the clamping device you'll need for every job you undertake. In many cases, you can improvise a clamp or holding jig to do a better job than any commercial clamp you can find. Here are a few suggestions:

- Clothespins and alligator clips can be used to hold small parts for soldering or gluing. Hold one handle of the clothespin or clip in a vise, or screw it to a block of scrap wood or to the workbench.
- For clamping circular work, a rope tourniquet can be fashioned that will hold the work as securely as a band clamp. Make several wraps and tighten the tourniquet by twisting a stick or rod in one loop of the rope. For holding such work as a rung being replaced between chair legs, a single loop of rope with a stick twisted in it holds securely.
- Rubber bands are handy for clamping smaller circular work for gluing. Or, you can make clamps for larger work from old auto inner tubes.
- Wedges and brace pieces can be used to clamp wide flat work for sanding and gluing.
- To hold a round bar or metal pipe for drilling or alignment, make a holder by bolting two parallel pieces of pipe together, then place the round work in the curved space made by the two joined pieces of pipe.
- For some work, merely stacking weight on the pieces will hold them while glue sets.

8
Timber-Cutting Tools

More and more energy conscious Americans are cutting their own winter fuel for wood-burning stoves, fireplaces and furnaces. If you're one of that growing army to invade the woods and forests, you'll want to choose good, safe, dependable tools to turn trees into toe-warming firewood.

Your selection of timber working tools will depend on how much wood you cut and where you cut it. Keep in mind the designed functions of various tools as you pick and choose those that let you gather your winter wood safely and efficiently. Saws are designed to cut across the grain, severing the wood fibers at right angles to the way the tree grows. Axes do their best work obliquely, at an angle to the grain, and should be selected for edge-holding ability and balance. Wedges split the wood along the grain, forcing apart the wood fibers.

If you saw up limbs and small trees, and perhaps split an occasional log, you can get along very well with hand tools. A good quality bow saw or buck saw is adequate for light

sawing. A long handled sledge and a couple of steel wedges, along with an axe, can handle most splitting chores. You can acquire these tools brand new for less than $50, and may pick them up for considerably less at farm sales or community auctions.

You can do heavier duty wood cutting and splitting with only those tools listed above. But your hours in the woods will be more productive if you add a power saw to the list. For heavy timber work, you'll need sturdier (and more expensive) equipment.

Let's start with the biggest and most costly timber tool you're apt to purchase: the chain saw. Chain saws are powered by both two cycle gasoline engines and 115-volt electric motors. If most of your wood cutting takes place at distances beyond the reach of extension cords, you'll need the former.

But don't discount the usefulness of an electric chain saw. An electric saw costs considerably less than a similar

Timber working tools include, from the top clockwise: cant hook, chain saw, one-man crosscut saw, ratchet winch, log chain, sledge and wedges, double-bit axe, broad axe.

gasoline model, is lighter weight for the same length cutter bar and has a good many uses other than cutting firewood. Many builders own an electric chain saw to cut heavy timbers and framing members. This kind of saw also comes in handy when you're building fences of split rails or post-and-pole construction.

And, if you don't have access to a timber supply, you may be able to use an electric chain saw to save money on purchased firewood. Suppose wood cutters in your area charge $60 per cord (the equivalent of a stack of wood 4 by 4 by 8 feet, or 128 cubic feet of wood) for firewood cut to 18 or 24 inch lengths. By doing some dickering, you may be able to haggle the price down to, say, $50 per cord for wood cut into 8 foot poles.

The wood cutter has fewer saw cuts to make, and fewer pieces to handle when loading and hauling the longer wood. With an electric saw, you can convert 8-foot-long poles into stove or fireplace length wood for only a few cents' worth of electricity and a little time.

In much the same way, you may fell trees and saw wood into poles out in the timber, then drag or haul the poles to a central woodyard near an electrical outlet and use an electric saw to buck the poles into firewood. This lets you do the felling, limbing and preliminary cutting with hand tools and still gives you the benefit of a mechanized saw for most of the "sawing-up" chores.

Buy a quality electric saw with a 14 inch cutter bar, if you will use it to cut much firewood. Choose a tool with at least a 1.75 horsepower motor that is double insulated to prevent electric shock. For added safety, select a saw that has a trigger lock-out key to prevent accidental starts.

However, if you're taking to the woods, you will likely need a gasoline powered saw. This is particularly true if you're the sole member of your wood cutting crew. Again, choose on the basis of quality. A first line chain saw will cost in the neighborhood of $250; a cheaper model only a few dollars less—and there's a great deal of reliability difference in the two.

Commonly-used tools to take to the woods are chainsaw (with combination screwdriver/ wrench for tightening chain tension), axe, hammer and wedges for splitting.

Clear area around base of tree of brush, sticks and rocks before starting to saw.

immediately stops the chain should the saw kick upward or backward.

Most first line saws built today have anti-vibration handle mountings, and rubber cushioned handles. From the standpoint of user comfort, this is a valuable feature, although vibration still is transmitted.

Other features are mainly a matter of personal choice, or what is included in the saw package you wish to buy. Some chain bars are equipped with sprockets in the nose; some saws have "automatic" sharpeners built in.

Control positions vary from saw to saw. The best way to get familiar with a new saw is to have the dealer perform a "show-and-do" bit, then stand by while you practice. Don't worry about what the dealer thinks of "walking" you through the starting and sawing procedures with the machine.

When you get the saw home, go through the owner's manual until you can instantly find each and every control on the machine. Then, practice the start-up sequence a few times without actually firing up the engine: pump the manual chain oiler; turn on the ignition; depress the compression release button (if your saw has one); lock the throttle in the open position, pull the choke and brace the saw firmly with the chain well away from your leg and other objects.

Unless you're doing very heavy-duty timber work, a saw with a 16 inch bar is large enough. You can safely fell trees up to 30 inches in diameter with a saw of this size, and you'll appreciate the lighter weight when you've been in the woods for three or four hours.

A 16 inch saw with a three cubic inch displacement engine weighs about 15 pounds. That doesn't sound like much weight to tote around, but after a half-day of hard sawing, even a lightweight saw will put you in touch with muscles you didn't know you owned.

If you're buying your first chain saw, check with professional loggers and wood cutters in your area. Which saw do they prefer? Why? The pros will point out features they like about their favorites and—just as important—give you clues on dealer reliability.

What features should you look for in a gasoline-powered saw? First, check the engine size in relation to cutter bar length. A 16 inch saw should be powered by at least a three-cubic-inch engine. An automatic chain oiler should be high on your checklist, too. And buy a saw with an anti-kickback brake. This safety feature is attached to a "wrap-around" bar just in front of the forward handle, and

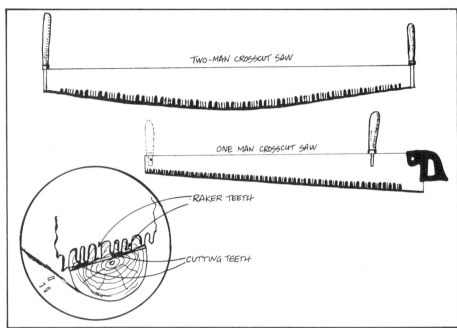

Manual crosscut saws are made for both two-man and one-man operation. One-man crosscuts can be fitted with a handle for two-man sawing.

After you've done this often enough that the sequence comes more or less automatically, you're ready to yank the starter rope. The engine will start with a terrific roar, and with the throttle locked wide open, the chain starts turning immediately.

When using a chain saw—electric or gasoline powered—keep in mind that those cutter teeth on the chain will chew through flesh and bone as readily as through wood. If you'll be sawing steadily for a considerable time, you may want to wear ear plugs to screen out the saw's higher decibels. The Occupational Safety and Health Administration (OSHA) lists chain saw noise as potentially damaging to hearing.

Remember that engine-driven chain saws require the engine lubricating oil to be mixed with the fuel. The oil-gasoline ratio is critical. The owner's manual will tell you the proper mix to use in your saw's engine. To insure that the oil is mixed well, it's a good idea to first mix the oil with about a fourth of the total amount of gasoline, then pour this mixture into the rest of the fuel. Each time you refuel the saw, shake the gasoline container several times to make sure the oil is mixed evenly.

Because the engine runs most of the time in a cloud of sawdust, the carburetor air filter on a chain saw should be cleaned often. Remove the filter carefully, so no sawdust or chips fall into the carburetor, and blow the dirt from the filter with compressed air. Most air filters have rubber or composition gaskets; soaking them in solvent will soften and damage this material.

Don't throw away your hand wood-cutting saws, even if you do most of your firewood work with powered saws. If you have a strong-armed partner to take to the woods, you can cut a lot of wood in a day's time with a two handled crosscut saw.

Or, you can go it alone with a one-man crosscut—if you can find one of these tools. You may have to search some to find a manual crosscut saw, even in timber country. One-man saws are equipped with a handsaw type handle, and are not as likely to bend and buckle when pushed and pulled from one end. They are shorter than two-man saws—about five to 5½ feet—and are made of heavier metal.

Two-man crosscuts are 5½ to seven feet long, and have cutting teeth alternated with rakers to remove sawdust from the kerf. These saws are of thin, tempered steel and, in the hands of experienced sawyers, can slice through a large tree trunk in a remarkably short time.

For cutting smaller trees and limbs, a bow saw with a Swedish steel blade held in a metal frame hacksaw fashion is a handy one-man tool. A bow saw typically has a thin blade, with little or no "set" in the teeth. This makes them a less than ideal tool for heavy cutting, but you'll find a great many uses for such a saw: pruning, triming, cutting small firewood, etc.

A buck saw is similar to a bow saw, except that the blade is slightly heavier and is held in a wooden framework that also serves as a saw handle.

Felling a Tree

Whatever kind of saw you use, the procedure for getting a standing tree safely on the ground is the same. If all trees grew perfectly straight, with symmetrical placement of their branches, well away from other trees that might snag and

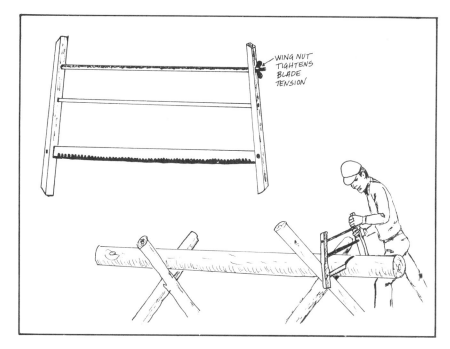

WING NUT
TIGHTENS
BLADE
TENSION

Bucksaw, as the name implies, is used most often to buck logs into firewood lengths.

hang another as it fell, sawing down timber would be a fairly simple matter. You'd merely make a notch or undercut in the direction you wished the tree to fall, then move to the opposite side of the trunk and make the felling cut (or backcut) and the tree would topple precisely where you wanted it. Unhappily, trees don't all grow exactly vertical, with evenly spaced, uniform limbs. They lean and crook and have heavy, lopsided branches.

A felling wedge, made of hard rubber, plastic or wood, is almost a necessity when you're sawing down standing trees. You *can* use a steel wedge, but these can be pretty hard on your saw, should the saw teeth come in contact with the wedge.

As the saw cuts into the tree on the felling cut, insert the wedge in the kerf opposite the notch and give it a couple of taps with the sledge. Saw some more, then tap the wedge again. This widens the saw kerf behind the blade, and serves two important functions: (1) it prevents the tree trunk from rocking back to close the kerf and bind the saw; and (2) it "pries" the tree over in the direction you want it to fall. You probably won't need to use a wedge with most smaller trees. Study the illustrations for the correct position of the notch, felling cut and wedge or wedges when cutting trees with different felling problems.

Swedish steel bow saw can be used for light and medium-duty firewood cutting; also comes in handy for pruning and trimming chores.

Plan a safe escape route before felling a tree, regardless of the kind of saw used. Here, the woodcutter steps behind a neighboring tree as the sawed tree starts to topple. Be on the watch also for dead limbs that may break off the tree as it starts to fall.

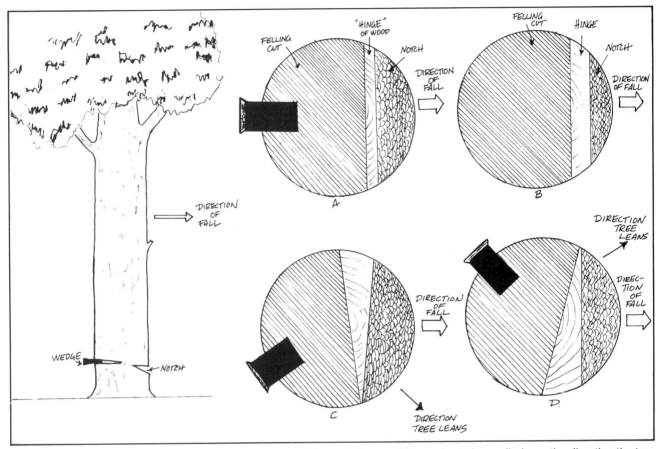

Different trees pose different felling problems, due to heavy limbs or the direction the tree leans. Above, A represents a straight tree with uniform limbs; it can be notched and felled in about any direction desired. B, a leaning tree should be felled in the direction it leans, if at all possible; cut a shallow notch because the tree will start to fall sooner than one that stands more nearly vertical. C, to "pull" a tree away from the direction it leans, make the notch cut in the direction you wish the tree to fall, then make the felling cut as shown, sawing in more on the side toward the direction of lean and use a wedge to help push the tree over in the direction you wish it to go. D, is the reverse situation of C, when a tree leans in the opposite direction.

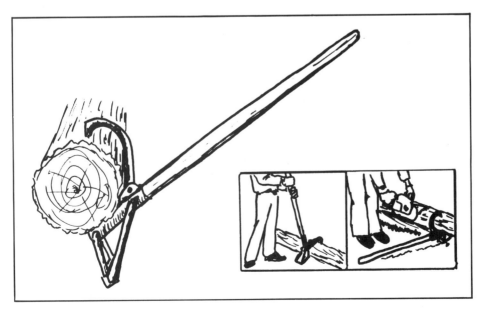

A log lifter helps raise logs off the ground for sawing off firewood cuts.

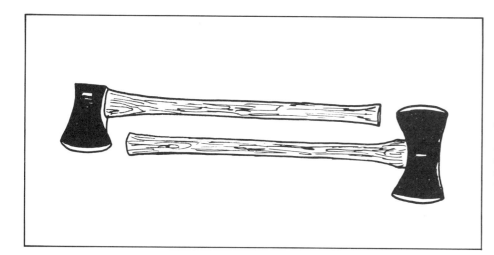

Whether a woodsman chooses a single- or double-bitted axe is mainly a matter of preference and which he becomes accustomed to using. An axe with a 3½ to four pound head and a 36-inch handle is the best choice for timber work.

Bucking up a Tree

Once you have a tree on the ground, the most immediate chore will probably be to lop off smaller branches. The author uses an axe to clear away smaller limbs at the *top* of the fallen tree, then works back along the limbs to the main trunk, sawing firewood-size limbs to length as he goes. This is a procedure born of one-man wood-cutting, where no helpers were available to help pry the heavy tree trunk off the ground. This method leaves the main part of the tree as one long log that can be moved or blocked up more easily than can the trunk with all limbs attached.

The trunk should be supported off the ground while being sawed into firewood lengths, for two reasons: it lessons the likelihood that the saw will bind in the kerf as the weight of the trunk closes the gap behind the blade, and it reduces the hazard of sawing into dirt or rocks and dulling the saw. The top or smaller end of the trunk is much easier to hoist off the ground than is the butt end. You may want to build or buy a "log lift" tool, such as that shown in the accompanying sketch.

When cutting off limbs, stand on the opposite side of the log. When chopping larger pieces, make sure the area of axe swing is clear of brush and other obstructions that might deflect the tool.

Most firewood pieces can be split with two wedges, one started in the butt (lower) end of the log and the other used to open the crack thus made.

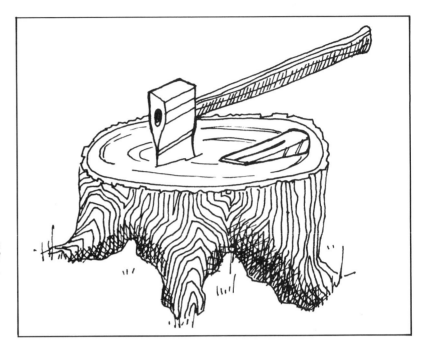

Handier than a sledge for splitting chores is the splitting maul, with one hammer face and one wedge-shaped cutting face.

Choosing and Using an Axe

For most people who spend much time cutting wood, their axe is almost as personal a tool as a favorite pocket-knife. The long handled, double bitted chopping axe is the most familiar symbol of the North Woods lumberjack. However, axe types, sizes and styles are mostly a matter for personal choice and what you are accustomed to using.

For heavier work—felling trees, chopping logs or splitting wood—choose an axe with a 36-inch handle, whether you prefer a single or double bitted head. A head weight of three to 3½ pounds is ample for most work. A lighter axe doesn't deliver enough power; one much heavier strains arm and shoulders.

The axe blade should be of tempered steel of medium hardness. Too soft steel lets the edge get out of shape each time you hit a dead limb or hard knot. Too hard steel will chip, and is difficult to sharpen with a file and oil stone. If you can find one, choose an axe tempered to medium hardness. If your only choice is between two extremes of too hard and too soft, choose the softer steel and carry a file and stone for frequent touch-ups.

Clear the area of anything that might catch and deflect the axe before you begin. When lopping off limbs, stand on the opposite side of the log from where you're chopping. Keep your axe sharp and your footing solid.

Splitting Wood

The revival of interest in wood burning has spawned a host of mechanical wood splitters. All of them cost a great deal more than a splitting maul and a pair of steel wedges.

Most hardwoods (which make the best firewood) have a well defined grain that splits readily. You don't need brute force to split a fireplace log, but you do need to know where to place the splitting wedge or wedges to start the crack properly.

The tools you'll need to split most wood are a splitting maul or sledge, two steel splitting wedges each about three or four pounds in weight, and an axe. A splitting maul is the preferred tool for both driving wedges and widening the crack created by the wedges. This tool has a hammer face on one side of the head and a heavy, wedge-shaped cutting face on the other. A splitting maul typically has a head weight of eight or nine pounds, with a three foot or longer handle. Many variations of this tool are made—including one with a set of levers on either side of the cutting face—but a straightforward splitting maul like that pictured is the best choice for the money.

An axe by itself is not a satisfactory splitting tool, because the thin blade is designed for cutting, rather than for forcing apart wood fibers. However, an axe is handy for finishing the splitting job and for cutting stray splinters that hang on after the wedges and splitting maul have done their work.

Split logs from the bottom up, in the same direction the tree grew. Start the first wedge in the butt end of the log, with the wedge across the heart of the piece. Tap the wedge with the splitting maul (or sledge) to seat it, then deliver sharp blows to the wedge. Drive the wedge into the log until about an inch of the wedge protrudes. On particularly stubborn logs, such as those cut where the tree forked or where a large limb grew, you may need to use a second wedge in the crack made by the first.

Billets of wood are easier to split if you work with the grain. A, the butt cut generally is easier to split if the wedge is started in the upper end of the log (the top end as the tree grew), because the tough, whorly grain at the base resists the wedge. In B, the log can be halved or quartered to leave the limb stub on one stick of firewood. The situation at C shows a billet cut from the crotch or fork of two large limbs; the simplest way to split this log is to start the wedge as shown, then split the other side of the fork in the same manner.

Be careful not to strike the wedge with an axe or the cutting edge of the splitting maul. The maul need not be sharp, but it should not be nicked and chipped, either.

Other tools that come in handy in timber work:

- A peavey or cant-hook, to roll and twist logs; also to dislodge trees that have become hung up in other trees.
- A ratchet hoist or rope fence stretcher, to encourage leaning trees to fall where you want them.
- Safety clothing, such as metal toed shoes, a hard hat and heavy work gloves.

CONCRETE & MASONRY TOOLS

Concrete, stone, brick and block have almost limitless applications in building and improving a home and its surrounding area. With poured concrete, you can get a lot of durable construction for the time, labor and money invested. The decorative and practical uses of brick, stone and blocks of various kinds and materials can add beauty and value to about any homestead.

Many of the tools used in preparing for and performing concrete and masonry work are those used in other handyman pursuits. Hammers, nails, saws, levels, squares and measuring tapes all see service in building forms for poured concrete. Wheelbarrows, shovels, hoes and rakes normally used for yard and garden chores can be pressed into duty for concrete and masonry projects.

In this section, however, we want to concentrate on those tools and equipment used primarily to mix, pour, float and finish concrete; to cut, break and lay brick, stone and block; and to fasten things to masonry walls already constructed.

9
Mixing It Up

Concrete is basically a mass of sand and gravel held together by a cement-water paste that has hardened. The paste is made with portland cement and clean water.

But strong, durable concrete is more than a haphazard mixture of those ingredients—sand, gravel or crushed stone, water and portland cement—that make up the material. The aggregate (sand and gravel) used should be clean, free of dirt, loam or organic matter. The water also should be clean, and near neutral in acidity. In general, water that is fit to drink is fit to use for concrete making.

You *can* buy the ingredients and mix your own concrete. And this may be the way to go for small jobs, where a cubic yard or less of concrete is needed. But today, nearly everyone in the U.S. lives within serving distance of a ready-mix or transit-mix concrete company; and the truth of the matter is, ready-mix concrete is not only much easier than mixing by hand, but in most regions, it's also cheaper.

However, most ready-mix firms charge a minimum per load, and many charge extra for distances beyond a certain radius from the plant. For smaller jobs, you may elect to mix the concrete you'll need in a revolving drum mixer, in a wheelbarrow, in a large box built for the purpose, or simply on a smooth, flat surface.

In days past, many people built wide, low sided boxes in which to mix concrete, masonry cement or plaster for small and medium sized jobs. With today's materials cost, though, you can buy a wheelbarrow for about what the lumber would cost for a mixing box; and the wheelbarrow is definitely more transportable.

If you are mixing sand and masonry cement to lay brick, block or stone, you have little choice. This mortar must be mixed at the site, and because the mortar usually is made stiffer (with less water in the mix) than concrete, a revolving drum type mixer doesn't do an adequate job. If you are laying up a lot of masonry—building a fireplace, for instance—you may want to rent or borrow a paddle-wheel type mixer to stir up the mortar. But for smaller jobs, or where you'll only be laying a few courses of brick, block or stone each day, the mortar can be mixed in a wheelbarrow in batch sizes to suit the speed of the mason.

For most purposes, masonry mortar is made with three parts fine sand and one part masonry (not portland) cement. For wheelbarrow mixing, measure out the desired amount of sand and spread it out in the wheelbarrow. Then, measure the appropriate amount of masonry cement and spread it over the sand. Mix with a square end shovel or hoe until all the sand has been coated with cement.

Then add water slowly, while mixing the mortar, until the "mud" is of the right consistency. Each mason has his own methods of testing mortar for the right amount of water. Generally, the mortar should be stiff enough to adhere to the vertical sides of brick, block or stone, but plastic enough to let the masonry materials be well bedded in the mortar.

Other texts (such as *Successful Practical & Decorative Concrete,* by Robert Wilde) go into detail on mixes and proportions for portland cement for various uses. While we will stay mainly with the tools you need to do the job here, the following table may be helpful:

Materials required per cubic yard of concrete for various uses				
Use of Concrete	Sacks of Cement	Sand, cu.yd.	Gravel, cu.yd.	Largest size gravel
Thick sections not subject to freezing; footings, foundations	5	2/3	3/4	1½"
3 to 4 in. thick concrete: walks, driveways, steps, patios	6¼	2/3	3/4	1½"
Thin concrete, 1 to 2 in. thick; tanks, lawn furniture; sculptures	8	2/3	3/4	3/8"

NOTE: Each 94-lb. bag of portland cement contains 1 cubic foot.

Measure it

Whatever mixing method you use, you'll need some way to measure the dry ingredients—sand, gravel and cement—and the water. Mixtures by weight are more accurate than mixtures by volume, but not as convenient for most projects. With practice, you can measure ingredients fairly accurately with a shovel. But to begin with, you should measure each element of your concrete mix—whether you will be mixing by hand or in a rotating-drum mixer.

You can build a box 1 foot high, 1 foot wide and 1 foot long (one cubic foot volume) to measure aggregate, since each bag of portland cement contains one cubic foot. But your use of hand mixed concrete will likely be for small, infrequent projects, and you may not want to go to the trouble of building a box.

A galvanized 2 or 3 gallon bucket makes a handy sized measuring device, and has more alternative uses than a one cubic foot box. Fill the bucket with each ingredient—sand, gravel, cement—and level it off each time. Measure the correct amount of water also.

Hand-Mixing Tools

If you need only a small batch of concrete—say to set a clothesline pole or fence post, you may want to mix it by hand either on a clean, flat surface or in a wheelbarrow.

Even a small garden type wheelbarrow is a better mixing apparatus than a flat deck or driveway. But for very small amounts of concrete, you may have to make do with what you have handy. Either way, the mixing procedure is the same.

First, put the measured quantity of sand on the mixing surface and spread it out in a thin layer. Then, spread the measured amount of cement over the sand. Use a square end shovel or garden hoe to mix the sand-cement mixture. A shovel is handier, because you can turn the mix more easily. Turn and stir the sand-cement until it is of a uniform gray color, then spread the required quantity of gravel on top.

Mix the sand, cement and gravel thoroughly with the shovel or hoe. Don't use an ordinary garden rake. The rake tines will tend to separate the larger gravel from the rest of the mix. Turn the complete mixture at least three times—more if brown streaks show.

Once all the dry material has been coated with cement powder, use the shovel or hoe to form a shallow depression in the center of the pile. Add the water slowly in the hollow. Then, turn the dry material at the rim of the depression into the center, and continue mixing until the mix is of a plastic consistency.

If you have mixed the concrete in a wheelbarrow, it's a simple matter to wheel the load to where it is to be poured. Concrete mixed on a flat surface may have to be carried by shovels or buckets.

For small batches of concrete, you may want to use a

Steps in patching a cracked sidewalk are: A) Chip out all broken and cracked concrete and undercut the groove so new concrete will "key in" for better holding power; B) Wet down the concrete and the ground under it to keep it from absorbing too much water from the new concrete; C) Fill and tamp concrete into the crack; and D) Use a wooden float to smooth the new concrete and float larger pieces of aggregate below the surface. If a smooth finish is desired, use a trowel after concrete has dried some.

bagged dry mix—such as "Sakrete"—ready to mix with water. However, this is an expensive method to use if you're pouring more than a couple of cubic feet of concrete. Still, the convenience may offset the cost, in some instances.

For example, during a visit to an old family cemetery where several of my ancestors are buried, I noticed that several smaller headstones had fallen over. I returned to the cemetery with a sack of pre-mixed dry concrete, a spade (for digging a small footing), a square end shovel, a wheelbarrow, a pointed trowel and a bucket (for dipping water from a nearby creek). In a short while, the tipped over tombstones were bedded firmly in a concrete base. I took the wheelbarrow and other tools to the creek, rinsed them well and was on my way back home in less than an hour. All this is just a way of illustrating how modern-day masonry materials can be used.

Concrete Mixers

For all but the smallest batches of concrete, you'll want to lay hands on a concrete mixer powered by an electric motor or gasoline engine. These are made in sizes to mix from one to six cubic feet of concrete per batch, and some smaller units have wheelbarrow type frames, wheels and handles to allow easy transport.

If you're doing only an occasional mixing job, consider renting or borrowing a mixer. Most rental centers have trailer type mixers that can be towed by an auto with a standard bumper hitch.

If you plan to buy a concrete mixer, shop around to see if you can find a serviceable used machine. A new mixer represents a considerable investment—$250 to $400 for a 2½ or 3½ cubic foot model with an electric motor.

But new or used, the machine you buy should be durable, efficient and of a size that suits your rate of work. Just to mix a one cubic foot batch of concrete, the mixer must slosh around about 150 pounds of material—and you have to shovel it.

The most common concrete mixer is the rotating drum type, either belt or gear driven by an electric motor. If you're pouring concrete beyond the reach of electric power lines, you may need a mixer powered by a gasoline engine. When you choose a concrete mixer, take into account the size of your project and the help you'll have available. A 2½ cubic foot capacity mixer can keep two or three people busy.

A short handled, square end shovel is useful in spreading and leveling concrete.

Compact concrete mixer handles two-cubic-foot batches and breaks down for transport or storage. You may prefer a mixer with wheels.

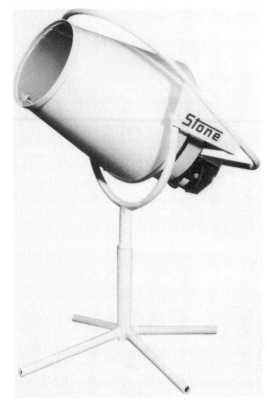

Each operator has his own favorite method of loading materials into the mixer. You'll get faster mixing if you shovel all of the gravel into the drum and add about half of the required water, then let the mixer rotate for a minute or so before adding—in order—the sand, cement and the

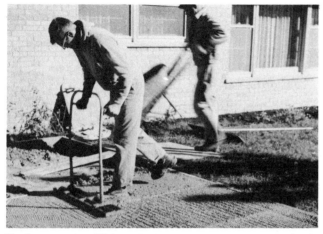

For large areas of flat concrete, a scraper-tamper gets fresh concrete securely in place.

A deep-bodied construction wheelbarrow is useful if you're moving much concrete. For small batches, a garden wheelbarrow will serve.

rest of the water.

After all the material has been placed in the drum, continue mixing for three to four minutes, then tip the drum to discharge the concrete—either directly into the forms or into a wheelbarrow.

If several minutes pass before you mix the next batch, shovel about a fourth of the required gravel for the next mix into the drum and add half of the water—rinsing the edges and inside drum surfaces as you add the water. Avoid sloshing water or wet concrete on the mixer's electric motor or belts. Newer, better made mixers have the motor and belt drive encased in a plastic housing.

Clean the mixer drum and frame well after each use period; even if you're only breaking an hour or so for lunch. At the end of the day, shovel several scoops of gravel into the mixer drum and add enough water to the gravel so the mixture makes a sloshing sound. Let this gravel-water mix scour the inside of the drum while you hose down the frame and wheels of the mixer. Use a scraper or wire brush to remove hardened concrete. Don't bang on the drum with a hammer—the dents you make will only collect more concrete the next time you use the mixer. After the gravel and water has revolved for several minutes, dump it out and rinse the mixer drum with clean water. It's much easier to clean a concrete mixer often than it is to remove built up deposits of hardened concrete.

Most concrete mixers have grease fittings for lubricating the shaft and gears with a grease gun. Grease the mixer each day it is in use, and grease it well before storing the machine. Check to see if the electric motor has an oil fitting; if so, add just a few drops of 10-weight oil (not penetrating oil) each time the mixer is put into service.

Even with the most careful use, some water is likely to get on the V-belts that drive the mixer drum. Use a belt dressing stick to keep the belt from cracking and slipping in the pulleys.

Getting-Ready Tools

Building foundations, slab floors and other concrete fixtures that will need to support a lot of weight should be placed on footings poured to some depth below grade. You'll need regular digging tools—spade, pick, mattock, long handled shovel—for digging the excavation for these footings. In firm soil, the banks of the excavation often can be formed so that the footing can be poured with no other form needed.

Even if you're preparing to pour a driveway, sidewalk or patio, you will probably need to dig the dirt somewhat below grade, then partially fill the excavation with gravel or crushed rock. After the gravel is spread and leveled for the subgrade, over which the concrete will be poured, it should be tamped firm to compact the surface.

If the gravel will be more than a couple of inches deep, tamp it in layers of about two inches each. Special cast iron tamping tools are made for this purpose, but you can use a wooden fence post, a section of 4 by 4 timber or any heavy, square end timber.

Unless you are placing a plastic film or other vapor barrier under the concrete, the subgrade gravel should be moistened before the concrete is poured. You can do this with a garden hose and spray nozzle. This lets the concrete dry slowly for better curing.

Before you start mixing concrete or calling the ready mix truck, be sure that you have everything ready to go. Get together the tools you'll need to form and smooth the concrete, have all forms in place and well braced, have the footings or subgrade in condition and line up any extra help you will need. Concrete jobs—large or small—should be poured quickly and continuously from start to finish.

The subbase should be well tamped before concrete is poured for walks, driveways, patios, etc. You can use a cast iron tamper such as that shown, or use a heavy square ended timber.

10
Smoothing and Finishing Tools

Timeliness is a key factor in finishing flat concrete work. Concrete is fast setting and should be placed in the forms soon after mixing—within 30 minutes, at the outside.

While the results you get with finished concrete often depend as much on *when* you perform a job as on how and what tools you use, it's possible to get in too big a hurry for some operations—such as finish troweling. But, in general, you can pour a great deal of flat concrete—driveways, sidewalks, patios, slabs, etc.—with a minimum investment in tools, and produce professional results if you do each finishing job at the proper stage of the concrete's "stiffness." This is particularly true if you use transit mixed concrete, which will allow the entire "pour" to age and dry at about the same rate.

Most of the tools you will need are already on hand in most households—or can be made from materials you have. Key finishing tools—trowels, edgers, groovers—should be selected for quality, as well as for the size of job or jobs you have to do.

Shovel

You'll need a shovel for most work. More than one might be handy, but you can get along very well with a short handled, **square end shovel** for spreading and spading concrete. Concrete poured to depths of six inches or more—as in foundation walls for buildings—should be tamped or "spaded" as it goes into the form.

This can be done with a square end shovel, a spade or a board with a chisel shaped bevel cut in one end. Unless you will be pouring a great deal of concrete, there's little need to invest in specialized tamping and spading tools.

Work the spade or tamping board along the forms, up-and-down and back-and-forth. This moves the larger pieces of aggregate away from the forms into the mass of concrete, and gives a smooth, dense surface when forms are knocked down. Be careful not to dislodge any reinforcement steel during the tamping operation.

With slabs, walks and other flat concrete, the only tamping usually needed can often be accomplished by tapping

lightly along the length of the forming boards with a hammer. The bulk of the work with flat surfaces is in finishing the concrete.

Screeding

The first operation in smoothing and finishing flat surfaces is "screeding." After the concrete is placed and spread, level it off in the form with a straight edged board, called a **"screed."** It's best to use a 2 by 4 that spans the width of the form by two feet or so, to strike off and level the concrete immediately after pouring.

Move the board back and forth with a sawing kind of motion; at the same time, pull it along from one end of the work to the other. Keep the edges of the board on the outsides of the form. It's easier, particularly for wide surfaces, if there's a man on each end of the straightedge.

The first step in finishing flat concrete is to "screed" or strike off the surface with a straight edged board.

A darby is used to flat the surface of concrete flat work immediately after screeding. For large areas that are hard to reach with a darby, a long-handled bull float is used.

A small amount of concrete should be kept ahead of the screeding board, to fill in low spots. Use a shovel to rake concrete into larger hollows. As the screed is pulled along, it should be tilted slightly in the direction of movement to form a cutting edge.

If the first pass of the screeding board produces waves or ridges in the concrete surface, go back and do it over. In most cases, you will need to screed the surface twice. Start at the same end as before, but move the board back and forth in shorter "sawing" movements.

Floating — First Pass

After screeding, smooth the surface with a wood float—either a **hand float** (for smaller slabs) or a long-handled **bull float** or **darby.** This levels ridges and fills in small hollows left by screeding. Floating also submerges coarse gravels so that hand floating and troweling can produce a smooth, level surface.

You can buy a darby—a tool that is merely a long, flat piece of wood, aluminum or magnesium with a handle on top. Or you can build a bull float from a piece of 1 by 4 board, of whatever length you wish. Most bull floats are

from 30 to 48 inches long. Attach a long handle (a piece of 2 by 2 lumber, a long pole or anything else that is handy) to reach to the center of wide slabs.

After initial floating with a darby or bull float, delay further finishing until the concrete is fairly stiff. Test the concrete surface occasionally while you wait. Hand-floating should be done while the surface is just beginning to lose the water sheen, but is still fairly plastic.

Hand Floating

Commercial hand floats are made of aluminum, magnesium or wood, in several sizes: 12 to 16 inches long and 3½ or 4½ inches wide. Again you can use a piece of 1 by 4 to make your own. Make the handle from wood, or use a handle from an old cabinet or door.

In some cases, hand floating should be done after the slab has been edged and grooved; especially where a rougher texture is desired and hand floating is the final finishing.

When concrete is to be finished smooth, floating prepares the surface for troweling and gives an even (but not very smooth) texture to the surface. For sidewalks and driveways, where a non-skid texture is needed, you may

An edger is a flat working surface with a lip on one side. Hold it flat on the concrete, with the lip along the forming boards.

A groover, or jointer, is about six inches long, with a cutting edge to make a lateral joint in flat concrete. Use a straight board as a guide. Push the groover across the concrete, putting pressure on the rear of the tool. Then, reverse the groover and draw it back across the same joint to smooth and compact the edges of the joint.

want to float the surface a second time, after some stiffening of the concrete has taken place.

Edging

Edgers come in several sizes and are made of various metals. Most are about six inches long and two to four inches wide, with a raised lip of ¼ inch to 1½ inches. For walks, driveways and patios poured about four inches thick, use a stainless steel edger with about a ½ inch lip.

Edging produces a neat, rounded edge that helps prevent chipping and cracking of the concrete, and also compacts and hardens the concrete next to the form. On work to be troweled, preliminary edging should be done after the surface has been floated, when the concrete has set enough to hold the shape of the tool.

Run the tool back and forth between the concrete and the forms, all the way along the sides of the walk, patio, etc. In some cases, you may want to run the edger lightly along the form after the final troweling has been done.

Grooving

Groovers (also called "jointers") are made of bronze or stainless steel, in a variety of sizes and styles. Handiest

to use are those about six inches long and two to 4½ inches wide, with a cutting edge on the bottom surface, extending from ½ inch to an inch.

Immediately after the edging tool has been run around the form, the slab should be grooved to help predetermine the location of and hide cracks in the concrete. Concrete poured in slabs often is prone to some cracking under the stress of expansion and contraction. Grooves in the slab at intervals help dictate where those cracks will occur. In general, concrete slabs should be grooved to about one-fifth of their thickness.

Use a straight edged board as a guide to make the grooved joints perpendicular to the long dimension of the slab. Start the groove by pressing down on the tool to push its cutting edge into the concrete, then move it forward while pressing on the back of the tool. After the initial joint is cut, turn the tool around and pull it back over the groove to produce a smooth finish.

If the concrete has stiffened to the point where the tool does not penetrate easily, use a hand axe or hatchet to score a line where the groove is to be made, then use the groover to finish the joint.

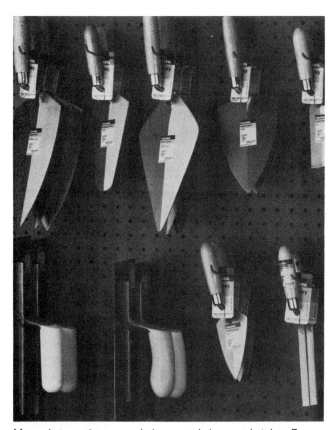

Mason's trowels are made in several sizes and styles. For finishing flat concrete, choose a 12 to 14 inch finisher's trowel. For laying brick, block and stone, select a 10 inch general purpose pointed trowel and a 5 inch pointing trowel.

Troweling

If there's one watchword in troweling flat concrete, it must be: don't start too soon. You cannot produce a really smooth surface until the concrete has begun to stiffen and most of the water sheen has evaporated from the top. On a hot day, where concrete is poured in direct sunlight, this may occur soon after the surface is floated. Or, on cool, cloudy days, it may be several hours before the surface is ready to trowel.

Test the concrete often. When only a slight dent can be made by pressing your hand on the concrete surface, the concrete is ready for troweling.

Initial troweling usually is done with a longer, wider tool. **Trowels** come in various lengths and widths—from 10 to 20 inches long and from three to five inches wide—and are made of carbon tempered or stainless steel.

For the first pass, use a flat trowel about 16 inches long, held almost flat against the surface of the concrete. A trowel that has seen some service is better for this function than a brand new one; its edges are rounded and less likely to bite into the concrete. Move the tool in long sweeping arcs over the surface, covering half of the previous arc on each new swing.

To get a very smooth surface, you will probably need to go over the concrete at least a second time. On this pass, use a smaller trowel—about a 12 by 3 inch tool—and raise the leading edge of the trowel slightly as the surface is troweled. The trowel should make a high-pitched ringing sound as the blade moves over the surface, if the concrete is set to the proper troweling consistency.

For large slabs, where the center of the surface cannot be reached from the edges, you will need to use knee boards (flat pieces of plywood work well). Usually, both hand floating and initial troweling operations are done in an area of the surface before the knee boards are moved to a new area.

Remember: using a steel trowel results in a very smooth surface that may be slippery when wet or frosty. Where more traction is needed, the surface may be finished with a wood float only—or perhaps roughened with a stiff broom after floating. Of course, if you are finishing a basement floor or an outdoor surface that later may be covered with vinyl tile or indoor-outdoor carpeting, you'll want to finish the surface as smoothly as possible—which means at least two passes with the steel trowel.

You can produce about any texture or pattern you wish in concrete surfaces; using only those tools you have around the house, in most cases. Generally, the softer the concrete is when it is worked, the more pronounced the texture. Here are some ideas; your imagination will call up others:

• A "swirled" pattern can be achieved by moving the final finishing tool—whether trowel or wood float—in short semi-circles on the concrete surface. Use a steel trowel after the concrete is fairly stiff for a light swirled pattern. For more pronounced swirls, use a wood float while the surface is still fairly moist.

- A long "wavy" pattern can be created by using a soft bristle push broom on the surface after the preliminary troweling. Or, you can use a large paintbrush or wallpaper paste brush to get similar but narrower waves.
- A stiff broom pulled across the surface after floating or troweling gives a rough, non-skid surface. The broom can be dragged straight across the slab, or swept in large circles to create a curved pattern.
- Use a groover or length of copper tube bent into a slight "S" shape to outline flagstone-like patterns in the concrete while the surface is still fairly plastic. After the flagstone effect has been scored, lightly trowel the surface again. Just before the concrete is too stiff to work, use a soft bristle brush to clean the dust and sand from the joints.
- Exposed aggregate patterns are among the simplest to make. Usually, this is done by letting the floated surface partially set, then hosing it off to expose some of the rocks and gravels. Use a fine spray with the hose nozzle. You can use a broom in conjunction with a garden hose to bring out in relief as much aggregate as you wish.
- You can create interesting effects by adding flat or round pebbles—perhaps of various colors or sizes—to the surface after you screed off the slab. You can mix large pebbles and small ones, use all white or all red pebbles, mix colors, use colored marbles—whatever your imagination suggests. Some home builders use this technique inside the house to accent entry ways or fireplace hearths.

Whatever finish you put on it, concrete needs moisture to cure properly. New concrete should be protected from too rapid drying out for at least five days. Cover floors, walks and other flat surfaces wth burlap, straw, hay, plastic film or other materials to keep water from evaporating too rapidly. If you use porous materials, such as burlap or straw, keep the surface moistened for the curing period.

Troweling leaves a smooth, hard surface. Hold the blade nearly flat on the surface of the concrete and swing it in long sweeping arcs.

For large areas of flat concrete, you may want to rent an engine driven power screeder to strike off the concrete; particularly if you're using ready-mix concrete, poured in big batches.

For good traction, you may want to form a pattern in sidewalks and driveways after floating or troweling. A stiff bristle push broom makes a coarse but attractive pattern.

Raked joints often are made with a special pointing tool.

11 Unit Masonry Tools

Unit masonry—stone, brick and an almost infinite variety of concrete block—can add practical and beautifying touches to any homesite. Walls, barbecue grills, garden pools and planters in rustic or formal construction can accent or "set off" different parts of the grounds.

Skilled masons put in years learning the finer points of their craft. So, a primer course in masonry materials and tools will not make an artisan out of an amateur. But the rudiments of unit masonry can be commanded by about anyone with a moderate amount of skill, intelligence and a few well chosen tools.

The range of materials—and the possible treatments of them—are almost limitless. You can construct useful, rustic masonry structures of rubble stone picked up from along a creek bed or hillside field; or you can use ultra formal arrangements of block and brick.

Stone and brick working tools: 1. breaking sledge; 2. hand driller's hammer, for driving brick sets and chisels; 3. brick hammer; 4. brick chisel; and 5. star drill.

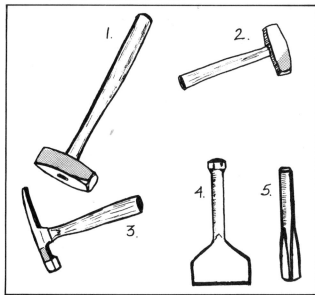

Poorly laid up masonry adds little to either function or appearance, however. Masonry work—as any sort of building work—is easier and more presentable when the right tools are used properly, with the proper materials for the project undertaken. Beyond that, design and style are mainly matters of personal taste.

One advantage of working with unit masonry—especially for the home handyman, whose time may be limited—is that it can be done at your own pace. While concrete should be poured continuously from start to finish of a project, brick, block or stone can be laid up in a "stop-and-go" fashion as time permits.

And you don't need a big investment in tools for most unit masonry work. However, regardless of how small or how simple the project, it is easier, quicker and better if you have the right tools and know how to use them.

You'll need most of those tools mentioned in Chapter 9 for hand mixing cement, plus a few additional implements made specifically for the job to be done. In larger projects, such as a tall brick or stone wall, you'll also need some carpentry tools—hammer, saw, measuring tape, plumb bob, level, square—to build a footing under the wall and keep the wall plumb and level as it goes up.

You may also need brick hammers, brick sets and chisels—along with a small hand sledge—for cutting brick or block to fit. In some cases, you may have need of a masonry saw as well. You can buy abrasive cutting blades that let you use a portable circular saw to score and cut masonry units, but if you have much work of this type to do, you will be better off renting or borrowing a heavy duty radial-arm masonry saw.

The tools you'll need most often are a good pointed trowel, a brick or stone hammer and an accurate level. Depending on the masonry project, you may also need a smaller pointing trowel, brick sets and chisels and one or more joint forming tools.

Trowels

Rather than the square bladed trowels used to finish concrete, unit masonry requires the use of a **pointed**

Rock-laying tools include level and plumb bob for keeping courses straight; rock hammer for chipping and breaking stone to fit; pointing trowel for handling mortar; piece of copper tubing and pointing tools for forming joints. You may also need a ball of string to keep long walls level.

trowel with a slightly flexible blade. Choose a tool with a 10 or 12 inch blade that is four inches wide or more at the handle end. The handle shank should be brazed to the blade, or made all in one piece with the blade. Avoid buying a trowel with the handle shank merely tack welded to the blade.

In addition to the larger trowel, you may also need a small **pointing trowel**, with a four or six inch long blade, for pointing up joints between masonry units and for use in tight places. Both trowels should have polished, heat hardened steel blades and hardwood handles. Some masons like to wrap the handle with electrical tape for a more comfortable grip.

Brick and Stone Hammers

Masons' hammers have one square striking face and one curved, tapered face that ends in a chisel-like point for chipping and breaking brick and stone. The head of a brick hammer typically weighs about 1½ pounds; a stone hammer is a pound or so heavier.

Buy a good, hardened steel hammer head. The choice of handle—whether hickory or tubular steel with a rubber grip—is mostly a matter of personal choice.

A **mason's scutch** is a hammer with two tapered faces. One end has the chisel point of the brick hammer; the other

tapers on all four sides to a point. Both ends are used for chipping and breaking brick, stone or block.

Brick Sets and Chisels

Brick sets and **chisels** are made from a single piece of steel comprising the blade, handle and struck face. Both types of tools come in several sizes, with blade widths from one to three inches. Both are handy for cutting and scoring bricks, blocks or stone. The principal difference in the two tools is that a brick *set* has the edge ground on both sides, much like a cold chisel; while a brick *chisel,* has a single bevel ground to form the cutting edge, more like a wood chisel.

Brick sets and chisels should be struck with a hand drilling sledge, not a bricklayer's hammer.

Jointing Tools and Methods

Depending on the type of pattern you want in the mortar between the units of masonry (brick, block or stone), you will need some sort of tool to make the joint and harden the mortar.

Your choices of tools on the market are many—**jointers** come in various shapes and widths, each designed to form a particular kind of joint. See the accompanying sketch for

Rock is best cut with a hammer by nibbling off a little at a time, rather than trying to break off big chunks.

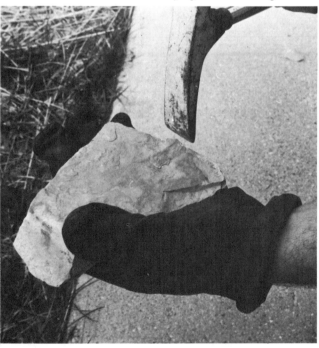

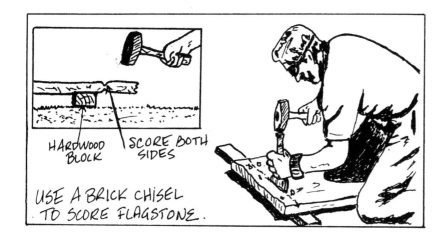

HARDWOOD BLOCK   SCORE BOTH SIDES

USE A BRICK CHISEL TO SCORE FLAGSTONE.

To cut flagstone, use a brick chisel to score the rock on both sides, then support the stone on a board or block and break the flagstone along the scored line by tapping with a rock hammer.

the various kinds of mortar joints, and the shape of tool needed to make them.

A **flush joint** is used to compress the mortar and remove any excess from the wall; usually used with concrete or cinder blocks, and sometimes on brick work.

A **V-joint** can be made with a tool purchased for the purpose, or you can use the point of a trowel. You can also grind a piece of thin, flat metal for use to shape the joint. The main thing to remember is that the point of the V should be centered between the courses of masonry.

A **weathered joint** is made with the trowel point held at about a 30 degree angle to expose the lower edge of the top course of brick or block. A **struck joint** is made the same way, except that the trowel is held to rake mortar away from the top brick of the lower course.

A **raked joint** is made either with a special tool designed for the purpose, or with a homemade substitute. Many masons simply "rake" the mortar out with a screw head attached to a piece of 1 by 4 board. The board acts as a guide to control the depth to which mortar is removed.

A **swept joint** is a concave indentation in the mortar, made with a short length of pipe or tubing, or a round piece of iron rod. This is a good, weather-tight joint with enough mortar removed to outline the masonry units with a shadow line.

A **raised** or **tapped joint** has a convex bead of mortar extending beyond the line of brick or block. It's made by tapping the brick or block with the trowel handle just enough to squeeze out a small raised bead of mortar. The appearance of this kind of joint depends on the mortar bed being just the right thickness for the proper amount of mortar to be forced out of the joint. In some raised joints, the bead of mortar is "dressed" with a tool shaped like that shown in the sketch.

Types of mortar joints for brickwork:
Stuck, *made with a small pointing trowel held point down and raked along the joint;* **Swept,** *made with a soft bristle brush or old paintbrush;* **Extruded** *made by leaving the ridge of mortar that is squeezed out in laying and leveling brick;* **Raised,** *formed with a special tool, or a section of copper tubing that has been cut away;* **Flush,** *made by wiping the brick;* **V-joint,** *made with a special tool for the purpose, or with a piece of flat metal ground to a V point;* **Weathered,** *the opposite of a "struck" joint, made with a trowel;* **Raked,** *made with a square end pointing tool, or a screw driven part way into a flat board.*

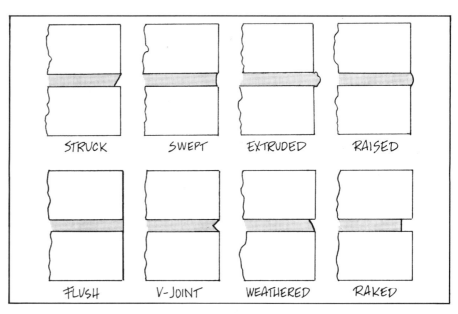

STRUCK   SWEPT   EXTRUDED   RAISED

FLUSH   V-JOINT   WEATHERED   RAKED

Leveling and plumbing tools

You'll need a good, accurate level for most masonry work. If you'll be laying up walls or other projects that call for long courses, a **mason's level** may be worthwhile. These tools are made of wood, from 42 to 48 inches long, and have spirit vials to indicate level, plumb and—sometimes—45 degree angles. However, if you're planning only one time use, or several smaller jobs, you can get along with a regular carpenter's level and a straight board 48 inches or more in length.

Also for long horizontal masonry runs, you'll need a mason's line (or cord). Better ones are made of linen or nylon. You can buy cotton line, but cotton is subject to excessive stretching, especially when damp.

A string level can be used in conjunction with a mason's line. This is a small one bubble level that clips to the line. When the line is stretched tight, the level shows true horizontal.

For most masonry work of any height, you may want to use a plumb bob to keep walls and corners plumb (vertical). However, for most work, an accurate level and a carefully leveled mason's line are all that is needed.

And, for most projects, you'll also need a folding rule or retractable tape to measure dimensions.

Masonry Cement

Cement used to bond layers of unit masonry together is not the same stuff as that mixed for poured concrete; it has a different job to do. Good, strong mortar must be carefully made so that it is wet enough so the moisture does not evaporate too quickly, but not so wet as to be "runny" and too easily squeezed out of joints.

Some professional masons like to mix their mortar from portland cement. You can do this, if you wish, by following this recipe:

- 1 part portland cement
- 1 part hydrated lime
- 5 parts clean, dry sand
- Enough water to give the mortar the consistency of putty.

Mix the dry ingredients first, until the whole mixture has a grayish-green color—no stripes of brown. Then add water, a little at a time, until the mortar is wet enough to spread readily, but not so wet that it is loose and soggy.

Mix thoroughly after each addition of water. It's important to add only a little water at a time. There's only a narrow margin in moisture content between mortar that is too dry and mortar that is too wet.

Laying a brick wall: Upper left, use a mason's line to keep bricks straight; spread mortar evenly and slightly thicker than the joint will be. Upper right, "butter" the end of the brick with mortar, lay the brick and tap to level and seat it in the mortar bed. Lower left, remove the mortar squeezed out of the joint (unless you will make extruded or raised joints) and return it to the hawk or wheel-barrow. Lower right, when mortar has set somewhat, use the proper tool to shape and compact the joint you desire.

Galvanized wall ties are used to anchor brick and rock veneer to frame walls.

But there's an easier way to go in most areas of the country. Special masonry cement is available in 70 or 80 pound bags, ready to be mixed with clean sand. Mix one part masonry cement to three parts sand, then mix in enough clean water to make mortar of the right consistency. It's much simpler than handling hydrated lime, which has a tendency to lump.

Laying Unit Masonry

Let's assume that you're building a low wall of 4 by 8 inch bricks; perhaps to separate the yard from the vegetable garden, or whatever. We'll further assume that you have previously built a substantial, level footing for the masonry structure, have stretched a level line to mark the first courses of bricks and are now ready to start building the wall.

Brick, clay tile and similar masonry should be moistened before being laid up, so that not too much moisture is extracted from the mortar. You can do this by directing a fine spray from the garden hose over the stacked bricks for several minutes, then letting excess water evaporate before laying the brick.

(Concrete blocks and fairly porous stone should not be dampened. Moisture makes these units expand. If they are laid up wet, when they dry out, blocks can contract and cause cracks in the mortar joints.)

If the wall is to be two feet high or higher, it should be two bricks thick or thicker. First, lay out the entire first course of brick on the footing, with the bricks spaced the same distance apart as the thickness of the intended mortar joint—usually about ½ inch.

If you are laying a two-brick-thick wall, lay the first course (header course) of bricks crosswise, or perpendicular to the long dimension of the wall. This lets you count the number of bricks you'll need in each header course.

Then, lay out the second course of bricks—still using no mortar—on top of the first row. If you're laying up a "common bond" wall, this second course of bricks will be laid longitudinally (stretcher course), or with the long dimension of the bricks parallel to the wall length. Count the bricks in this course, also.

If at all possible, arrange the header and stretcher courses so that few if any bricks have to be cut to odd lengths to fill in the spaces. In most brick walls of this type, every fifth or sixth course is laid as a header course, with many or all of the bricks turned crosswise to bond the wall together. Also, the bricks in each course should lap or span the bricks in the course below, so that vertical joints are staggered. (See the sketch on how to lay a brick wall).

Once you have made the dry run with the first two courses of brick (some masons call this "chasing out the bond"), you're ready to mix the mortar and start laying brick. Start at one end of the wall and spread a layer of mortar about ½ inch thick and long enough for three or four bricks. Don't put too much mortar down at one time, as it dries fairly quickly.

Place the end brick in position so that the edge of the brick squarely touches the stretched line. Tap the brick lightly with the end of the trowel handle to level and bed the brick in the mortar.

On second and succeeding bricks to be laid, you will need to apply a coating of mortar to the end of the brick that will abut the last one laid. This is a little tricky, until you get the hang of it. Dip up enough mortar on the tip of the trowel to "butter" the brick, wipe the mortar onto the end (or side) of the brick and slip the brick into position alongside its neighbor.

Lightly tap the brick to level and align it at exactly the right height, then repeat the process.

The procedure and use of tools is much the same for laying concrete blocks or cut stone. However, if you are using field stone of random shapes and sizes, you probably will need to do some choosing, chipping and cutting to get the stones to fit properly. Also, you will probably have to be more general about leveling and aligning each stone in the wall. However, each *course* of stone should be generally level, and stones in successive courses should overlap the joints of the course below.

Masonry tools require little maintenance, other than a good cleaning after each use and storage in a safe, dry location. If brick hammer faces become cracked or mushroomed, discard the tool and replace it with a new one. If the cutting edge becomes dull, it can be re-dressed.

Brick sets and chisels can be ground and sharpened, much as are single and double bevel chisels of other design. As nearly as possible, try to maintain the original angle on cutting edges when re-dressing them.

After each period of use, clean all tools thoroughly and wipe them with a lightly oiled rag. They'll be ready for service when you need them again.

12
Masonry Fasteners and Hangers

From time to time, most of us need to anchor something to a masonry wall—shelves, wall studding, cabinets, etc. This poses some special problems, since common nails and screws cannot readily be driven into concrete, brick and stone.

In times not long past, about the only option was to use a **"star" drill** and a **hand-driller's sledge** to chew a hole into the wall, then insert an expansion plug of lead, plastic or other soft material to hold a bolt or lag screw. The four cutting edges of a star drill resemble an oversized Phillips screwdriver tip, and the tool will make a hole in the hardest concrete. The drill is struck with the hammer, then turned slightly and struck again. Repeat this process until the hole is of the desired depth—or until the driller gives out.

You may still want to use a star drill to make a hole for an expanding sleeve type fastener. But check around before you start drilling. In the past several years, an amazing variety of fasteners and hangers have been developed to use with masonry. Some you can glue on, some you can drive directly into the wall without first drilling a hole. You have several options today.

Even if you use a plug of an expanding sleeve fastener —or another type that requires a pre-drilled hole—a portable electric drill and a carbide tipped masonry bit saves a lot of work and time over the sledge and star drill route.

For hollow masonry walls—block or tile—you can use toggle bolts, Molly anchors or other fasteners described in Chapter 2. These work the same way as they do with gypsum board, plaster or paneling. Merely use a **carbide tip drill** of the proper size to make a hole for the anchor through only one side of the brick or tile, then insert the fastener and tighten it down to expand the holding part on the inside of the wall.

If you're fastening studs or furring strips to a concrete wall, you may be able to use one of several types of anchors that attach to the surface of the wall with adhesive. These fasteners come with nails, bolts and clips, to accommodate a variety of objects, and are easier to use than fasteners that require a hole drilled in the wall. You merely spread the adhesive, allow it to dry to the "tacky" stage, then position the anchor. In a few hours, the glue hardens and is ready to hold.

Making holes in concrete calls for rugged drilling equipment. Use a steel punch or star drill to start the hole, then a carbide tipped masonry bit to complete the job.

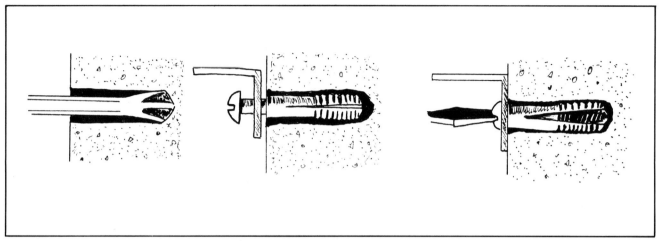

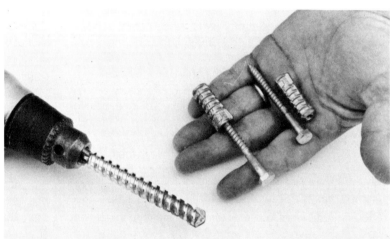

Lead expansion anchors hold securely in concrete or masonry walls.

Or, you may want to use specially hardened nails that can be driven directly into the masonry. Some of these nails have a spiral or screw shank, for extra holding power. Use a **hand sledge** or **driller's hammer** to drive these hardened nails—don't use a claw hammer.

There are two problems with using these so-called "concrete nails." One, if you're driving them into poured concrete, the nail tends to glance when it hits a piece of hard aggregate and breaks out a large chunk of concrete. Two, the nail must be struck squarely on the head, or it bends and glances.

Wear high-impact safety goggles and gloves when driving concrete nails or drilling with a star drill. In fact, that's pretty good counsel any time you're doing anything that might cause a piece of masonry to chip or break off.

There are several **power drivers** on the market, that can drive nails into masonry walls. One type uses a .32 caliber powder cartridge that is detonated by a firing pin and slams the nail into the concrete, mortar, brick or stone. These tools are dangerous to use unless you've had some

experience with them. That .32 caliber cartridge goes off with a terrific bang—the business end of the tool should be seated squarely on the masonry surface.

Another type of power driver uses a hammer as the motive force, to drive pins or threaded studs into the wall. The pin is held in a sleeve, which prevents it from bending or glancing as you drive it.

If you're hanging wall cabinets or other heavy objects on masonry walls, you'll want an anchor that stands up to the weight and leverage. In most cases, this involves drilling a hole in the concrete, then using one of several types of fasteners.

First, the hole. Carbide tip masonry bits make clean holes in about any type of material. Some masonry anchors require a ½ inch diameter hole; others call for a ⅜ inch hole. Decide on the type of anchor you will use before you buy the masonry drill bit, unless you will have use for more than one size bit.

You'll need a ½ inch or larger portable electric drill to do a satisfactory drilling job in masonry. A ¼ inch drill—unless it

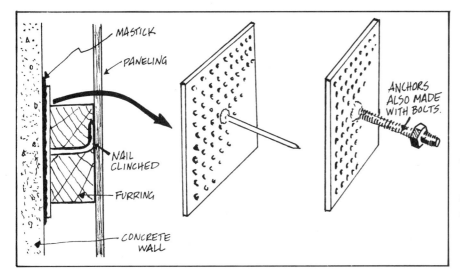

Labels on illustration: MASTICK · PANELING · NAIL CLINCHED · FURRING · CONCRETE WALL · ANCHORS ALSO MADE WITH BOLTS.

Anchor plates attach to concrete walls with cement, and are made with spikes or bolts. This type of anchor is handy when you're paneling over a basement wall.

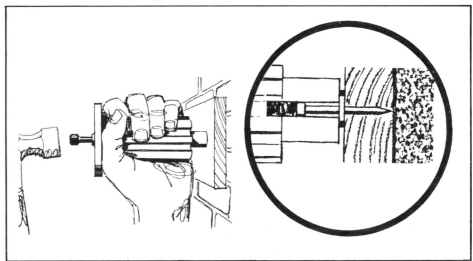

Power drivers direct all of the hammer's power to the head of the pin and hold the pin to keep it from bending or glancing. Position the driver perpendicular to the wall or other surface and hit the drive rod with a heavy hammer. (Courtesy of USM Corporation)

has a variable speed feature—turns too fast to deliver the power needed. You'll need to exert quite a bit of pressure on the drill to force the masonry bit into the concrete. A smaller drill could be damaged beyond repair by this kind of treatment.

One of the difficult things about drilling into masonry—especially into poured concrete—is that the drill often strikes a hard particle that causes it to drift or slip to one side of where you want the hole. You can help avoid this by starting the hole with a star drill (steel center punch will work, too), then boring the hole with the electric drill.

In poured concrete, made with chert or flint gravel, the masonry bit may not be able to cut through these superhard bits of aggregate without some help. If the drill stops going into the wall and begins to emit a high-pitched shriek, remove it from the hole and use a star drill or center punch to break the piece of gravel. Then, continue drilling with the electric drill.

Different types of anchors come with instructions on the size and depth hole needed. When you have the hole drilled to the proper depth, insert the expansion sleeve, split pin or whatever type anchor you are using.

Ordinarily, you will align the object to be fastened to the wall for a guide for where to drill the holes in the masonry. However, for reasons mentioned above, drilling into solid concrete is not always as precise as boring holes in wood. Here's a better way to line up the project:

Outline where the object is to be fastened, then drill the holes and set the anchors that you're going to use. Cut the heads off a couple of screws or bolts that fit the anchors and file a slight point on the head end. Thread the screw, temporarily, into the anchor, with the sharpened head protruding slightly from the wall. Hold the object you're hanging on the wall in position against the projecting points and bang it with the heel of your hand. This will leave dents where you need to drill holes in the object to be fastened to the wall.

When you choose the type of concrete or masonry anchor, keep in mind the weight, size and depth of the object to be fastened to the masonry wall or floor. Small items, such as picture frames and small shelves don't exert a great deal of pressure on the fastener. Wall cabinets, plumbing fixtures and such need more holding power.

Split pin type anchors expand to grip the sides of a hole drilled in masonry walls.

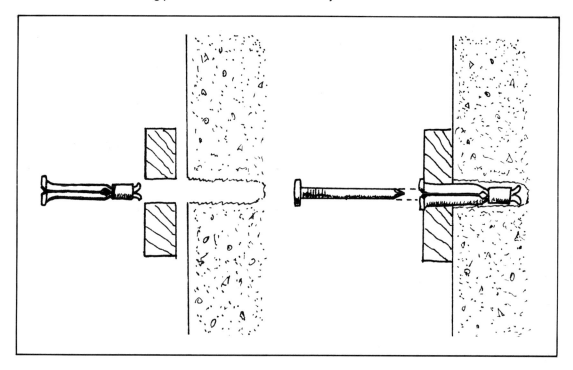

Section C
PLUMBING TOOLS

If you have a set of household tools—screwdrivers, open end and adjustable wrenches, slip joint pliers, round point shovel or tiling spade—you are already equipped to handle most commonly occurring plumbing emergencies. Unless you plan to go into the plumbing business, the tools you'll need beyond a few basic ones should be bought or more expensive plumbing tools rented as you need them.

Have a basic understanding of your plumbing system and how it works. When the bathroom is flooding, you call and pay a plumber, not so much for the special wrench he uses to shut the water off as for knowing where to apply the wrench. By studying basic plumbing principles and an inspection of your own plumbing system, you will know where to apply the wrench yourself.

Actually, the plumbing in your house is composed of several "systems"—some interconnected, some separate. In most homes there is a "cold-water" system, a "hot-water" system, and a "drainage (or sewer)" system. Depending on where you live and what type of water or sewage service you have, your home may also have a "water-well" system, a "septic-tank" system, a "hot-water-heating" system, and so on.

It's good preventive medicine to check over your plumbing system as completely as you can—before it springs a leak. Trace water supplies, the drainage system, and locate shut-off valves, drain traps, drain valves and other fixtures. You'll also want to pay particular attention to the different kinds of pipes, fittings and fixtures and the materials of which they are made. You'll need different tools and techniques to repair copper tubing, plastic pipe or galvanized steel pipe. An older home may have a cast-iron or clay tile drainage system, both of which involve special repair problems.

Have the tools you'll need on hand and in good working condition. For installing galvanized pipe, you'll need Stillson (pipe) wrenches; a pipe vise; pipe cutters, reamers and threaders. With copper tubing, you'll need a good tubing cutter and either a propane torch for making sweat fittings or a flaring tool for making flared joints. With PVC plastic pipe, you'll need a miter box and handsaw to cut the pipe squarely.

13 Getting a Grip on Things

It's tough to predict exactly which plumbing emergencies will strike and what tools you'll need to handle them. However, as a good part of plumbing consists of screwing and unscrewing threaded parts and fittings, we will discuss holding and gripping tools first.

As noted earlier, you will not need a great many specialized plumbing tools, even if you are planning a major plumbing project. And many of those tools you will need may already be in your tool box.

When buying plumbing tools—once again—**pay attention to quality**. With some, such as adjustable wrenches, you'll also want to consider the range of application. A pipe wrench (Stillson wrench) will find many uses other than those directly related to plumbing—holding and turning steel rods and other round stock, for instance.

So don't stint on quality, even if you will buy only a few tools specifically for plumbing projects. A good pipe wrench still costs less than a single visit by the plumber.

The main gripping tool for plumbing work is the pipe wrench. Tools shown in the sketch are, from the top, straight pipe wrench (Stillson); off-set pipe wrench; strap wrench; and chain wrench.

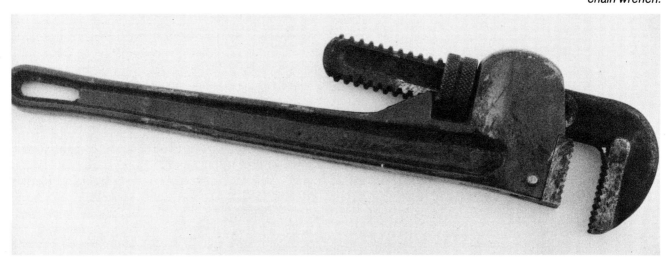

Pipe Wrenches

A **pipe wrench**—or "Stillson"—has adjustable toothed jaws that grip the hard, round surface of steel pipe as force is applied to the handle. On quality wrenches, the teeth are made of tough steel that will hold on the hardest pipe. Less expensive wrenches have softer teeth which become dull and slip on the smooth, round pipe.

Better quality pipe wrenches are designed so that some parts—such as the movable and fixed jaws—can be replaced. However, with normal use, you'll seldom need to replace a pipe wrench or any of its parts.

For most jobs, you'll need two pipe wrenches—one to grip the pipe and one to grip the round coupling. Good choices for most homeowners are a 14 inch wrench with jaws that open to two inches and an 18 inch wrench with a 2½ inch jaw width. Pipe wrenches are made in sizes from six to 24 inches, with the size referring to the overall length of the tool when jaws are open to the maximum width.

The toothed jaws of a pipe wrench are not exactly parallel, as are the smooth jaws of a monkey wrench or adjustable open end wrench. The outer jaw, or "hook" jaw, is adjusted by turning a knurled nut, and is designed

If you can avoid it, do not use a pipe wrench on nuts or other flat-sided fittings. The jawed teeth damage the shoulders of the fitting.

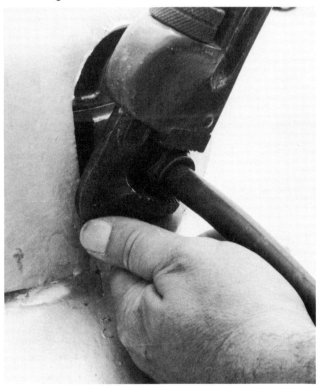

with a slight amount of play or "slack" which allows the teeth to grip a round surface tightly when the wrench is turned in the direction of the outer jaw.

And grip it does. In plumbing applications, a pipe wrench should be used only on steel or brass pipe; the jaws will crush copper tubing or plastic pipe. The teeth are designed to dig into the pipe and will leave marks. This doesn't matter much on thick walled galvanized pipe that will be hidden from view, but a pipe wrench should not be used on chrome-plated or polished fittings or pipe.

In general, flat-sided fittings—such as valves and pipe unions—should not be tightened or loosened with a pipe wrench. The jaws can damage the shoulders of these fittings. However, a nut, union or valve that has been damaged or rounded by improperly used wrenches or pliers can be loosened with a pipe wrench. You'll probably mangle the fitting so that nothing *except* a pipe wrench can be used on it again, but sometimes you have no alternative.

Some people never seem to get the hang of adjusting a pipe wrench. Set the jaws so that the pipe jams between them about halfway back, rather than all the way against the throat of the wrench. This way, when you pull on the wrench handle, the jaws tighten together and bite into the pipe.

A good pipe wrench is a rugged tool that will stand up to a lot of hard use, but not abuse. Don't hammer with or on the wrench. If you need more leverage to loosen a rusted nut, you probably can get by with using a "cheater" (piece of pipe) to extend the handle; but it's better to get a longer wrench.

Pipe wrenches need little maintenance. Keep the adjusting mechanism clean and free of dirt and grit. Lubricate the adjusting screw occasionally with powdered graphite. Wipe the tool dry before storing it.

Adjustable Open End Wrench

An adjustable **open end wrench** (often called a **Crescent wrench**, after its major manufacturer) has smooth parallel jaws that are infinitely adjustable between the narrowest and widest opening. It fits any number of standard and metric nuts, bolts and other flat sided fittings.

For most household uses—and the tool has many—a 10 or 12 inch adjustable wrench is a good choice. The jaws are angled at about 30 degrees from the handle, which lets you use the wrench in many tight spots where a standard open end wrench would not do the job. By flipping the wrench over and getting a new grip, the nut or fitting usually can be loosened or tightened a little at a time.

The adjustable wrench is simple to use. The key is to adjust the wrench so it fits tightly on the nut or bolt. The

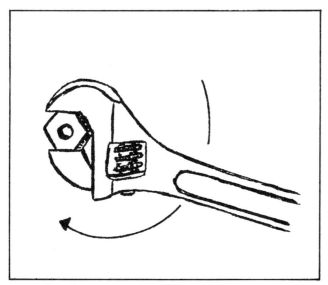

Adjustable open-end wrenches provide a wide range of capacity in one tool. Turn the wrench in the direction of the movable jaw, if possible.

Some of these "tongue-and-groove" type pliers have curved jaws designed to grip pipe. Others have straight toothed jaws. A 10-inch pliers has a jaw capacity of about two inches, and is a good choice for most household chores.

Locking Plier-Wrenches

Locking **plier-wrenches** (often called **"Vise Grips"**) come in a variety of sizes and have an almost limitless number of uses. The compound leverage system of a locking plier-wrench lets the tool function as pliers, wrench, portable vise or clamp.

The locking plier-wrench has a fixed upper jaw. The lower jaw can be adjusted by turning a knurled nut at the end of the fixed handle. A locking lever on the movable handle clamps the jaws onto an object of about any shape, so long as it will fit between the tool's jaws. These tools are made with both straight and curved jaws.

Similar tools are made with different types of jaws—C clamp, pipe clamp, sheet metal clamp, chain clamp,

movable jaw is adjusted by rotating a knurled screw. Place the wrench over the nut or fitting to be tightened or loosened, then tighten the adjusting nut until the jaws fit snugly.

One caution—no matter what kind of wrench you use—pull, rather than push the wrench handle, if at all possible. If you must push the handle, do it with the heel of your hand and your fingers held so that they will not be smashed should the wrench slip.

Don't hammer on a wrench handle, and don't use a piece of pipe or another wrench to extend the leverage of any wrench. Maintenance of an adjustable open end wrench is similar to that of a pipe wrench.

Pliers

Many plumbing jobs do not call for the "biting" power or leverage of a pipe wrench. For some tasks, ordinary combination pliers can be useful; for unscrewing smaller pipes and fittings that have been loosened with another tool, for instance.

But ordinary slip joint pliers do not have enough gripping power for many projects. They can slip on tight nuts or fittings, damaging the work and your knuckles.

A better choice of tool for most pipe work is the **expandable pliers** (often called **"Channelock" pliers**, after their major manufacturer, or **water pump pliers**).

Expansive pliers have toothed jaws that adjust to several different opening widths. The better tools of this type have a number of channels or grooves cut on one half of the tool, which engage projections on the other half.

Locking plier-wrenches are handy for many jobs, and can even serve as a second pipe wrench in plumbing chores. Set the adjustable tool to grip the round pipe about two-thirds of the way back on the jaws, then lock the jaws onto the work. This model, by Channelock, has a finger-tip release feature.

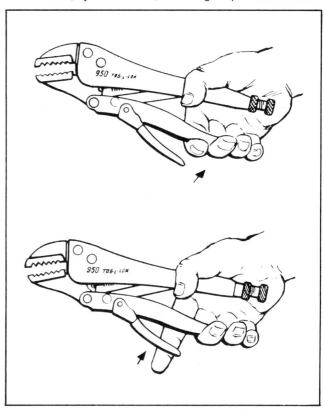

etc.—all with the same adjusting and locking feature. The **chain clamp locking tool** can be used in lieu of a pipe wrench or chain wrench to hold pipe, or can be used in conjunction with a machinist's vise to make a passable pipe vise. (It also can double as an oil filter wrench.)

While a locking plier-wrench has many applications about the household, and may be one of the handier tools you will own, it is only a fair substitute for open end, box end or adjustable wrenches for that purpose.

Locking plier-wrenches come in standard sizes from five to 10 inches.

Vises

A **pipe vise** is used primarily to hold pipe and other round stock. It differs from an ordinary machinist's vise in that its toothed, angled jaws (or chains) grip a pipe and prevent it from rotating. This is an important function when you are cutting, reaming or threading galvanized pipe.

However, for occasional use, the most practical kind of vise for you may be a **machinist's vise** equipped with auxiliary pipe jaws. A machinist's vise can be used for a great many other jobs; whereas the alternative uses of a pipe vise are limited.

You can also hold pipe in an ordinary **flat jawed vise**, with the aid of a pipe wrench. Adjust the wrench on the pipe, then cramp the handle of the wrench against the side of the workbench. Another way to use a flat jawed vise to hold pipe is to fasten temporary wooden jaw inserts on the vise.

If you plan to cut, thread, bend and join quite a lot of brass or galvanized steel pipe, you may want to buy or rent a vise specifically for use with pipe. If so, choose one that has its own stand of three sturdy but collapsible legs, with a locking platform between. This type of vise can be set up where you have room to maneuver long sections of pipe.

Select a vise that will handle pipe up to two inches in diameter, if you're buying it; even if you do not initially plan to work with pipe of that large a size.

Pipe vises are made in several different designs; better ones use either a yoke or chain clamping device. Some, as mentioned, are mounted on their own tripod-like stands; some clamp or bolt to a workbench. Some have quick-tighten, quick-release mechanisms. In addition,

A pipe vise is handy for plumbing jobs, but not absolutely necessary. You can clamp pipe in a machinist's vise and keep it from turning by cramping a pipe wrench against the bench, as in the drawing at left. Or, you can add wood inserts to the jaws of a machinist's vise.

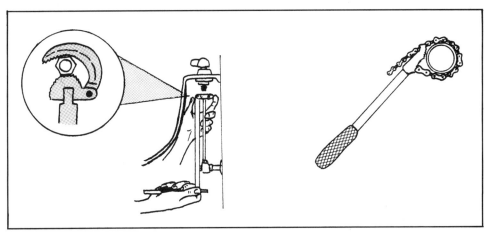

A basin wrench, left, is designed to get at hard-to-reach nuts, as those behind sinks and lavatories. The head swivels to either tighten or loosen nuts. A chain wrench, at right, uses a bicycle type chain to grip pipe, and often pinch hits as a second pipe wrench.

many pipe vises have channels for bending pipe of various sizes.

Other Gripping Tools

In addition to the tools mentioned earlier—most of which have uses outside the plumbing area—you may need some specialized gripping and holding tools for particular jobs. Often, if you have only temporary need of a specialized tool, it's better to rent or borrow, rather than buy.

A **basin wrench** has toothed jaws that are mounted at right angles to one end of a long steel handle. The tool is designed specifically to reach up into the close quarters beneath a sink or lavatory and tighten or loosen the nuts holding the faucet or fixture in place.

To use the wrench, hold the shaft parallel to the supply pipe, hook the jaws around the nut and turn the handle. One of the jaws can be flipped over so the tool can be reversed to either tighten or loosen the nut.

Your most likely position for using a basin wrench is flat on your back beneath the sink. You'll usually need a light under there, too; a flashlight with a magnetic holder comes in handy.

Adjustable spud wrenches are smooth-jawed tools with adjusting mechanisms similar to those of pipe wrenches. They are made in straight end and offset types, and are designed to fit the flanges of unions, valve bonnets, drain nuts on tubs and sinks, and other flat, hexagonal fittings.

Unless you will be doing a lot of plumbing, don't invest in one of these tools. They are handy, but you can accomplish most functions of this wrench with an adjustable open end wrench of the proper size.

Chain wrenches are made in a variety of styles and sizes, and are versatile tools. The chain is attached to a handle so that when the chain is wrapped around a pipe (or any irregular surface) and pressure is put on the handle, the chain tightens and bites into the pipe.

A chain wrench can be used in places too tight to maneuver a pipe wrench. In fact, many handymen prefer a chain wrench-pipe wrench combination, rather than a pair of pipe wrenches.

A **strap wrench** is similar to a chain wrench in operating principle, but uses a hard nylon belt to grip the pipe, rather than a toothed chain. When pressure is put on the handle, the strap tightens and turns the pipe by the friction of the belt.

Strap wrenches are used primarily to install chrome plated and polished pipe and fittings, where a pipe wrench or chain wrench might scratch and mar the finish. You can get along without a strap wrench and still install scratch free fixtures by using several layers of cloth between the pipe and the jaws of a pipe wrench.

Valve seat wrenches are special tools used to remove seats from valves and faucets. Two types are in general use.

One is a straight square steel bar 8 to 10 inches long, with a fitting for square valve seat holes on one end and a fitting for valve seats with octagonal holes in the other. A wrench is used to turn this tool.

The other valve seat wrench is made with the same fittings on either end, but the steel bar is L-shaped and can be turned without the use of a wrench.

To remove a valve seat, dismantle the valve or faucet by removing the cap nut and spindle. Insert the valve seat wrench (either the square or octagonal end, whichever is needed) into the hole in the valve seat and unscrew it. We'll have more on valve and faucet repair in Chapter 15.

There are many other kinds of special gripping and holding tools—some are good, some are merely gadgets. Look around and talk to plumbers to see what special tools make a particular job faster or easier. Chances are you'll discover a handy implement or two not mentioned here. But chances are even better that for 99 percent of the work the professional plumber uses the tools described above.

14
Cutting, Reaming and Threading Tools

When it comes to cutting tools, a basic knowledge of the material to be cut is helpful; as is some planning of the job before the work starts.

Accurate measurements taken before any cutting is done prevents the waste of time and materials. Careful planning can let you get along with fewer joints and fittings—another saving in time, as well as money.

Smaller jobs of pipework can often be supplied by lengths of pre-cut pipe purchased with the threads already cut. If your plumbing job is a more complex project, involving the use of several parts, joints, fittings and fixtures, you probably will want to make at least a rough sketch showing dimensions and the kind and location of fittings to be used. Again, careful planning and accurate measurements are musts.

When measuring and cutting pipe, be sure to take into account the distance the pipe will screw into the couplings and other fittings on its ends. The same is true of plastic pipe and copper fittings.

For virtually all cutting, reaming and threading jobs, you will need some way to hold the pipe firmly. A pipe vise, as mentioned in Chapter 13, is handiest, but not absolutely necessary.

Cutting Pipe and Tubing

For an occasional job of pipe cutting, a **hacksaw** will suffice. It's not as handy as a pipe cutter, but it's cheaper and has more alternate uses.

Use a medium to fine toothed blade (18 to 24 teeth per inch) and work carefully to avoid catching and breaking out teeth or breaking the blade. Generally, the thicker the material being cut, the coarser the saw blade. Use a file edge to make a notch where the pipe is to be cut. This not only marks the place, but helps to start the saw blade in exactly the right place.

Mount the blade in the saw frame with the teeth pointing forward, or away from the handle, and stretch the blade tightly in the frame. Use even pressure on the saw

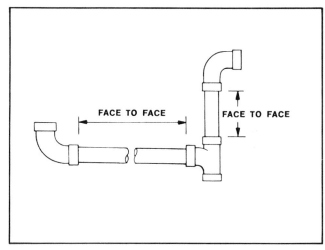

Accurate measuring is critical to pipe-fitting. The best way to measure plastic pipe, as shown, is by the face to face method, which requires that you add the necessary length for pipe entering the sockets of fittings. For plastic pipe, the socket depths are:

Pipe size	Socket depth
1½″	¾″
2 ″	⅞″
3 ″	1½″

Galvanized steel pipe commonly is also measured face to face, then the distance the pipe screws into standard fittings is added to the measurement. Be sure to add the extra length for fittings on both ends of the pipe. Fitting screw-in distances for standard galvanized fittings are as follows:

Pipe size	Fitting depth
½″	½″
¾″	½″
1 ″	⅝″
1¼″	⅝″
1½″	⅝″
2 ″	¾″

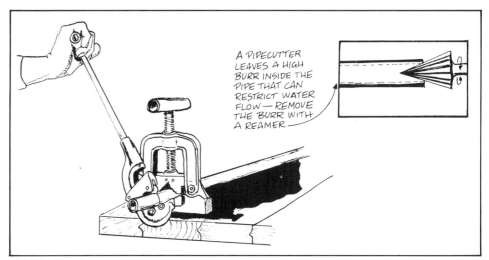

A wheeled pipecutter leaves a high burr inside the pipe that can restrict water flow. Remove the burr with a pipe reamer, as shown in the inset sketch.

A PIPECUTTER LEAVES A HIGH BURR INSIDE THE PIPE THAT CAN RESTRICT WATER FLOW — REMOVE THE BURR WITH A REAMER

and make long, slow strokes, releasing the pressure on the backstroke. If you are cutting steel or iron pipe, use a lubricant made of equal parts of light machine oil and kerosene.

If you have much steel pipe to cut, you'll be time and work ahead if you buy or rent a **wheeled pipe cutter**. A quality cutter is fairly expensive to buy, but with reasonable use, should last indefinitely. You may be able to rent or borrow a pipe cutter from your plumbing supply house. Some mail order firms also loan tools to customers.

A pipe cutter leaves a smoother, squarer end on the pipe than does a hacksaw. These tools are made in several designs. The standard one most homeowners will find useful is a one wheeled cutter model with a hand screw to tighten the cutter as it is turned or rotated on the pipe. The cutter head has a pair of small rollers that bear against the pipe and hold the hard steel cutting wheel

exactly perpendicular to the surface of the pipe.

To use the pipe cutter, place the tool carefully on the pipe (held firmly in a vise) so that the cutting wheel engages the pipe at exactly the place to be cut. Tighten the wheel snugly against the pipe by screwing the handle clockwise. Apply threading or cutting oil and turn the cutter 360 degrees around the pipe, tightening the handle a little each turn to force the cutting wheel into the pipe, until the pipe is cut in two.

A standard pipe cutter cannot handily be used to cut installed pipe; there's seldom enough room for a 360 degree swing. One **ratchet action cutter** on the market lets you cut pipe anywhere you can move the handle as much as 10 degrees—between joists, inside walls, under sinks, etc. This type of pipe cutter is handy for removing a section of defective pipe, but the tool costs about $50.

Copper tubing can be cut with a hacksaw; but again,

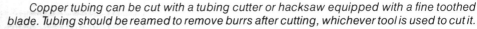

Copper tubing can be cut with a tubing cutter or hacksaw equipped with a fine toothed blade. Tubing should be reamed to remove burrs after cutting, whichever tool is used to cut it.

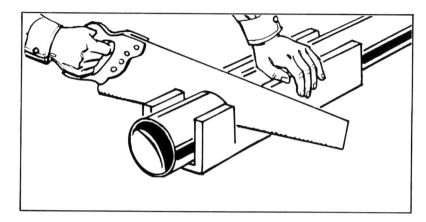

Plastic pipe can be cut with a hand-saw; use a miter box to cut the pipe squarely. (Courtesy of Sears, Roebuck)

the job is easier and more precise if you use a tubing cutter—a smaller, lighter version of the wheeled pipe cutter. Be careful not to turn the handscrew more than half a turn at a time, to avoid bending or flattening the thin walled tubing.

Plastic and bituminous fiber (Orangeburg) pipe can be cut with a crosscut handsaw or hacksaw. Use a miter box or other guide to make a square 90 degree cut in the pipe.

Reaming Pipe and Tubing

Pipe and tubing cutters, and to a lesser extent, hacksaw blades, leave a burr inside the pipe. This burr, or lip should be removed so as not to restrict the flow of water in the pipe. (See Illustration)

Most **tubing cutters** have a retractable reamer, that can quickly remove burrs from the soft copper tubing. Steel pipes take tougher equipment.

Several types of **pipe reamers** are on the market, including those with their own ratcheted handles. More practical for most homeowners is a square shanked conical reamer that fits an ordinary bit-brace. To use the reamer, mount the shank in a bit-brace chuck and insert the point of the reamer into the end of the pipe as far as it will go. Keep the reamer parallel to the pipe and rotate the brace slowly in a clockwise direction. Stop reaming as soon as the burr has been removed.

If the pipe is to be threaded, reaming ordinarily should be done after threads are cut. For only a few pieces of pipe, you can use a round or half-round file to remove the burrs.

On plastic pipe, any burr left by the saw can quickly be removed with medium sandpaper.

Threading Pipe

A **pipe threader** consists of a steel central holder—called the "stock"—in which thread cutting guides (called

"collets") and dies can be clamped. Some models have a pair of long steel handles extending on opposite sides; others have a single handle with a ratchet action.

To use the tool, select the proper size collet and die for the pipe you want to thread. Some thread cutters have adjustable guides, rather than removable collets. Loosen the cover plate on the stock (usually held down with a

Pipe threaders use a tapered die to cut threads in steel pipe. (Courtesy of Bill Mason)

thumb screw or wing nut) and open the cover plate. Insert the proper sized threading die and tighten the cover plate.

On the opposite side of the tool, fit a collet sized to match the pipe diameter—or if the thread cutter has an adjustable guide, set it for the pipe diameter. The guide, or collet, slides onto the pipe ahead of the thread cutting die and holds the die straight on the end of the pipe.

Place the die on the end of the pipe, and push the tool until it makes firm contact with the end of the pipe.

Check to make sure the die is aligned correctly, then turn the threader slowly clockwise, exerting considerable pressure until the tool starts to cut into the pipe. Stop and squirt cutting oil liberally on the die and pipe.

Continue turning the thread cutter clockwise for half a turn, then turn it back counter-clockwise about a quarter of a turn to clear metal chips and shavings. Repeat this half a turn clockwise, quarter turn counter-clockwise, applying cutting oil on the die and pipe often.

When the end of the pipe is flush with the outside surface of the die, stop and turn the thread cutter counter-clockwise to back it out and off of the pipe. If the die is screwed on further, the end of the pipe that projects through will have straight threads, rather than tapered threads. Pipe threads are supposed to be slightly tapered, so they will tighten securely in the fittings.

Shake the chips and cuttings from the die and brush them from the pipe threads. Wipe the thread cutter with a lightly oiled cloth before putting it away.

Cutting Cast-Iron Pipe

Unless you live in one of several places where a homeowner must contend with archaic building codes, you probably will not be using cast iron drain piping for new plumbing—not with copper and ABS plastic so much lighter and easier to work with.

But in times past, cast iron was widely used for drain piping, and is still specified by building codes of some municipalities. It's durable stuff, and if you own or rent an older house, it probably has cast iron drains.

A regular wheeled pipe cutter won't touch it. You will have to use something else to cut cast iron. There are special chain-clamp cutters that break cast iron pipe with one swing of a long handle, but since you'll probably be repairing or modifying a drain system that is already in place, these may not function in the close spaces you'll need to work.

For "service weight" cast iron, you can score a cut about $1/16$ inch deep all the way around the pipe with a hacksaw, then use a cold chisel to finish breaking the pipe at the scored mark. Use a cold chisel with about a ¾ inch wide blade and a fairly blunt cutting edge.

For "extra heavy" weight cast iron pipe, you probably will need to use a cold chisel all the way. Work the chisel

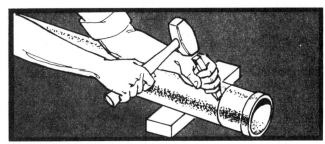

Cast-iron pipe is scored with a chisel, then tapped with a hammer to break the pipe along the scored line.

around and around the cut, gradually striking the chisel harder and harder to separate the pipe. However, don't hit the chisel too hard before a good, deep scoring mark has been made in the pipe. Cast-iron pipe can shatter.

Vitrified clay pipe is cut in much the same way, but use a sharper cold chisel than with cast iron.

Other Cutting and Threading Tools

In some special situations, you may need a **threading tap**, to cut threads inside pipe or holes in metal. A tap resembles a machine screw, with four slots down its side. The end of the tap is smaller than the body, as the tap is screwed into a pipe or pre-drilled hole, its own threads cut threads in the softer metal.

The method of use of a tap to make interior threads is similar to that of a die to make external threads. The key, to making the tool work, is to drill the proper size hole (or use the proper size tap for the pipe being threaded) and lubricating the cutting threads. The most likely use you will have of a machine thread tap—as far as plumbing is concerned—is to thread a hole in cast iron pipe to accommodate a new drain line; perhaps when you are installing a utility room sink or stall shower.

A **flat file** is useful for smoothing and squaring the end of a pipe; particularly one that has been cut with a hacksaw. Hold the end of the pipe in a vise or on a flat surface, and file squarely across the end.

Valve seat refacing tools are used to cut or grind the seat of a faucet or valve that has been scored by leaking water. Generally, it's a better bet to remove and replace the valve seat than to try to re-face it, but some older valves and faucets do not have removable seats.

Don't fool with the T-shaped valve seat refacers sold in the so-called repair kits in dime stores and discount houses. They seldom do the job.

Instead, try to borrow or rent a professional tool with interchangable cutters. These tools cost more money than usually can be justified by the homeowner who only needs to repair one or two faucets, however.

It's cheaper (and usually more satisfactory) to replace the entire valve or faucet.

15
Assembling Pipe and Fittings

Plumbing, as any trade, has its own tools and its own curious terminology. For instance, thin walled copper tubing, when installed as part of a plumbing system, is called "pipe"—as in cold water pipe.

Part of the jargon—and you don't need to learn much of it—comes from the fact that a half dozen or more kinds of pipe are used in modern plumbing; with probably a dozen different methods of connecting them. You also will not need a great many of the specialized tools that plumbers use to make the connections.

Selecting the materials you will use from the wide assortment of pipes and fittings available is not as baffling as it may seem at first. However, you should be familiar enough with different materials and components to tell the difference between, say, copper tubing and CPVC plastic pipe, and know how and why to install a particular fitting in a particular place.

Some materials complement each other; some compete with each other. For instance, copper placed in direct contact with steel quickly corrodes from electrolysis, often to the point that the pipe or fitting can fail. This problem is solved by joining copper to steel with a fitting of non-conducting material compatible with both copper and steel.

Which material you use in your plumbing projects will be dictated partly by your budget, as well as by the function of the components. If you are doing repair or add-on jobs, the existing material may determine what you use to some extent. You can use one type of material for an entire job, or mix and match materials to cut costs or meet specific needs.

If you live in a town or other political subdivision with building codes, bone up on the rules before you get too far along with your planning. If the local code specifies certain materials for some systems, you'll need to use them to observe the letter of the law. It doesn't necessarily mean that material is better than others, however. Rules of this kind are usually made by humans with strong personal preferences—or perhaps a brother-in-law in the plumbing supply business.

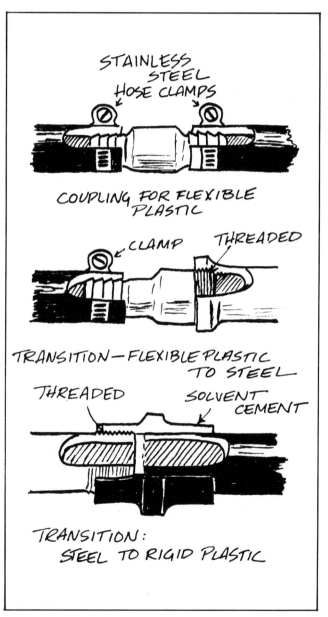

Fittings are made for connecting different types of pipe together.

The methods and tools used to join pipes and fittings vary with the material used. Galvanized steel, black iron and brass (seldom used these days) pipe usually is threaded and assembled with threaded fittings. Copper tubing can be joined by soldering (sweating), flaring connections or compression joints. Plastic pipe often is joined with solvent cement; although some types of plastic pipe can be threaded. Cast iron pipe, depending on the type, can be joined either by threaded fittings or lead caulking. Some pipe, such as bituminous fiber or asbestos cement used for sewer lines, is joined together with friction couplings.

If you are adding to an existing plumbing system, investigate the possibility of using "transition fittings" to join new plastic or copper to older galvanized steel or cast iron piping. If you are planning a major new plumbing project (and local codes do not prohibit their use) consider copper tubing or plastic pipe for both hot and cold water supply lines, and plastic for drain, waste and vent piping. These materials are lightweight (plastic weighs only five percent as much as steel pipe of the same internal diameter) and easy to work with.

Joining Plastic Pipe

It's possible to install the entire drainage, waste and vent systems of a building with only a miter box, handsaw and a couple of pieces of medium grade sandpaper—plus a measuring tape, of course. Plastic, in addition to being quick and easy to install, is especially well suited for drain and sewer lines or septic tank lines. It is resistant to corrosion, soil acids and repels tree roots as well as any other type of material.

Kinds of Plastic Pipe			
Material	**Type**	**General Uses**	**Joining Methods**
ABS (Acrylonitrile-Butadiene-Styrène	Rigid	Drain, waste and vent; soil pipe	Solvent cement; clamp fittings
CPVC (Chlorinated polyvinyl Chloride)	Rigid	Hot and cold water service threaded; clamp fittings	Solvent cement;
PE (Polyethylene)	Flexible	Cold water supply; Gas service (where permitted)	Insert fittings; clamp fittings
PVC (Polyvinyl-Chloride)	Rigid	Cold water service; drain, waste, vent; electrical conduit; gas service	Solvent cement; threaded; clamp fittings

Make sure you're buying plastic pipe and fittings of the quality and material you need. See that the material is marked with the manufacturer's name or trademark, pipe size, plastic compound or code, pressure rating and the standard to which the pipe is manufactured (usually an ASTM standard). In addition, better quality pipe has been tested by the National Sanitation Foundation and will carry the NSF seal.

Flexible plastic pipe can be cut with a handsaw, backsaw or hacksaw. In a pinch, you can even cut it with a knife, but a saw is better. Rigid plastic can be cut with a tubing cutter or saw. If you're using a saw, cut the pipe in a miter box to get square ends, then ream the inside of the pipe with the reamer on the tubing cutter or a knife.

Plastic pipe and fittings most often are joined by a solvent cement which results in a "welded" bond between pipe and fitting. This is a simple operation, but care should be taken to make sure fittings are properly aligned.

Measure and cut the pipe to the correct length (including the distance the pipe will enter the fitting) and adjust the fitting in the correct position for assembly. Mark both the pipe and the fitting so you can quickly put them in position after applying the cement. The cement sets in just a few seconds, and the joint is forevermore permanent.

To joint plastic pipe and fittings, buff the area of the pipe that is inserted into the fitting with sandpaper; apply the solvent cement to both the pipe and coupling; and insert the pipe into the fitting and turn about a quarter-turn. (Courtesy of Sears, Roebuck and Company)

Remove the fitting from the pipe end and check to see that the inside burr has been reamed down. Make sure the pipe is clean and free of water and oil. With a piece of sandpaper, roughen the pipe slightly for about an inch back from the end. Check the inside of the fitting to make sure it also is clean.

Then, quickly apply a thin coating of cement (with the dauber in the cement can) to the inside of the fitting and the outside of the pipe. Don't put too much cement inside the fitting; any excess will be squeezed into a burr when you install the pipe.

Assemble the joint quickly after the cement is applied. Turn the fitting a quarter-turn or so, and line up the marks you made earlier.

Wait about five minutes before moving the pipe to make the joint at the other end of the pipe or fitting. The cement dries quickly, but the joint can be weakened if the parts are moved before it is set.

Flexible plastic pipe often is joined to fittings and pipe of other materials by a "transition" fitting. The most common type is a short piece of metal or hard plastic that is inserted into the end of the plastic pipe and held in place by a clamp very much like the clamps on auto heater hoses. The other end of the fitting typically is threaded to accept a valve, pipe coupling or other metal fitting.

The transition from rigid plastic to steel or copper can be made in several ways. Rigid plastic can be threaded in much the same way as is steel pipe, but cutting threads weakens the pipe considerably. If possible, some other method should be used to join rigid plastic to fittings of other materials.

One such fitting incorporates an O-ring type seal, similar to a compression fitting for copper tubing. A flange nut fits over the seal and the end of the plastic pipe, and when tightened, compresses the seal against the pipe. The other end of the fitting is either threaded to take threaded pipe or fittings, or has a sweat type joint to take copper tubing.

One caution: where transition fittings involve a sweat joint on one end, make the sweat connection first and allow the fitting to cool before attaching the plastic pipe. Heat from the soldering torch can warp and damage plastic.

Joining Copper Tubing

Copper tubing, while costing more than galvanized steel pipe of the same size, is a popular choice for water supply piping. It's easier to install than steel. You simply measure it, cut, ream and join it together by one of three or four different methods.

Copper tubing is available in sizes from ¼ to ¾ inch, and in two types: rigid (hard-drawn) and flexible (soft-

drawn). Rigid copper comes in 10 and 20 foot lengths. Flexible tubing comes in coils of 12, 30 or 60 feet.

If you are replacing defective pipe or adding to an existing water system, you may prefer to use flexible copper tubing. It can be snaked around obstacles and led through walls, floors and ceilings without joints or fittings. This cuts down on the possibility of a leak in an awkward location.

Even so-called flexible tubing can buckle or kink when sharp bends are made, however. If you need to make sharp bends, use a **tubing bender**. The most convenient type is a wound, spring steel cylinder that resembles a screen door spring.

For new construction plumbing, rigid copper is more often used, with elbow fittings to make neat 90 and 45 degree angles in the system. It's prettier, but right angle bends cut water pressure more than long sweeping bends made with flexible tubing.

Either type of copper tubing can be joined with any one of three commonly used joints. However, because the tubing has thin walls, it should not be threaded.

Sweating (or soldering) is the most widely used method of joining copper pipe and fittings. To make sweat joints, you'll need a tubing cutter (with reamer), some steel wool, an old toothbrush (for applying soldering flux) and a portable propane torch.

Tools you'll need to make copper sweat fittings are propane torch, a toothbrush for applying paste flux, lead-tin wire solder, and steel wool.

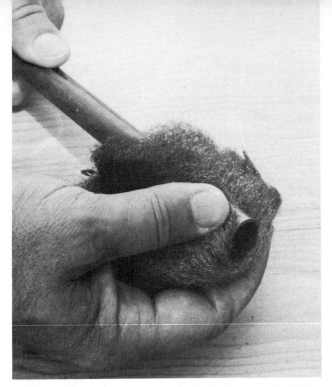

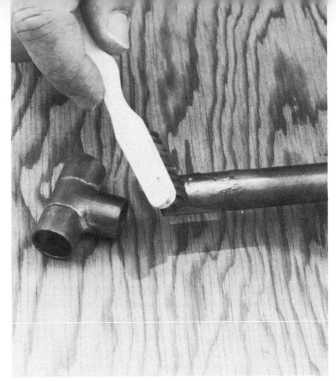

Shine the end of the copper pipe and the inside of the fitting with steel wool before applying flux.

Apply paste-type soldering flux liberally to pipe and fitting.

You will also need a supply of paste-type soldering flux and a spool of wire-type solder that is 50-50 lead and tin, or a solder that is 40 percent tin and 60 percent lead. Either will do the job; the 60 percent lead product is slightly cheaper. Unless you can find no other solder, don't use the rosin core or acid core types. They will work, but need higher temperatures to flow properly.

Measure and cut the copper tubing (which becomes "pipe" or "line" when soldered and installed) with a tubing cutter. Slip the fitting to be sweated over the pipe end. It should go on easily, but fit fairly snugly.

(Note: if you are sweating a valve onto copper pipe, take the valve apart before starting the soldering process. The heat can damage valve washers and packing.)

Remove the fitting and clean the inside end that will fit over the pipe with steel wool. Also clean the end of the pipe back about an inch. Don't try to remove too much material from either the fitting or the pipe—merely buff it good with the steel wool.

Next, using an old toothbrush, apply a liberal coating of paste flux to both the inside of the fitting and the end of the pipe. Don't worry about using too much flux. Any excess will boil away, with no harm done. Too little flux can result in a weak joint.

Now, reassemble the joint, making sure the fitting is aligned properly. Clamp the pipe in a vise or brace it on a brick or other non-flammable object. If you are making a sweat joint next to a wall, floor or other finished surface, use several layers of aluminum foil to protect it.

To light the propane torch, first, strike a match, *then* open the valve—just a crack. The results of leaving the valve open while you search for a match—particularly in

a confined space—are apt to be noisy and serious. When the torch lights, open the valve slowly until the flame burns steadily about two inches long. Opening the valve further will only burn more gas, without providing a more adequate soldering flame.

Play the torch flame on the fitting and pipe, but not directly on the joint. Heat the heaviest piece of metal first (usually this is the fitting) then the lighter part. Test the temperature of the fitting by touching the tip of the solder to it. If the solder melts immediately, the metal is hot enough. When the solder melts readily on both the pipe and fitting, place the tip of the solder wire against the joint. As the solder melts, it is drawn into the joint by capillary action—even if the joint is uphill. Keep feeding the solder until a bright ring of solder appears all around the joint.

If you are making more than one joint on the same pipe or fitting, go right to the second joint immediately after the first is completed. When the joint—or joints—is finished, let the pipe and fitting set undisturbed for several minutes.

That's all there is to it—except, don't forget to turn the torch off after the last sweat fitting is made.

Metal ring compression joints can be made in copper pipe and fittings with only a tubing cutter and an adjustable open end wrench. This type of joint is made with a flange nut, a wide brass ring (that resembles a wedding band) and a fitting—coupling, elbow, valve, faucet, etc.

These compression joints are often used to connect faucet supply tubing to cut-off valves. To make this type of joint, cut the tubing squarely with a tubing cutter and remove any burrs or ridges. Slip the flange nut and brass ring over the end of the tube, then insert the end of the tubing and the metal ring into the fitting. Tighten the flange

Heat the copper fitting first, then the pipe to soldering temperature. Do not play the torch flame directly on the joint.

Feed solder into the joint until a bright ring of solder appears all the way around the joint. Let the pipe cool some before moving it.

nut down over the ring and onto the fitting. You won't need to use a great deal of pressure to make this joint water tight. Merely tighten the nut as tightly as you can with your fingers, then turn it another quarter turn or so with the wrench.

A similar compression joint employs a rubber O-ring or composition washer type of seal.

Flare joints can be made in copper tubing, but the fittings used restrict the size of the pipe considerably. On the plus side, flare joints can be made quickly with just a few tools: Flaring tool, flat file and open end wrenches.

Flare joints are often made in copper tubing used for natural gas or LP gas service lines, where sweat fittings would not be appropriate for obvious reasons.

To make a flare joint, cut the copper tubing squarely, then slip a flange nut over the end of the tubing. Place the end of the tubing in a flaring tool and form a bell shaped flare on the end of the pipe.

Several types of flaring tools are on the market; most of them relatively inexpensive. The handiest type has an anvil-like body with flared holes to accept several different sizes of tubing. The tubing is clamped in the tool, with the end of the tube flush with the top surface of the anvil. Then, a screw-driven, cone-shaped ram is mounted directly over the end of the tubing and tightened slowly to flare or bell the end of the tube.

This bell fits over a corresponding cone shaped surface on the flare fitting. When the flange nut is tightened on the fitting, the flared end of the tubing seats firmly against the fitting.

Making a successful flare fitting is not particularly difficult. The key is to cut the tubing squarely on the end and

remove all burrs and ridges. If necessary, use a wide flat file to get the end of the copper tube absolutely square.

(Be sure the flange nut is slipped onto the tubing *before* the tubing is flared.)

You *can* make flared joints in rigid plastic, thin walled

Metal compression ring fittings are quick and easy to make, as in this supply pipe joined to a valve. The flange nut is slipped onto the pipe, then the metal compression ring is placed on the pipe and the flange nut screwed down on the body of the valve.

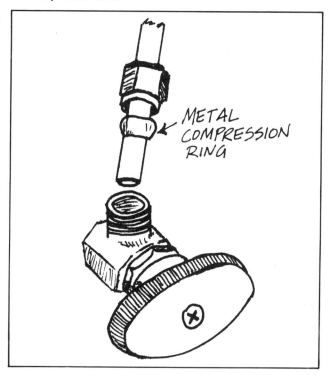

METAL COMPRESSION RING

SINK TAIL PIDE

WALL FLANGE

SLIP JOINT NUT

COMPRESSION WASHERS

P-TRAP

Flexible compression joints typically are made with drains and trap fittings from sinks and lavatories. A flexible washer or O-ring seal is tightened by a T-flange nut to make a leak-proof joint.

Making lead joints in cast iron pipe is fairly involved. First, a caulking tool (or yarning iron) is used to pack oakum into the joint, then molten lead is poured in on top of the oakum. After the lead hardens, it is expanded and sealed against the pipe with a caulking tool.

brass and stainless steel pipe, also, but there are usually better methods of connecting these materials.

Joining Steel Pipe

Galvanized steel pipe, with its attendant thread cutting and an almost infinite number of threaded fittings, is the traditional stuff that gives us the stereotyped image of a plumber. Cartoon caricatures of plumbers show them carrying pipe wrenches; although many of these workmen may use copper flaring tools and plastic solvent cement more often than Stillsons.

Despite the work required to make steel pipe connections, compared with installing copper or plastic, it is much stronger and tougher than either of those materials. And, in most regions, steel is cheaper than copper and may be cost competitive with plastic in most common sizes. Even if you use copper or plastic for most of your plumbing, you may want to use steel pipe in areas where the pipe is exposed and subject to possible damage—as in a garage or basement workshop.

Galvanized steel and black iron pipe are almost universally joined by threaded fittings. Gripping the round pipe and fittings is a job for pipe wrenches and chain wrenches, as described in Chapter 13.

However, there's more to making a pipe joint than simply screwing a threaded section of pipe into a threaded fitting. Never make up a pipe joint *dry*. The male threads of the joint should be coated with a pipe joint compound (called "pipe dope" by most plumbers) which acts as a sealer, lubricant and rust inhibitor.

Some plumbers use a thin Teflon tape instead of pipe joint compound.

After measuring, cutting, threading and reaming the

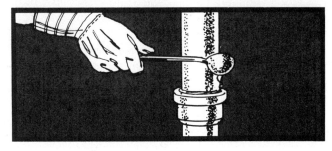

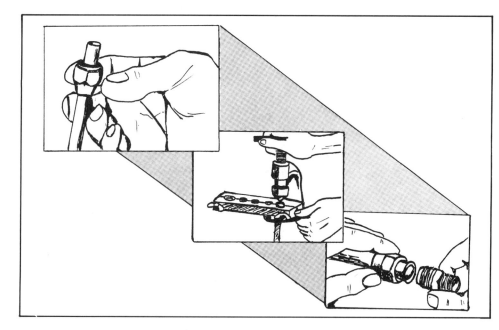

Flare joints in copper tubing are easy to make, but restrict water flow more than sweating or using metal rings. To make a flare joint, slip the flange nut over the pipe, flare the pipe in the correct flaring tool and tighten the flange nut on the fitting.

pipe—as described in the previous chapter—apply the pipe dope and screw the pipe and fitting together hand tight—usually about four or five turns. Then, complete the tightening with pipe wrenches—or a pipe wrench and chain wrench combination. If you use two pipe wrenches, adjust one to fit the pipe and the other to fit the couplings.

You don't need to exert a great deal of pressure on the joint. Threads on the pipe and inside the fitting are tapered to jam firmly together as the joint is tightened. The pipe joint compound also helps to seal the joint. Making up a joint too tightly expands the female threads. If, for some reason, the joint should need to be backed off slightly, it will leak.

Give some thought to the weight of the pipe and the water it will carry when assembling and installing steel pipe. Support the pipe to avoid strain at the joints.

When screwing a valve or faucet onto the end of a pipe, use an open end wrench or other smooth jawed wrench on the end of the valve next to the pipe. This avoids placing a strain on the body of the valve, which could damage it.

You *can* bend galvanized pipe, and most plumbing supply firms have heavy duty pipe benders for the purpose. Also, some pipe vises are equipped with channels for bending pipe. However, for most household plumbing, making up pipe with fittings is more satisfactory than bending. A 21 foot section of pipe, bent into a huge "L", is unhandy to replace, once the house has been finished around it.

Joining Other Types of Pipe

The "shiny" chromed and polished pipe and fixtures that stay in view in kitchens and bathrooms can usually be installed with an adjustable open end wrench, a screwdriver and perhaps a strap wrench to give a scratchless grip on polished pipe. Chrome plated brass drain piping goes together with compression fittings that, in most cases, need be no more than hand tight.

Such materials as cast iron and vitrified clay drain and waste pipe require a few special tools, but not many.

For instance, you'll need a **caulking iron**—or yarning iron—a sort of blunt ended chisel, to drive oakum and lead into caulked joints in cast iron pipe. These tools are made in several shapes and sizes, to suit the particular pipe size and joint used. If you only need to repair and tighten old joints, one caulking tool should last from now on.

If you are installing cast iron pipe with caulked joints, you will also need a plumber's furnace, a cast iron melting pot and ladle to melt and handle the lead. But it's easier and less messy—and just as effective—to join cast iron pipe with no-hub joints. These consist of neoprene rubber sleeves, a sheet of stainless steel and screw clamps like those used on auto radiator hoses. This material also makes a good patching kit for most kinds of pipe. (See Chapter 16.)

Vitrified clay pipe can also be joined with oakum caulking. However, the caulking in this case is held in place by cement mortar, rather than molten lead. There are alternatives to caulking clay pipe, as well. In most areas, clay pipe is now available with polyvinyl chloride gaskets on the spigot end of the pipe. The joint is pressed together by friction.

For one reason or another, you may have to work with cast iron, vitrified clay or bituminous fiber drain and sewer pipe. But if you have any choice in the matter, choose plastic. It's lighter, faster, easier and—in the long run—cheaper.

16
Maintenance and Repair Tools

Sooner or later, even well designed, well installed plumbing systems are going to need maintenance. Toilets become clogged and faucets leak, even in new houses. And the longer a house is lived in, the more likely that one or more components of the plumbing will need repair.

Fortunately, the average homeowner can remedy most plumbing problems with a few tools and a basic knowledge of the most likely cause of trouble. Preventing and curing problems is not that difficult, if you understand how plumbing systems work and why they sometimes fail to work properly.

Chances are, you already have on hand most of the tools you'll need to perform most routine plumbing maintenance and repair. You can fix a leaky faucet with a screwdriver and open end wrench. A section of leaky pipe can be temporarily patched with some neoprene gasket material, hoseclamps and a screwdriver.

Here are a few specialized tools you may want to acquire against an emergency that happens on Sunday afternoon when hardware stores are closed and plumbers are not available.

Shovel

A shovel as specialized plumbing repair equipment? Yes, a shovel. Whether your home has its own septic tank system or is connected to a central sewer line, a good share of your plumbing is underground. The odds are pretty good that a shovel will play an important role in some aspect of plumbing repair.

A ready-mix concrete truck backs across your septic tank lateral field when the ground is soft. You'll need a shovel to dig out and replace crushed lateral lines. A section of clay tile in your 50-year-old sewer line slips out of

A round-point digging shovel with a low angle handle makes for best digging—should you have to excavate a sewer or water line.

Maintenance tools include a force cup, and perhaps chemical drain cleaners. You'll also have occasional use for a plumber's snake and a shovel.

alignment and water starts backing up in your basement. Shovel, again.

Buy a long handled, round point digging shovel, with the handle set at a shallow angle to the blade (called a "low-lift" shovel). To dig, push the blade straight into the earth with your foot, putting your full weight on it, if necessary. Make a second shovel cut about three inches behind the first, then pull back on the shovel handle to break out the clod of earth. Don't put so much pressure on the long handle that *it* breaks.

Then, continue digging by taking four to six inch bites to shovel blade depth as you work. If you're digging out a water line or sewer line, you'll want to dig a trench slightly to one side of the pipe, then shovel away the dirt on top of the pipe.

For digging long trenches, a tiling spade comes in handy. Buy one with a 16 inch blade and a short D-handle. In stony or very hard soil, you may need to use a pick or mattock to loosen the soil.

Force Cup

Clogged drains or fixtures, if they aren't too badly stopped up, can usually be opened with a "plumber's friend," or force cup—a large rubber suction cup with a short wooden handle.

Suppose water fails to drain from a kitchen sink. If the sink is nearly full, bail out some of the water before using the force cup. Leave enough water to cover the rubber part of the cup, however.

Make sure the drain plug is removed from the sink. However, if you're working on a double sink, you will need to stopper the drain in the other sink tightly. (If you are working on a lavatory with an overflow near the top of the basin, have someone hold a rag or sponge over the overflow opening while you work on the drain with the force cup.)

Hold the force cup at an angle as you place it under the water and onto the drain opening. This lets the air—or part of the air—escape from the rubber cup. Then, with the opening of the cup firmly over the drain, "pump" the tool to send a column of water back and forth in the pipe. After four or five pumps, pull the cup free of the drain quickly. This sucks some of the material loose from the clog and helps free the blockage.

Caution: never use a commercial caustic drain cleaner on the sink while you are working with the force cup. Some of the solution could splash into your eyes, with painful results.

Once the drain is cleared, let the water flow through it for several minutes. If it's a kitchen sink, subject to build-ups of grease, pour a big pot of boiling water through the drain to dissolve any remaining grease. **Note:** Don't use boiling water if you have drain pipes of ABS or PE plastic.

If the drain doesn't unclog after about five minutes of treatment with the force cup, that tool probably will not do the job. Put the force cup aside and use another remedy. Wipe the rubber cup clean after use. Grease and oil cause rubber to deteriorate.

The force cup should also be the first attack on a toilet bowl clog, and usually will do the job.

The force cup is the first line of attack on clogged drains and toilets. If the clog doesn't budge after a few minutes with this tool, it probably will not do the trick.

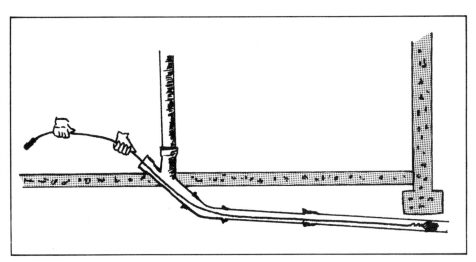

A plumber's "snake" should be inserted into the drain or sewer line until it makes contact with the obstruction, then revolved to catch the clogged material and withdraw it. Before you open the sewer or drain clean-out plug, bail as much water as possible from the system.

Sink Trap Clean-out

Most sink clogs are caused by material collecting in the U-shaped trap in the drain directly beneath the sink. Removing and cleaning this trap is the logical second tactic in clearing a clogged sink drain.

Forks, spoons, toothpicks, swizzle sticks—all sorts of things find their way down a kitchen sink drain, and a good many of them lodge in the trap. There they rest, collecting odd bits of garbage and grease, until the drain is tightly clogged.

Most sink traps are connected with flexible washer type compression fittings; easily disconnected with an adjustable open end wrench (not a pipe wrench) or smooth jawed "Channelock" pliers. Place a bucket beneath the drain trap, then loosen both flange nuts nearest the trap. **Note**: before you remove the trap, bail as much water as possible from the sink.

Plumber's "Snake"

If the drain trap is clear, the clog is obviously further downstream in the system; most likely where the sink drain line joins the "soil stack" or main drain pipe. Do not reinstall the trap right away.

A "snake" or clean-out auger is a flexible metal tool, similar to a speedometer cable. Snakes come in lengths up to 25 feet. Longer models are made of flat, spring steel tape. Run the snake into the drain line at the downstream trap connection, rotating the tool slowly as you push it into the pipe.

This usually will clear the clog. The main soil stack, of three or four-inch pipe, seldom becomes clogged itself. If it does, or if the stoppage is in the soil waste line that runs laterally to the sewer or septic tank, you will be having problems with all sinks and toilets—not just the kitchen sink.

After using a snake on a soil stack or sewer line, uncoil it and leave the tool where the sun will dry it and kill off bacteria. Then, recoil the snake for storage, wiping it clean as you go.

Air Flask

If the drain from the kitchen sink happens to have a swag, or low spot, grease can gradually collect there and clog the drain. At times, a plumber's snake will simply slide through this semi-congealed grease without removing it. When the snake is withdrawn, the goop oozes back to again clog the drain.

The best long range cure for this ailment is to make sure the drain has the proper slope for its full length. But you can temporarily clear the drain with compressed air, either from a portable air compressor or an air flask or tank. Seal the drain pipe around the air hose as completely as possible, and let the compressed air push the grease into the main soil stack, where it can be washed down the sewer.

Compressed air works very well if you are sure that grease is the culprit. However, if the clog is of more solid material, you can damage drain pipes with air pressure. Always try a plumber's snake first.

Closet Bowl Auger

A shorter, stiffer version of the plumber's snake is called the "flexible closet auger." Toilet bowls become stopped at times—some more frequently than others, due to rough surfaces or poorly designed traps.

Usually, the problem with clogged toilet bowls is a wad of toilet tissue lodged in the trap. A shot with the force cup may be sufficient to clear the stoppage.

If it isn't, you may need to use a closet auger. Start the hooked end of the flexible snake through and twist on the crank as you advance the auger into the trap. When you feel the crank tighten, pull the tool back to bring out the obstruction.

The only permanent solution for a chronic problem stoppage is to replace the toilet bowl with one that operates better.

Fixing Pop-Up Valves

Pop-up stopper valves in bathroom lavatories and tubs are a definite improvement over rubber plugs—when they work. Newer types of pop-up valves can be removed for cleaning without dismantling the control linkage. On older types, you may have to loosen a ball joint with an open end wrench at the rear of the lavatory or bathtub.

A pop-up valve that does not hold water in the sink or tub often can be re-adjusted to seat tightly. To do this, loosen the thumbscrew or setscrew on the lifter rod and move it up or down until the valve closes properly. Some valves that have become worn beyond adjustment can be replaced. Others will require a completely new pop-up assembly—or the venerable rubber plug.

Clogs in lavatory and bathtub drains almost invariably are caused by hair. In sinks or showers where shampooing takes place you may want to set up a regular maintenance schedule of drain cleaning.

A special short-handled "snake" called a toilet bowl auger dislodges bad clogs in the toilet.

Emergency Drain Pipe Repairs

Leaks in the drainage system, where water is not under pressure, are fairly simple to repair, unless a section of pipe is damaged. Several epoxy type patching kits on the market let you make durable, long lasting repairs to drain pipe.

Leaky **lead pipe** can be repaired, almost indefinitely, with a poultice made of cloth and wet plaster. Let the pipe dry, then apply plaster to the pipe, all the way 'round and

Remote controlled pop-up drain valves in sinks and bathtubs often can be adjusted to working order without replacement.

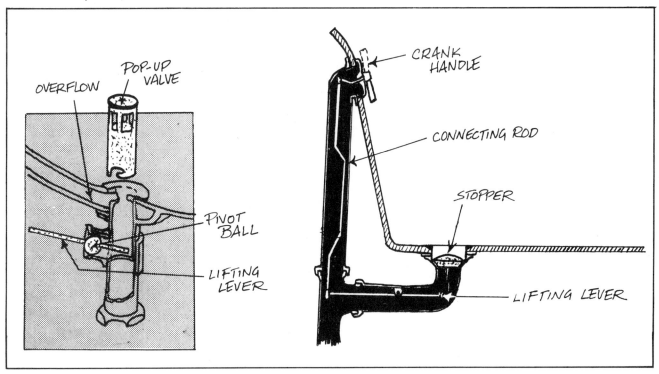

for about four inches above and below the leak. Wrap the wet plaster with a "bandage" of clean cotton cloth.

Apply another layer of plaster and make another turn of cloth, winding the cloth tightly over the plaster. Continue this procedure until the patched sleeve is about an inch thick. It's a rather crude looking remedy, but will hold for years, if properly applied. It's about the only way to patch a curved section of lead pipe—short of replacing the entire section.

Lead caulked joints in cast iron pipe are subject to seeps and leaks as a house settles and causes small cracks to open in the caulking. Usually, these can be repaired by expanding the lead in the joint with a caulking iron, as described in Chapter 15. If the leak cannot be stopped by expanding the lead, you may need to re-caulk the joint.

Plastic pipe leaks can be temporarily patched with one of the methods shown for steel water pipe. Smaller leaks often can be sealed by cutting a curved section from another piece of plastic pipe, then cementing it over the leak.

Leaks in thin wall **copper** or **brass pipe** usually are caused by corrosion; perhaps by electrolysis when a steel or iron object is placed in contact with the pipe. If this is the case, the pipe probably will have become so fatigued that it would collapse under any kind of pressure patch. About the only sure remedy is to replace the section of pipe.

Repairing Pressurized Pipe

Pressures in hot and cold water supply pipes typically are 40 pounds per square inch or more—enough force to squirt a stream of water over your house. You'll need more than adhesive tape and chewing gum to patch leaks in them.

Several methods of patching are shown in the accompanying sketches. For more permanent repairs, you will need to remove the defective section of pipe and replace it with a new one, if the leak is very bad.

For **threaded pipe**, the simplest way to do this is to cut the defective section in two with a hacksaw, then unscrew the two pieces from the adjoining fittings without disturbing any other parts of the system. Cut and thread *two* pieces of pipe to replace the one removed, screw them into the fittings at either end, and make the final connection in the middle with a pipe union.

Copper tubing leaks can often be repaired successfully if the pipe is in good shape and the hole is not too large, by soldering the hole closed. First, the pipe must be drained and valves opened to allow the heated air to escape, then the pipe is heated with a propane torch and lead tin solder used to seal the leak.

Holes larger than about 1/8 inch in size may be difficult to solder successfully. Patch them with a curved section of copper tubing, of the same diameter as the pipe being repaired. Split the patch so that it fits snugly over the leaky

Temporary repairs to leaky water pipes can be made with neoprene or rubber gasket material held in place with whatever you have handy.

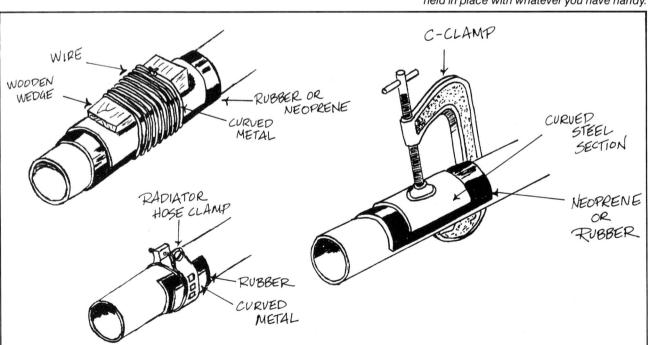

section of pipe. Use the same flux and solder technique as described in Chapter 15 for making sweat joints.

Repairing Leaky Valves and Faucets

Leaks in faucets and globe valves can usually be repaired simply by replacing the disks or washers that fit down on the seat to close the valve. Faucets and valves leaking around the stem can be repacked with commercial thread packing.

To replace a faucet washer, turn off the pressure (by closing the nearest shut-off valve to the faucet) and take the fixture apart; removing parts as they come into view.

Start by removing the handle; which usually is held to the stem by a screw on top. On some faucets, the screw is concealed by a decorative metal or plastic cap which must be pried off to reveal the screw. With the screw removed, use the screwdriver handle to tap the faucet handle off the stem.

On some faucets, a decorative housing (called an "escutcheon") may be fitted over the packing nut. Remove this housing, if the faucet is so equipped, then remove the large nut that holds the stem and packing in place. Use smooth jawed wrenches on these nuts—a pipe wrench will damage the corners.

Remove the valve or faucet stem by screwing it all the way out. It helps to slip the faucet handle back onto the

stem for leverage. Don't use pliers or vise grips on the valve stem.

Turn the valve upside-down. The washer is held to the bottom end of the stem with a small screw. Replace the worn washer with a new one of the same size, replace the washer screw and reassemble the valve by reversing the procedure outlined above.

While you have the valve or faucet apart, check the condition of the valve seat by running your fingernail around its surface. If the seat is pitted or corroded, you'll probably have to replace it—might as well do it now. Valve seat facing tools are available (as described in Chapter 14), but refacing old, corroded valve seats—even with a professional quality seat reamer—is strictly a "maybe" proposition. It's better to replace the seat with a new one.

Pump Repair

Individual water-well systems have one of several types of pump and pressure tank combinations. Most common for deep wells is an electric submersible pump and a pressurized water tank.

Replacing a burned-out pump is a major—and expensive—undertaking. But some ailments of the system can be cured rather easily.

Pressure water tanks are designed to operate with an

Parts of a washer-type faucet, at left. To change the washer in this kind of faucet, first loosen the handle screw at the top of the valve stem, as at No. 1. Sometimes, this screw is concealed under a metal or plastic decorative cap which must be pried off. On some faucets, as in No. 2, an escutcheon covers the packing nut. This escutcheon or housing may be held in place with a nut of its own. Remove it to expose the packing nut. 3. Loosen and remove the packing nut. 4. Remove the valve stem by unscrewing it all the way out. The washer is held in place at the bottom of the valve stem with a small screw.

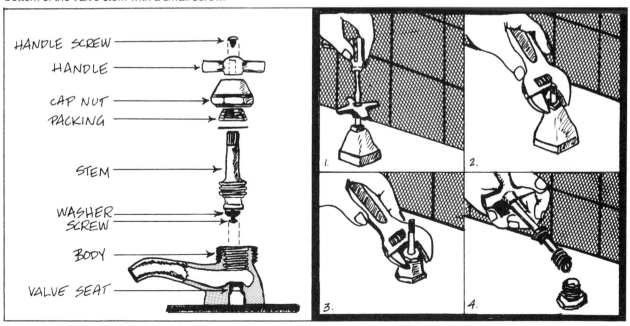

"air-bubble" that is compressed as water is pumped into the tank. Since water is not compressible, if this air pocket were not incorporated in the system, the pump would need to run almost continuously when water is being used. Newer submersible pumps "bubble" in some air with the water to maintain the proper mixture of air and water in the tank.

However, should the air charge be lost, the tank becomes "water-logged" and the system will not operate. This generally can be cured by shutting off the pump, draining the tank and recharging the tank with air. Some pressure tanks have an air valve in the top, which allows air to be pumped in with a regular tire pump. Others require that the tank be drained and re-charged by disconnecting the water inlet fitting.

At times, the pressure switch goes haywire, so that the pump is not turned on when the pressure drops to the normal start-up point. Another common ailment is a sticking check valve (the valve that allows water through in one direction only) that lets water drain back from the tank into the well. Tapping on these fixtures, or on the pipe near them, may "unstick" them and restore proper operation.

The pressure switch also is sensitive to cold. The switch may not function even if the water in the pipe is not frozen. An electric space heater, heat tape or pan of hot water usually restores the switch to operation in a few minutes. Don't use a propane or gasoline torch on the pressure regulator or the pipe nearby.

Use a Chemical Drain Cleaner?

Despite TV commercials, not all plumbers encourage liberal use of chemical drain cleaners. Chemicals can be helpful in keeping small drain lines free of clogs, but their use in clearing a drain that has become stopped is doubtful.

For one thing, if the chemical *doesn't* unclog the drain, you have the added problem of trying to work with a drain full of caustic chemicals.

There are two types of products manufactured for use with clearing drains: acid and alkaline. Acid costs more, but is generally more effective. It's also more dangerous to use. The base of most acid products is sulphuric acid; which can dissolve grease and hair—and human skin.

The commercial household drain cleaners usually sold at supermarkets and drug stores are of the alkaline type.

They are fairly effective in opening a drain that is only partly clogged and flows sluggishly. However, these products are not as effective as acid in breaking through clogs that have a sink drain completely blocked.

Neither type of drain cleaner should be used in toilet bowls. They both can damage the wax seals in toilets.

Caution: Never mix acid and alkaline drain cleaners; the two products are at opposite ends of the pH scale and can literally cause an explosion if mixed. If you have used one type of drain cleaner without success, don't go buy the other type and pour it into the drain.

Preventive Maintenance

Most plumbing ills are much easier to prevent than repair,—another good argument for getting to know the plumbing system in your home, and inspecting it regularly.

- A screen over the top of the vent stack (the drain system vent that extends through the roof) will keep wasps and mud daubers from building nests in this most necessary plumbing fixture.
- Make sure that copper pipes are not in contact with other metal—to avoid the problem of electrolysis and corrosion. Copper pipe hangers are available; as are copper nails and screws to install them.
- Drainage system clean-outs strategically placed simplify clearing clogs if they do occur.
- Grease and used cooking oils should be disposed of in other ways; not poured down the sink drain.
- A regular cleaning of lavatory, bathtub and shower drains to remove matted hair can prevent a clog in these fixtures.
- Faucets should be closed tightly—not so tightly that the washer or valve stem is damaged, but tightly enough so that water doesn't leak through. Even a small stream of water pushed at 40 to 50 pounds of pressure can literally cut the material of a faucet washer, or even the soft metal of a valve seat.
- If you're replacing drain traps on kitchen sinks and bathroom lavatories, buy new ones with a clean-out plug in the bottom of the trap.

For these and other maintenance procedures, you will need few tools and only a few minutes of time. But they can save you the necessity of using specialized tools and several hours for repairs

ELECTRICAL TOOLS

There are few homeowners who do not use or come in contact with electricity and electrical equipment. Now most can install, use and maintain electrical appliances, equipment and wiring systems without a great deal of background in electrical theory. A few terms used to describe and measure the work electricity does will be helpful. To define terms used in the measurement of electricity, we perhaps can make a rough analogy to water in your plumbing system.

The well pump or city water tower maintains a water pressure or "push" measured in pounds per square inch. Similarly, an electrical generator or storage battery "pushes" electrical current into a line, which is measured in **volts.**

When you open a faucet in a water pipe, the water flows out at a certain rate, usually measured in gallons per minute. The rate of flow depends on the pressure in the line, the size of the pipe and the distance the water is pumped through the pipe. The equivalent flow through an electric wire, measured in **amperes**—or **amps**, for short—also depends on the voltage in the line and the resistance (measured in **ohms**) in the wire itself. Generally, larger electrical wires—like larger water pipes—have less resistance to flow.

If you leave the faucet open for a certain length of time, a given amount of water will flow through the pipes and out the faucet. Water is measured in gallons. With electrical power, the measurement is in **watts**; the product of **amperes** (flow) multiplied by **voltage** (pressure).

You will need few specialized tools to perform minor electrical jobs in your home. With an average tool kit, you can completely wire a house and install all the switches, receptacles and outlets. You can do even major wiring jobs with two or three good screwdrivers, a combination slip-joint pliers and a needle nose pliers with a side cutter, a pocket knife, a small hand drill and a hacksaw.

A few extra tools would make the job easier, however. A long shanked auger bit or twist drill comes in handy for making wiring access holes through joists and beams. A reel of "fish" tape may be needed if you are using conduit or have to "snake" wires through finished walls. You will also need a conduit bender if you plan to run wires inside thin-wall metal conduit.

17
Pliers and Cutters

Depending on the amount of electrical repair and installation you perform, you will need to cut wire, strip insulation from wire and bend, fasten and splice both solid-conductor and stranded wires. For small, infrequent jobs, these functions can be performed with a knife and pliers.

Bigger jobs may require tools to cut metal conduit, metal-armored electrical cable or surface wiring (raceways). While there are specialized cutters for these, a hacksaw with a fine toothed blade will serve very well.

Here are gripping and cutting tools you'll find useful in performing electrical work; listed in order of their most frequent use by most homeowners.

Combination Pliers

Ordinary slip-joint (standard) pliers can handle a great many wiring jobs, and are the type of pliers most likely to be included in your present tool kit. The wide, toothed jaws of combination pliers let you get a firm grip on wire for splicing or pulling the wire through a wall.

However, the cutters on these pliers do not make as clean a cut in wire as do the cutting jaws on other types, which we'll describe shortly.

Knife

You can use a knife to trim the insulation from electrical wires. A pocket knife works very well for small jobs and occasional use, as does a utility knife.

The knife blade should not be extremely sharp. You will use it to trim the insulation only; you don't want to nick the wire itself. Shave the insulation off with the same kind of stroke you'd use in sharpening a pencil. If you're using a

Pliers probably see more service than any other tool when it comes to electrical work. Buy good ones.

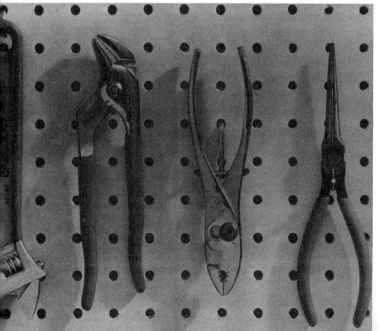

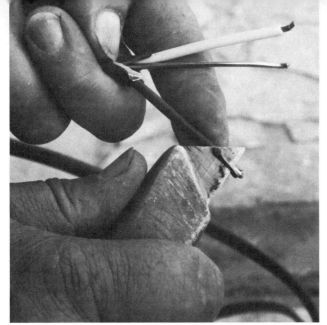

Trim insulation from wires with a knife in a sort of pencil sharpening stroke.

With pliers without spring openings, hold them with the third finger or little finger positioned inside the handle, to open the pliers. Use the side cutters on needlenose or lineman's pliers to cut wire, rather than the shear on combination pliers.

utility knife, select a blade that has seen some use—perhaps one that has been used to cut plaster board.

Woodworking Tools

If you are replacing or adding to your house wiring, you will need a few woodworking tools to measure, drill holes and make cutouts in paneling or other wall coverings.

A hand brace or power drill equipped with a long auger bit or twist drill can make holes in studs and joists for the wire to be slipped through. Use a drill only slightly larger than the diameter of the wire or conduit. Any hole will weaken wood framing members to some extent; choose a drill size to remove as little material as possible, but still make a hole large enough to allow wire to be pulled through.

For cutting openings in walls and ceilings for electrical boxes and switches, you'll need either a compass saw or electric saber saw. A utility knife (with a sharp blade for this purpose) can be used to cut plasterboard and ceiling tile. Measure and cut carefully, so that the cover plate or fixture conceals the opening.

Needle-nose Pliers

Among the handier pliers for several uses are the skinny nosed pliers with a sharp cutter near the pivot. Buy a quality tool. Some of the inexpensive pliers are not constructed of hardened steel; the jaws soon become scarred and rounded. Make sure the jaws align tightly when the tool is closed.

Needle nose pliers are handy for forming loops in wire ends to fit terminal screws. They also can get into tight places—as in outlet or switch boxes—where larger pliers cannot reach.

These pliers are made in lengths from five to eight inches, with jaws from 1½ to 2½ inches long. Some models have the jaws curved at a right angle to the handles. Some incorporate a coil spring to hold the jaws open.

Small nosed pliers find many uses around the house. They are particularly useful in radio and television repair, and auto ignition work. A rubber band slipped over the nose converts this tool instantly into a "third hand" clamp for soldering. If you fish, you probably own a needle nose pliers now that is one of the more indispensable items in your tackle box.

Lineman's Pliers

Lineman's pliers, also called electrician's pliers or "side-cutters," are a handy tool to own if you'll be doing much wiring. The broad serrated jaws grip firmly on wire and the side cutters make a neat job of cutting wire. Most models also have an insulation crusher built in, which can be used to crush and strip insulation from wires.

Lineman's pliers are made in lengths from 4 to 10 inches. A six inch tool is the handier choice for most

Electrician's or lineman's pliers have insulative coatings on the handles, but don't put too much faith in the insulating quality of plastic handles. Make sure current is off when doing electrical work.

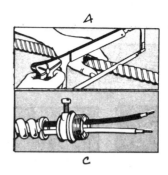

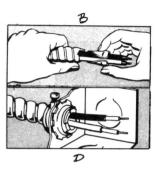

To cut BX armored cable with a hacksaw, hold the saw at an angle and cut through just the armor. Cut through one section, then twist the armor to break it. Remove the armor to expose the waterproof paper around the wires. Insert the bushing between paper and wires. Then slip the connector over the wires and tighten the lock screw onto the bushing. Insert the connector through knockout hole of the box and screw the locknut to the connector. (Courtesy of Sears, Roebuck & Co.)

round-the-home work…and the tool will find many uses other than electrical work.

Caution: So-called "electrician's" tools—pliers, cutters, screwdrivers—often are made with insulative coverings on the handles. Others have plastic dipped handles mainly for comfort. Don't depend on insulated handles for safety and protection from electrical shock. A drop of sweat or a small hole in the insulating material can be hazardous. Follow the rule of professional electricians: work on wires only with the current *off*.

Hacksaw

Specialized tools are made for cutting conduit (pipe cutters), armored cable (aviation shears) and other materials used in electrical work. However, a hacksaw is a valuable tool for most of these jobs—and you're more likely to find optional uses for a hacksaw.

Use a fine toothed hacksaw blade—24 or 32 teeth per inch—to cut thin-wall conduit and the steel armor plating on BX cable. A coarser toothed blade is more likely to catch and break when used on thin materials.

Special Cutting Tools

A look around most electrical supply houses will turn up several specialized tools for cutting wire, stripping insulation and bending and shaping wire. Some of these tools are useful; some fall more into the category of gadgets.

If you're doing a significant amount of wiring with armored cable (where electrical wires are encased in a spiral wound steel casing) you may want to buy, rent or borrow a heavy duty **metal snips** designed to cut the ar-

mor. If you *buy* such a tool, choose one with compound leverage and a straight cutting head. This tool will have more application in other jobs—such as sheet metal work—than will a similar tool designed specifically to cut BX cable.

A lighter weight version of metal shears is the **diagonal cutter**, a pliers-like tool with angled cutting blades. However, diagonal cutters only cut; they cannot be used as other pliers for holding or twisting wire, and—since a diagonal cutter is only marginally better than the side cutter on a linesman's pliers—you probably can get along very well without this tool.

A variety of **wire stripping tools** are made, for cutting, bending and stripping the insulation from electrical wire. An inexpensive model, such as that shown in the illustration, is adequate for most homeowners' uses. Professional electricians often use a larger, more expensive tool for stripping wire insulation—but then, they use the tool every day.

If you buy a wire stripper, even an inexpensive model, choose one with several different functions. The most versatile tool—like that shown—will strip insulation from several sizes of wire, cuts wire cleanly and also can be used to crimp solderless connections onto wire. The wire cutter end of the tool can also be used to cut small screws without damaging the screw threads.

In short, even if you are wiring a house or re-wiring an older one, choose those specialized electrical tools that have application in other areas of home repair and maintenance. Unless you plan to hang out your shingle as an electrician, you don't need many tools to strip, cut and bend electrical wires; so choose tools that will have other uses, once the wiring job is done.

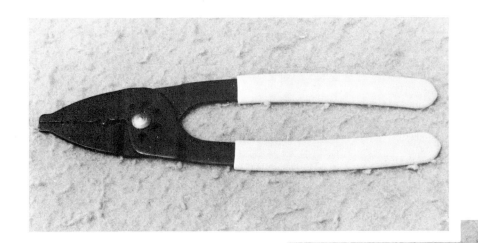

An inexpensive wire stripping tool can perform several functions, such as stripping insulation from several sizes of electrical wire, cutting wire and cutting wood screws without damaging the threads.

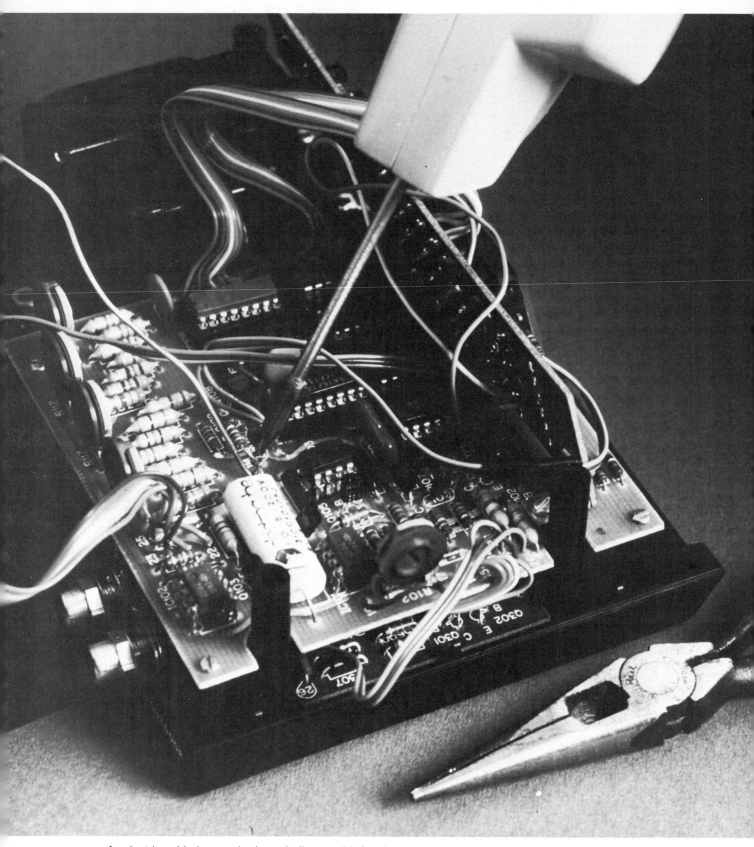

An electric soldering gun is almost indispensable for electronics work, and very handy for household electrical chores.

18 Making the Connection

Whether you are repairing, replacing or adding to the wiring in an older house, wiring a new house or addition, the best bet is to run electrical wire with few or no splices. This takes a little planning, but actually saves time and materials on the job.

For another thing, in-line splices—even carefully made ones—are just one more opportunity for trouble. Taped over wires and cables are not as well protected as unbroken ones. It's better wiring technique and safer to run the wire from the fuse box or circuit breaker to the first receptacle in the circuit, then run another unspliced length to the next outlet in the circuit, and so on.

The tools you will use to run and install electrical wire and receptacles are those gripping and cutting tools described in Chapter 17, plus a few others.

Claw Hammer

For driving staples, nailing up clamps and attaching boxes to house framing members, a claw hammer is the tool.

Bit Braces

Bit brace and long shanked ⅝ inch bit (or power drill and ⅝ inch twist drill). If you are installing the wiring inside metal conduit, you will also need a pipe reaming bit for the brace. (See Chapter 13 for a description of this tool.)

Screwdrivers

Two or three different sizes, to tighten screws and locknuts on outlets and other receptacles. A "stubby" screwdriver comes in handy in electrical work.

Fish Tape

To "fish" wire through walls or conduit.

Electrical Tape

Use plastic tape for most jobs. It's cleaner and faster to use than friction or rubber tape. It also takes up less space in boxes and does the work of both rubber and friction tape. For wiring subjected to a great deal of moisture, however, you may want to use rubber tape.

Soldering Gun

If you will be running and splicing wires where electrical current is available, use an electric soldering gun to solder those joints and splices that require it. If no power is available, you'll have to use a propane torch and old-fashioned soldering iron.

When soldering, first coat the wires with a paste type flux, so the solder will flow better. Heat the wires until the

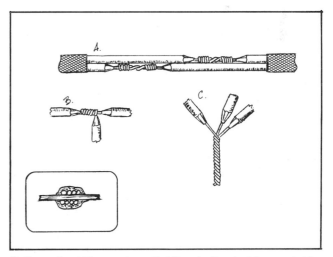

Splices should be made up tightly, whether inside or outside of electrical boxes. A. To splice a two conductor cable, splice each wire separately and stagger the splices so they will not be side-by-side. B. A tap splice is used to join a branch wire to another wire. C. Use a pigtail splice to join wires where there will be no strain on them. Inset, when soldering splices, use plenty of flux and be sure that solder flows well into all spaces.

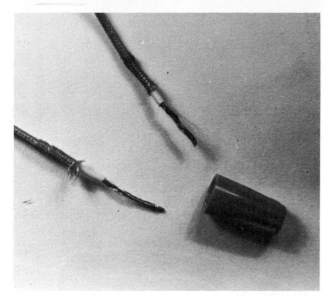

solder melts quickly and flows into every joint and crevice of the splice. Use an acid-core solder. Don't heat the wire so hot that the copper conductor anneals and becomes brittle, or the adjacent insulation is damaged.

Solderless Connectors

Solderless terminals and connectors come in several types. The terminals clip onto the ends of wires to fit screws on outlets and switches. One type of connector is a threaded clamp with a bolt or nut to connect two or more heavy duty wires. This type of connector generally is used for electric service connections and other heavy wiring where strain is put on the connection.

The other solderless connector type is an insulated cap that resembles a tire valve stem cap. It is made with internal threads and insulating material. To use it, simply join the ends of two wires and screw the connector over them. This type of connector will not stand much tension on the wire, however. And, although manufacturers say these connectors can be used without taping the joint, wrapping a couple of layers of plastic tape over the wires and connector is added insurance.

A Word About Wire

Electricity flows through metal wires—usually copper or aluminum—covered with insulating material. The insulation restricts the electrical current to the wire and prevents it from leaking off as it makes its journey from where it is generated to where it is used.

Electrical wire (called "conductor" by many electricians) is classified according to the diameter of the wire itself and the type of insulation that covers the wire. Wire size is measured by the American Wire Gauge (AWG) and refers to the diameter of the metal wire.

The higher the gauge number, the smaller the wire and vice versa. Single strand wires are made from No. 60 (the smallest, thinner than a human hair) to No. 0000, (the largest). For reasons of safety and resistance in the wire, wires smaller than No. 14 are seldom used to conduct house current, although Nos. 16 and 18 may be used for thermostats, doorbell circuits and other low voltage systems.

Flexible stranded wire (called "cord") is commonly used for lamp and appliance cords subject to moving and flexing.

Since it would be unhandy to run individual wires throughout a building, electrical cable is made up of two or three wires (sometimes more) encased in an insulative or protective shield. The insulative shield of the entire

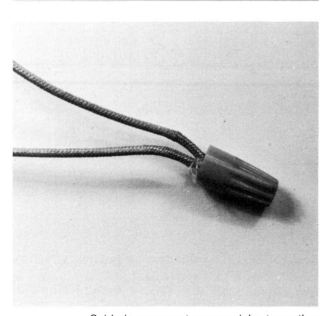

Solderless connectors are quicker to use than soldered splices. These connectors are advertised to be used without taping, but tape them just to be safe.

cable is in addition to the insulation around individual wires, of course.

The insulating material around wire varies, depending on the intended service of the wiring and the conditions to which it will be subjected. The protective sheathing that encases wires in a cable varies, also.

Flexible armored cable. Often called "BX" (which is a trade name), flexible armored cable contains two or three insulated wires in a spiral-wound galvanized steel armor. This is one of the more widely used types for house wiring, but must be used indoors in dry locations and be connected only to metal receptacle boxes.

Non-metallic sheathed cable. Also called "Romex," this type of cable is for interior uses in dry locations. It contains either two or three wires enclosed in a braided fabric or plastic sheath, and can be used with metal, plastic or porcelain boxes. Unless codes or local conditions prevent its use, non-metallic cable is much cheaper and easier to install than either armored cable or wires run through metal conduit.

Plastic-covered cable. This type of electrical cable is enclosed in a smooth plastic sheath, and can be used for outdoor and underground service, as in wiring a yard light.

Surface wiring. Several brands and types of surface wiring—often called "raceways"—can be installed on the surface of a wall or ceiling, rather than inside the wall. Raceways have wires encased in metal or non-metallic channels. Both rigid and flexible types are made. Some incorporate outlet receptacles and switches. Some are made of enameled metal that can substitute for the baseboard at the juncture of walls and floors.

If you are revamping the wiring in an older house or adding to it, where you would otherwise need to make several wall openings, investigate the wide selection of surface wiring available. You'll likely find raceways that harmonize with the decor of a room. However, you cannot very handily run a raceway strip from one room to another.

Conduit. Electrical conduit, or thin-walled metal pipe, often is used to hold electrical wires, either inside a wall or on surface installations. Conduit is not made with the wires already inside it, as are the cables described above. Rather, it is installed much in the same way as is steel plumbing pipe, after which the wires are fished through the pipe.

The main purpose of conduit is to protect the wires from damage, as when a nail is driven into a wall. Also, the metal conduit provides a continuous ground for the house circuit. You can prevent accidental damage by running non-metallic cable at the same height in all walls, and then remembering where the cable is located. And you can meet the grounding provision by using three wire non-metallic cable and attaching the third (bare) wire at each junction to make a continuous ground.

So, unless you live in an area where electrical codes require the use of conduit, you can save a lot of time and money by foregoing this feature. Non-metallic sheathed cable meets all standards of the National Electric Code, if properly installed.

Whatever type of wire, connectors or receptacles you use, make sure they carry the "UL" seal of approval from Underwriters Laboratories.

"Fishing" a Wire

"Fish tape" is a stiff, flat metal wire used to "snake" electrical wires and cables through conduits, partitions and ceilings. The tape will need a hook on at least one end, which can be made by heating the end of the fish tape with a propane torch until the wire becomes red hot, then bending the end of the tape with pliers to make a hook of the correct size.

For fishing wires through walls and ceilings, you may need two pieces of tape—one about 13 feet long, the other about 20 feet long—with hooks on both ends.

Installing Non-Metallic Cable

Non-metallic cable concealed within a wall or ceiling must be fastened with cable straps (not staples!) every 4½ feet and within 12 inches of each outlet, switch and junction box. You can use plastic clamps to do the job in most cases. These clamps come with nails already in them.

Obviously, when you are wiring an old building and fishing wires through walls, floors and ceilings, you cannot attach a strap every 4½ feet for the full length of the cable. Use enough clamps or straps to hold the cable securely so that no strain is put on the wiring at junction boxes, however.

For exposed wiring, the cable must run on a supporting surface (stud, joist, rafter) and be fastened every three feet with clamps or straps.

In either concealed or exposed work, a cable strap or clamp should be placed on the cable within 12 inches of every box.

To attach non-metallic cable at boxes, strip the cable sheathing back about eight inches with a knife. Be careful not to damage the insulation on the wires.

Fasten the screw clamp connector to the outside of the cable sheathing just behind where it has been cut. Use a screwdriver to knock out the knockout hole in the box. Insert the cable and its connector in the hole and screw the locknut tightly from inside the box. Run the locknut down finger tight, then use a screwdriver to finish tightening by pushing on the wings or lugs on the locknut.

You may or may not want to install outlets and switches at the same time you run the cable to boxes. In new construction, you probably will wait until wall coverings are up. Whenever you do it, here's how:

- Strip the insulation back to expose about ½ inch of each wire, using a knife, lineman's pliers or wire stripping tool, as described in Chapter 17.
- Use needle nose pliers to bend the end of the wire into a loop to fit around the screw terminal. Be sure to attach the loop in the direction in which the screw turns when you tighten it. Otherwise, the loop will spread open.
- Use a screwdriver to tighten the terminal screw snugly on the wire loop.

Two and three wire electrical cables have color coded wires. The wire with black insulation is the "hot" or feed wire in alternating current electrical systems. The wire with white insulation is the "neutral" wire. (However, both black and white wires are "hot" when the circuit is closed.)

On three wire cables, a bare copper wire is always the "ground" wire. A third wire in some cables is wrapped in red insulation for three wire installations, such as 240-volt circuits.

Always connect wires of the same color together. And always connect the white wire to the chrome screw in outlet receptacles. Attach the black wire to the brass screw. Receptacles and switches built for three wire applications also have a grounding screw, usually painted green, to which the bare ground wire is connected.

If splices are to be made—either inside or outside of boxes—connect white to white and black to black. The only exception to this rule is when you may need to connect wires of different colors when wiring three and four way light switches.

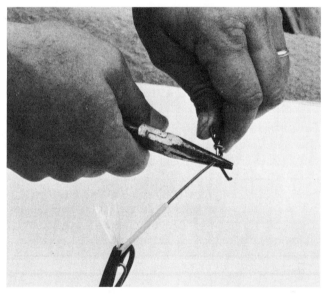

Start a splice by joining wires and bending an L-shaped hook in each wire, with enough wire in the end part to make the splice. Hold the joint where the wires come together with pliers and wrap first one side of the splice, then the other. Use plastic electrical tape to wrap at least two layers over the entire splice—more is better.

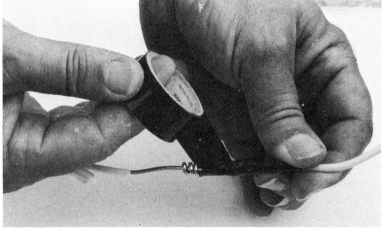

150

19
Testing and Safety Equipment

While this chapter does not pertain strictly to tools, the author feels that since electrical tools and usage of same have been discussed in previous chapters—safety in working with electricity, and testing completed work for its safety, is something which must be covered.

A healthy respect for the hazards of electricity is wise. Most professional electricals have it—or soon acquire it. They have learned—sometimes from painful lessons—not to take short cuts. They never assume anything when working with electrical current, and take no one's word for the safe condition of the circuit. Some professional electricians remove fuses and put them in their pockets while working on house wiring, or tape circuit breaker switches in the "off" position. It's a good way to prevent a circuit from being energized accidentally while working on it.

The National Electrical Code is the "bible" for assuring safe wiring practices, materials and devices. However, the Code is not a "how-to" manual on electrical wiring. Rather, it specifies standards of materials to be used in particular installations and under various conditions. The 450 page guide is available from most electrical suppliers, or can be ordered from the National Board of Fire Underwriters.

Whatever work you are performing on an installed electrical system, do it *only* when the current is definitely *off.* All house circuits are fed from a service panel, either a fuse box or circuit breaker panel. When you are working on an individual circuit, remove that fuse or open that particular circuit breaker. If you are working on several circuits, pull the main fuse or shut off the main entrance switch on the breaker. **And remember:** the connections on the line side of fuse boxes and circuit breakers are live, even if the fuse is pulled or the circuit breaker switch is off.

Circuit Breakers

The electric company's wires come into the house to a service or distribution panel. On most newer houses, the service panel employs circuit breakers to protect the house wiring from short circuits and overloads. On older houses,

the service panel may use fuses, which will be discussed shortly.

The circuit breaker type of service panel eliminates the need for fuses. If a circuit overloads or shorts out, the breaker opens automatically to stop the flow of current. To restore service (after the cause of the short has been corrected) you simply flip a switch. Because of this convenience, the circuit breaker has largely replaced the fuse in most home electrical systems.

When installing new circuits or replacing old ones, make sure the ampere rating of the circuit breaker matches the size and type of wire installed. In turn, the wire should be sized to handle the amperes and wattage of the total lights, fixtures and appliances to be operated on that particular circuit.

Procedures for checking shorts and overloads are the same for circuit breakers as for fuses, described below.

Most older homes, and some latter day built ones, utilize fuse panels for the distribution and protection of wiring circuits. A fuse is merely a short metal wire or strap that melts when a predetermined amperage of current flows through it. The wire is generally encased in a glass, porcelain or metal shell.

Fuses are of two types: plug and cartridge. A **plug fuse** is the more familiar type, with a body that resembles the screw base on a light bulb. (Never screw a fuse into a light bulb socket). The metal wire is viewed through a glass window, to determine if the fuse is intact or if the wire has melted or "blown."

A **cartridge fuse** is cylindrical in shape, usually three to four inches long, with metal contacts at each end. These fuses typically are used for heavier circuits. Fuse boxes often have this type of fuse as the main disconnect fuse between the service panel and the incoming utility wire.

Fuses are designed to "blow" at a certain amperage or flow of current through the circuit. Always replace a fuse with one of the same amperage rating, after you have determined why the fuse blew. You *can* screw a higher amperage fuse into the socket, but this is a dangerous practice.

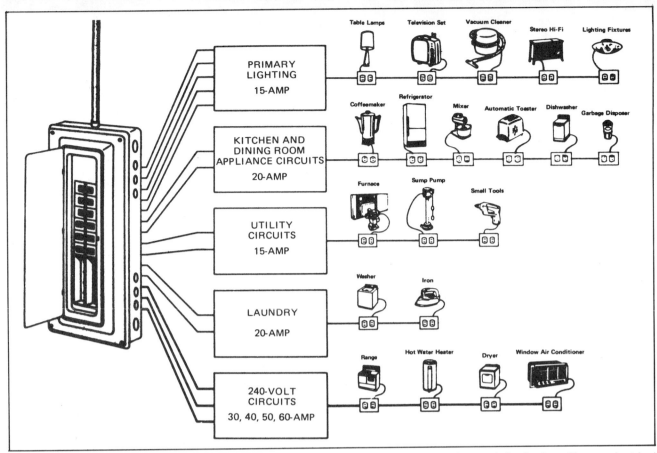

Circuit breaker panels are used most often for safety and distribution of house electrical circuits.

Before you replace a blown fuse (or reset a circuit breaker), find out why the fuse blew in the first place. If you don't find and correct the problem, a new fuse will also blow. Replacing it with a higher amperage fuse could cause a fire in the shorted wiring or fixture.

If the fuse blew just as you plugged in or turned on a tool or appliance, that particular appliance may have increased the total circuit load enough to exceed the amp capacity of the fuse—a sort of a straw that broke the camel's back. Or, the appliance itself may have a short circuit. Either way, unplug the appliance before replacing the fuse or resetting the circuit breaker.

An appliance used with a long extension cord often can "draw" more amperage than the rated capacity of a fuse or circuit breaker due to resistance in the wire. If you must use an extension cord, use a heavy duty type with a high amperage rating. The larger wire has less resistance to the flow of current.

If you cannot locate the reason for the circuit overload, and the new fuse still blows, do not use the circuit until all wiring, fixtures and appliances on it have been tested.

Testing Circuits

If a fuse continually blows, it may indicate a short in the circuit or a defective fixture, lamp or appliance. You can test fuses and circuits with a neon test light, as described below, or you can make your own tester.

To discover the reason the fuse blows, turn off all lights, wall switches and disconnect all cords and appliances in the circuit you suspect. Then, take a 100 watt light bulb and screw it into the fuse socket that gives problems. If the bulb lights with nothing plugged in or turned on, there's a short in the circuit. If the bulb does not light, there's undoubtedly a short in one of the lights or appliances in the circuit.

To find out if the problem is a light or lamp, leave the bulb in the fuse socket and plug in all lamps—one at a time—then turn on each light until the bulb in the fuse socket lights but the lamp doesn't. You've found the shorted light.

Fans, toasters and other appliances may not give you an accurate test with this method. Generally, however, if these appliances work properly while the bulb in the fuse socket shines brightly, there's no short in that particular appliance.

Homemade Wiring Tester

When you are wiring a new house, adding a new circuit or rewiring an existing house, you will want to test the circuit(s) before connecting them to the service panel. There are several testing instruments on the market for doing this, but you can make your own low voltage tester fairly easily.

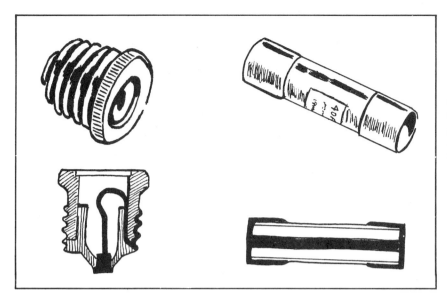

Fuses are of two types: plug (left) and cartridge (right). Plug fuses commonly are used in distribution panels for household current. Cartridge fuses are more often used in high amperage circuits.

In fact, with your homemade tester, you can test the wiring—including the ground—before switches and outlets are installed, while the wiring is still open and troubles are easy to correct. Here's how to do it:

Use a 6 or 9 volt dry cell battery and a bulb to match. The type battery and bulb used in hunting lanterns work very well. Make sure the circuit wiring is not connected at the service panel yet, of course. Then, connect the white and black wires at the beginning of the circuit to the two terminals of the battery. The battery described above has screw caps on the terminals, which makes the connection a simple matter.

With the wires connected to the battery terminals, go to the first receptacle in the circuit—outlet, switch or junction box. Locate the wires coming into the receptacle and touch either the black or white wire to the metal outer shell of the lantern bulb, and the opposite wire to the contact at the bulb's base. You can use either wire—white or black—in either position. (It's handier, but not necessary, to solder short leads to the bulb's outer shell and base contact.)

If the circuit is intact, the bulb should light. If it does, lightly join the wires at this first receptacle—black-to-black and white-to-white—and go to the second box in the circuit and repeat the lantern bulb test.

When making the temporary connections, don't twist the wires tightly together to make this test. You only need them in contact, and any twisting could damage the wire for later installation.

Make sure that no white wire or bare ground wire touches a black wire in your temporary connection. Repeat this test for all receptacles in the circuit.

If the bulb fails to light at any point in the circuit, check your temporary connections "upstream" in the circuit. At the same time, at each receptacle, you can check the ground—either on metal armored cable, conduit or bare wire grounding systems. To do this, connect the *black* circuit wire to the outer shell of the bulb and touch the bulb's base to the metal box (where armored cable or conduit are used) or to the bare ground wire (where three wire nonmetallic cable is used.)

You can repeat this low voltage test after all outlets and switches have been installed and all connections are made up permanently, but before the circuit is connected at the service panel.

Note: When making these tests, if a spark flies when you connect the battery to the black and white wires at the beginning of the circuit, do not connect the circuit. If there is a spark at the battery, there's probably a short somewhere

A dry-cell lantern battery and bulb make an inexpensive homemade circuit tester.

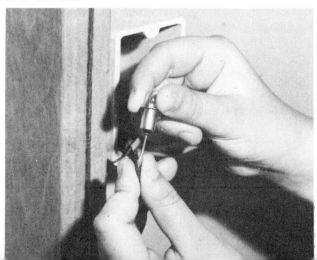

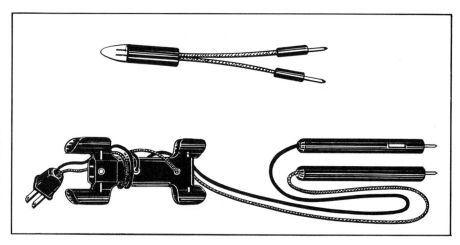

Neon circuit testers can locate current leaks in appliances, motors and cords; test fuses and perform other testing chores. Instructions on how to use the instrument are included with it. (Courtesy of Sears, Roebuck)

in the system. Check it out by connecting only one battery terminal to one wire (either black or white) of the circuit cable. Connect the shell of the bulb to the other battery terminal, then connect the opposite circuit wire to the base of the bulb. If the bulb lights—even dimly—the circuit has a short.

The place to start troubleshooting a short in the circuit is at the receptacle boxes. Check to make sure that no bare wires are in contact with metal boxes, or that no bare black wire is in contact with a bare white wire. Next, suspect any line splices that may have been made in the wire.

Occasionally, but not often, insulation can be damaged on wires inside a cable. This most often happens when a sharp kink is pulled in the cable during "fishing" through walls or conduit. If you cannot locate the short by testing each individual wire, this may be the case.

Neon Test Light

For testing circuits that are already connected, a small neon glow lamp with a pair of insulated wire contact leads is often used. It also can be used to test fuses.

To locate blown fuses with the tester, hold the insulated tips and touch the pairs of terminals to the terminals of the fuse panel. If the light glows, the fuse is good. If it doesn't, replace the fuse.

You can also use this type of tester to find current "leaks" in appliances and motors. Suppose you want to check whether the housing of your automatic washer might give you a shock. Place one lead of the tester against the washer and the other lead against a water pipe or other positive ground. If the light glows, there is current flowing. If the washer cord has a two pronged plug (an ungrounded plug), turn the plug around so that the prongs are reversed in the outlet. Repeat the test. If you still get a light, there is probably a short in the appliance.

Other Testing Equipment

A host of testing equipment is made, to measure volts, amperes and resistance (ohms) of electrical installations and equipment. However, with those testing devices—

both homemade and commercial—mentioned above, you will be able to test house wiring circuits and appliances for safe operation.

A simple, inexpensive ohmmeter often comes in handy, for measuring resistance to current flow. This instrument has two insulated leads, similar to those on the neon test light, and a needle that indicates the resistance in ohms (or megohms) on an increasing scale from left to right.

For service and repair work on both alternating and direct current electrical and electronic equipment, you may want to acquire instruments to measure current change through tubes, transistors and other components; or to measure the cycle frequency in alternating current.

However, it is beyond the scope of this book to go into detail on the more sophisticated testing and measuring equipment.

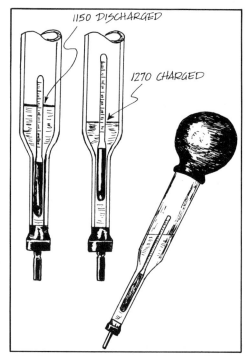

A hydrometer is used to read the specific gravity of electrolyte in wet cell storage batteries. Part of the battery electrolyte is drawn into the hydrometer with the syringe-type bulb on top. The scaled hydrometer float sinks to a certain level in the fluid, depending on the specific gravity of the solution. A reading under 1200 shows a low charge.

MISCELLANEOUS TOOLS

In this section is a collection of those tools, implements and materials that do not neatly fit into the categories of woodworking, concrete and masonry, plumbing or electrical work. It includes such non-tool items as workshops and workbenches.

Some of the tools described here have an almost unlimited variety of uses and applications about most homes. Among these are steel wool, awls, ladders and utility knives. Others will not be particularly useful, or even desirable, for all homeowners to acquire. Some, such as glass cutters, are useful only for a specific job—but have no satisfactory substitutes for their designed function.

20 Workshops and Benches

"A place for everything and everything in its place." If that adage was not coined with tool storage in mind, it should have been. Once you begin to assemble a selection of tools, you'll need a place to store them. And, once you start building and repairing items around the house, you will need a specific, well defined work area for efficient, convenient production.

The kind of tool storage you need will depend on the number, kinds, sizes and frequency of use of the tools you own, in most cases. A well arranged workshop, with workbench, drawers, hangers and cabinets for tool and materials storage, is the ideal.

But not all of us have the finances or space to afford the ideal. For some, the best storage possible may be the corner of an apartment closet, or part of one wall in the garage. For others, with more room, a complete workshop may be planned as a building separate from the house. Most homeowners find their own situation somewhere between: they have somewhat more room than a broom closet, but cannot justify a fully equipped separate structure.

Whatever kind of work/storage you have or build, it should provide for the arrangement, handy selection and safe protection of tools. You'll be surprised at the dollar investment you can make in tools, even by buying a piece now and then as you need it. It's only common sense to keep tools in good working condition and stored in a dry, handy place.

It's not recommended—either for tools or their user—to dump a hodge-podge assortment of implements into a drawer, then to scramble through the tangle to find the tool you need. All tools should be protected from rust and damage, which means that some should be protected from each other. Saws, planes and other cutting tools should be stored where they will not come into contact with other metal. Files, rasps and chisels should be stored individually, rather than tossed together where they will bump and bang into each other.

If the only possible location you have to store tools is a damp place—as an unheated basement—consider in-stalling a dehumidifier. At least, keep tools clean and covered with a film of rust inhibiting oil.

The Work/Storage Area

If possible, the tool storage and work area should be in close proximity to where you will be completing most projects. It's not convenient to have tools stored in the attic and do most of your work in the basement, or vice versa.

Most homeowners and apartment dwellers can set off some space—however small—for tool storage and a work area. The time and trouble of moving furniture, getting out tools and materials, then having to undo everything when a project is about half finished does not contribute to either workmanship or the enjoyment of a craft. It doesn't take much of this kind of hassle to convince the home handyperson that a special place to work and keep those tools is needed.

When planning your work/storage area, give some

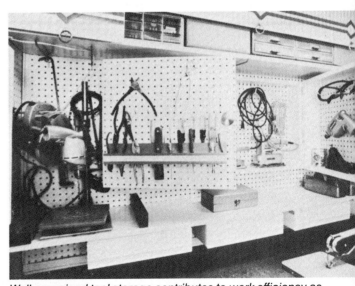

Well-organized tool storage contributes to work efficiency as well as work safety.

This 7-foot workbench is made of a solid core door top, mounted on drawers in the frame.

thought to where—as well as how—the space is to be arranged. The ideal, as mentioned, is a separate workshop, well located and fully equipped. This lets you work on projects in "stop-and-go" fashion as time permits, without having to break everything down and put it away. Basements, garages and back porches are often used for work/storage areas inside the house.

If possible, the work/storage area should be equipped with its own entrance, so materials and supplies can be delivered and stored with little inconvenience to the rest of the household.

However, some people have no options. The only solution may be to use a spare bedroom, or a corner of the family room. The area should be—or made to be—fairly rugged. Carpeted floors and wallpaper will not stand up to much workshop activity.

Wherever you decide to locate your work/storage area, give some thought to the noise and mess that are unavoidable with some jobs. Other members of the household tend to be opposed to having sawdust tracked through the house, and neighbors may not care for hammering or the whine of a power saw.

Workbenches

Workbenches, sturdy tables or stands, with nearby tool storage are where most home handymen do their work. The design variations of a workbench are almost as numerous as the people who build them. Good ones—designed and built to serve the needs of the handyperson—are in themselves tools of frequent use and inestimable value.

In planning your work/storage space, you will need to give a great deal of thought to the kind of work you do most frequently. This consideration will also partly dictate the size and type of workbench you install.

You can buy a complete workbench, with storage drawers, wood vise, bench hooks and other features that most people find useful. Or, you can build one to your own specifications—a good project for a beginner.

Some homeowners buy two unfinished drawer chests about waist high, then attach the bench top—either of 2 inch lumber or an old solid core door. Some "recycle" wood desks from used furniture stores or garage sales. For others, who must make temporary use of limited space, a pair of sawhorses with 2 inch boards laid across them may be the best bet.

Whatever the origin, shape and size of the bench you employ, it should allow for tools, materials and supplies to be stored close at hand. With a permanent workbench—even a small one—and a well defined tool storage area, you can leave partly-completed projects undisturbed until you get back to them again—there's less wasted preparation time, if you complete a job on the installment plan.

This is doubly important for homeowners who have only odd bits of time to work in the shop. If you only have a

Peninsular placement of this workbench gives the workman access to three sides.

couple of free hours in the evening, you don't want to spend half an hour setting up and taking everything down and putting tools and materials away.

Tool storage in tight places can be expanded by the use of shelves, drawers, hangers and cabinets. A piece of pegboard, with hooks and hangers, can provide a great deal of tool storage space along part of a wall. Keep an eye out for old kitchen cabinets—perhaps from a remodeling job—to install in your shop. Stand alone metal or wooden pantries also can be useful.

If you have the time, talent and inclination, you probably can design and build a workbench and the attendant tool racks, cabinets and drawers that suit your space and purposes better than anything you could buy—new or used. The resulting shop and storage area will be specifically designed to fit the kind of projects you undertake most often.

By laying out and building your own work/storage system, you can make departures from common practice that will contribute to your efficiency. For example, in shops with ample tool storage space, similar tools customarily are stored together; standard screwdrivers in one drawer compartment, Phillips screwdrivers in another, etc. However, if space is at a premium in your shop, you may want to store those two or three screwdrivers you use most often close at hand, and keep the screwdrivers used less frequently in another location.

For another thing, building the components of a workshop is excellent practice for a novice woodworker. You learn to cut, fit and join work pieces that do not require the more exacting skills demanded by smoother cabinetwork or furniture making.

Power Tool Workshops

A well-laid-out shop makes work more productive and enjoyable, and this is doubly true when power tools are employed often. Whether your shop will be in the basement, garage or a separate structure, plan the layout carefully. Once power tools are bolted down or built in, it's a major undertaking to transplant them to a more convenient location.

The place to start is with an accurate scale drawing of the workshop area. Include such features as doors, electrical outlets, windows, posts, stairways, etc. Your placement of power tools, the workbench and tool cabinets—as well as storage for lumber and other materials—will be dictated at least partly by these features.

The workbench is the central feature of most shops. It should be located first, in a position that affords good light-

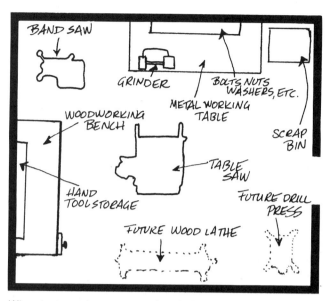

When laying out a power tool workshop, make provisions for any major tools to be added in the future.

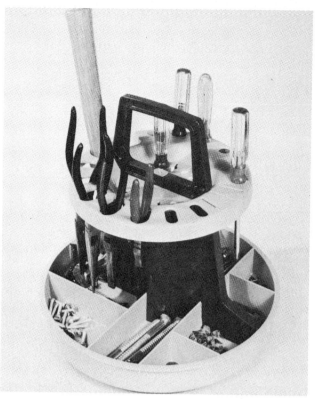

Tote boxes and tool caddies are useful for carrying tools to jobs that must be done outside the shop. This Rubbermaid tool toter features a Lazy Susan type revolving tray.

ing and handy hand tool storage. Locate the bench so that long workpieces can be accommodated by the vise (or vises).

Power tools should be situated where you will have ample room to work with stock of various lengths. The table saw (or radial arm saw) should be accessible from both sides; a central location is usually best for this machine.

If you have a relatively small workshop space, you may need to position saws, shapers and jointers so that longer pieces of work can be handled through an open window or door.

If your shop will have both wood and metal working tools, you may want to set up two separate "zones" for the different functions. For example, a long workbench (or two benches) may be equipped with a wood working vise at one end and a machinist's vise at the other, with wood and metal working tools arranged at opposite ends of the bench.

Or, you may want to use the same zone idea for various functions, and keep some work procedures more or less isolated from others. For example, you may use one part of the shop for planning, layout, cutting and assembling work, and another area for finishing, painting and varnishing.

As you lay out your workshop, don't forget to make provisions for power tools planned for the future. A jig saw or drill press to be purchased later should be allowed for now, while you're doing the shop planning.

It's helpful to study the layout and arrangement of several different workshops; noting tool storage ideas, power tool placement and other features. But don't feel that there is any one "best" way to lay out a workshop. As you study shop layouts, borrow those features that seem to suit your purposes; disregard those that would be awkward or impractical for your own situation.

The key point here is that your work/storage area should be designed to best serve you and the jobs you will be doing.

21 Shop Tools With Handles

There are a number of hand tools which, for one reason or another, did not find their way into an earlier section of this book. This chapter and the next are roundups of miscellaneous tools that sooner or later rate space in many homeowners' tool boxes.

Some of these tools are used *primarily* for particular jobs on particular materials, but are not commonly considered as tools for carpentry, plumbing or other home projects. For instance, knives are most often used to whittle, carve and shape wood, but are not especially in the carpentry and woodworking tools category.

Still, the tools described below and in Chapter 22 are very useful for some jobs, and virtually indispensable for others. Here, we discuss tools with handles: knives, ripping bars, tinsnips, awls, etc.

Knives

Knives come in assorted shapes and sizes, and are designed for a wide range of functions. Chances are good that you now own one or several knives of some description: pocket knife, utility knife, carpet knife, fishing or hunting knife. And, odds are, the tool sees frequent services.

One of your first knives may have been a **pocket knife,** or pen knife. It may be one of the "many-tools-in-one" foisted off on youngsters as "Boy Scout knives" or "Swiss Army knives," but it is a prized implement. And any young person who is given a new knife soon manages to find an amazing variety of uses for the tool: whittling, making hickory whistles, probing for splinters in unwary toes, playing mumblety-peg.

Most who came into ownership of a fine clasp knife early in life still regard the tool as a most useful implement. The author carries a two bladed pocket knife that has been a regular resident of his trouser pockets for more than 25 years. It is used often—and misused occasionally—but is kept clean and keen edged.

A pocket knife is particularly useful for cutting or whittling on curved or irregular surfaces. It can often be used in places where other cutting tools cannot do the job or would take longer to do the same job.

When carving or whittling wood with a knife, the same basic principles apply as govern the use of other cutting tools. Cut with the grain wherever possible, and not against it. Move the blade at an angle, with one end slightly ahead of the other, to cut closer to a line.

In heavy cutting and whittling, always cut away from your body. With a non-locking clasp knife, be careful not to put pressure on the end of the blade in such a way that it might close on your hand.

Look for quality—in both the blade steel and the construction—when you buy a pocket knife. Knife blades are sharpened and shaped into relatively thin and blunt tapers, from the back of the blade to the cutting edge. Consider the use you will most often put the knife to. A knife blade ground with a long, thin edge is useful for fine carving; but for heavy service, you need a blade with an edge bevel

Knives come in many shapes and sizes; some for general work, some for very specialized jobs.

The two halves of a utility knife are held together with a screw. Spare blades can be stored inside the handle.

A utility knife is especially useful for cutting roofing felt, asbestos shingles, vinyl and linoleum floor coverings, fiberboard and sheetrock wall coverings. It also is often included in wallpapering kits, for use in trimming paper. If you own a utility knife, you will find dozens of other uses for the tool.

You *can* sharpen a utility knife blade, by holding the blade at about a 30 degree angle and moving it lightly over a fine whetstone. But the replaceable blades are fairly inexpensive, and most utility knife owners discard a dull blade and replace it with a new, sharp one. The type of material often cut with a utility knife—tar paper, shingles, etc.—leaves a deposit on the blade that would complicate sharpening.

Carpet and **Linoleum knives** are made in a variety of styles and blade shapes. Most common are those blades fixed on wood handles. The cutting edge of the blade may be straight or hooked. Another type of carpet knife has a replaceable blade that is clamped in a guide, to cut carpeting smoothly along a wall or baseboard.

Unless you will be laying quite a lot of heavy floor coverings, you probably can get along very well with a utility knife.

Woodcarvers' knives, along with carving chisels and gouges, are specialized tools used to carve, sculpt, cut patterns, make models or furniture.

Some types of carving knives feature interchangeable blades of different shapes and functions. Others have fixed blades on wood handles. These are used to carve, whittle and chip wood.

that leaves more thickness of metal directly behind the cutting edge.

A **utility knife** with replaceable razor-like blades also finds many uses around the home and shop. This knife has a cast aluminum handle about six inches long, which holds the changeable blade. The handle is made in two halves, held together with a screw.

The blade (spares can be stored in the hollow handle) can be locked in the handle in one or two or three positions, depending on the type utility knife used. Some models feature a retractable blade. Some have substitute blades for sawing or scraping.

Professional woodcarvers use a variety of knives, chisels and gouges in their craft.

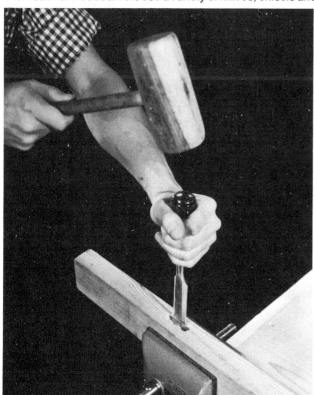

Putty knives—actually more trowel than knife–are useful for applying a great many adhesives and other materials, in addition to window glazing putty.

Tool maker's awls are precision tools used to scribe metal and patterns; points are interchangeable.

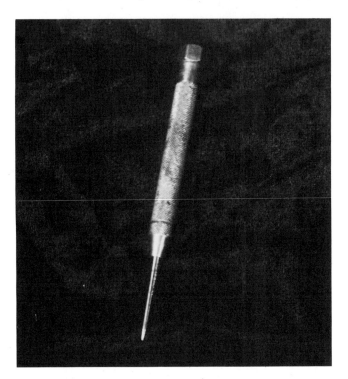

Carving chisels have flat, or nearly flat, blades and are used much in the same way as are larger wood chisels. **Gouges** for wood carving come in two types—paring and veining. Paring gouges are used to cut surfaces or ends needed to match in irregular shapes, as in moldings, pattern making or model making. The smaller, deep V or U shaped gouges are called "veiners." Larger ones often are called "fluters."

A **putty knife**—actually more of a trowel than a knife—is another one of those tools with almost universal application. It is designed to apply and smooth glazing putty around window panes—thus its name. But the putty knife in the average homeowner's tool kit probably sees more use around the home or workshop to apply plaster patches, vinyl flooring cement, wood filler paste, roofing tar and other non-glazing functions.

Better made putty knives have a polished, carbon steel blade that is hardened and ground with a bevel on one edge. Putty knives are made with blades of varying degrees of stiffness. Keep this in mind as you choose a putty knife for a particular use. Relatively stiffer blades are handier for scraping; more flexible blades are better for applying putty or paste.

All knife blades should be kept clean and sharp. Unless there's a particular reason for doing otherwise, maintain the original shape of the blade when grinding, filing or whetting a knife. You'll find more on sharpening knives in Chapter 23.

Awls

An **awl** is an icepick-resembling tool about six inches long, and can be one of the handier tools in your kit. You can use it to make starter holes for nails, brads and screws; scribe wood and other materials; and—in a pinch—you probably *can* use it for an icepick.

Actually, awls are made in several shapes for specific uses. Most have either screwdriver type plastic handles or more bulbous wooden handles.

A **scratch awl** has a sharp, conical point and is often used to scribe or mark wood or other relatively soft materials. It is also useful for making a small pilot hole for drills and augers; or, in soft woods, to make a starter hole for screws and other fasteners.

A similar tool is used to scribe metal. You can use an ordinary scratch awl to scribe and mark both metal and wood. But metal scribing usually is done with an awl with a sharper, needle point. Machinists and tool-and-die makers often use scratch awls with replaceable tips.

A **harness-maker's awl** is a leather-sewing tool, very similar in appearance to a scratch awl, but with a diamond shaped tip. This type of awl is used to make holes in leather and other heavy material. Waxed thread or leather lacing then is threaded through the holes.

Even a better quality awl is so relatively inexpensive and so universally handy that admonitions on its proper use must be offered with a grain of salt—particularly when the author himself often substitutes the tool for a small center punch, drift pin or probe. In the process, the awl's point becomes dull or damaged. When this happens, sharpen the

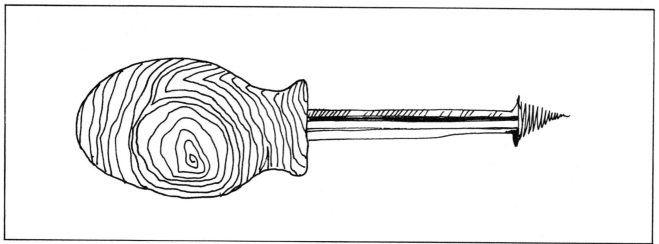

A screw starter, sort of an awl with tapered screw threads at the point, is useful for making starter holes in wood and other nonmetallic materials for screws.

tool on a grinder back to the long conical point, then hone the tip.

A **screw starter** is, in effect, an awl with tapered screw threads on the tip. It is used to thread starter holes for wood screws.

Nail Pulling and Ripping Bars

A variety of tools are made for ripping and prying apart woodwork and pulling nails. Nail pulling tools generally are of two types: "cat's paw" nail bars and chisel bars, both about 12 to 14 inches long.

The **"cat's paw"** is a straight steel rod with a curved claw at one end. It is used most often for pulling nails that have been driven beneath the surface of the wood. The claws are driven into the wood, astride the nail head, then the handle of the bar is pulled to lift the nail out of the wood.

A **chisel bar** has two claws—one at either end—and is ground to a chisel-like bevel on both ends. This bar can be used to pull nails, much in the same fashion that a claw hammer is used, and can also be driven into wood to split and rip apart the pieces.

A **ripping bar,** or **pinch bar,** is 24 to 36 inches long, with a deeply curved nail claw at one end and an angled, wedged shaped face at the other. This bar is used for heavy duty dismantling of woodwork, as in tearing apart building frames or concrete forms. The heavy claw can be used for pulling large nails and spikes. The angled prying end is used to force wood members apart.

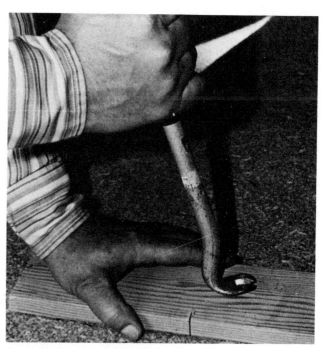

"Cat's paw" nail pulling bar, above; and a ripping bar.

A nail pulling bar is handy for pulling nails that have been driven flush with–or slightly below–the surface of wood.

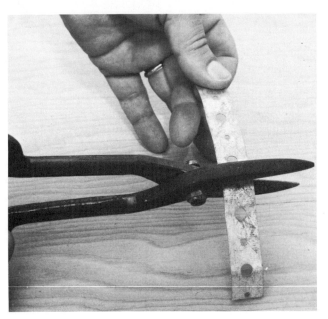

Tin snips can cut ordinary metals up to about 18 gauge. Shown are straight snips. The tool is also made with curved and hawk-bill cutting tips.

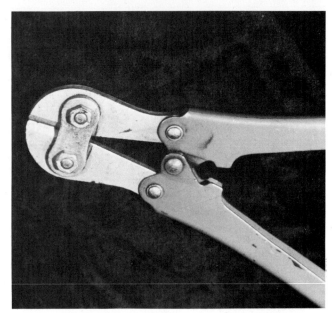

A bolt cutter uses compound leverage to exert tremendous force on the cutter head, to slice through steel rod, padlock hasps and other metal. (Courtesy of Bill Mason)

Wire Brush

A wood handled brush with steel bristles comes in handy for cleaning rusty tools, removing paint, cleaning soot from flues and other heavy duty uses. Obviously, the steel bristles are not suitable for any kind of finishing work.

You also can buy wire brush attachments of various sizes to use with electric drills and bench grinders. This makes a faster, more efficient way to buff tools than the use of a hand wire brush.

The metal bristles of all wire brushes are subject to rust unless the tool is thoroughly dried before storage.

Metal Snips

For average sheet metal cutting, a pair of metal or tin snips are about the handiest tool to own. Snips are made in three styles: straight, curved and hawk bill. The hawk bill snips will have either a right or left cut.

Straight snips, resembling a stubby pair of scissors, are used for cutting straight lines and outside curves; which encompass most home and workshop sheet metal cutting. **Curved and hawk bill snips** are needed to cut inside curves (started from a drill hole) and for close spaces where straight snips could not be operated.

For straight cutting, open the snips' blades wide and insert the metal all the way to the throat of the tool. Be sure the cutting edge of the blade is aligned with the line of cut, then squeeze the handles together as you would a pair of scissors. Stop cutting before the tips of the blades close completely and take a new bite. Cutting all the way out to the tip can leave nicks and burrs in the metal.

When cutting a wide sheet, let the right hand piece of the material bend down slightly, and pull the left part upward to allow room for the snips' handles to operate. Keep the cutting edge of the top blade over the line to be cut.

Don't try to cut standard sheet metal over about 18 gauge with ordinary tin snips. Heavier metal can be cut with a hacksaw, or clamped in a vise and sheared with a cold chisel.

When tin snips become dull, they can be sharpened with a file or whetstone, as described in Chapter 23. Use the file only on the bevel side of the blades. Before storing tin snips, apply a light coat of oil to the blades and a drop of machine oil to the pivot screw.

Bolt Cutters

Bolt cutters are long handled shears that employ compound linkage to exert a tremendous pressure on the hardened blades. This tool can cut through bolts, nails and metal rod, but is too heavy and awkward to be of much use in cutting flat metal.

A smaller version, also rigged with compound leverage, is handy for cutting medium weight metal—such as the armor on BX electrical cable—and also is maneuverable enough to cut flat metal.

Tongs

There are other handled tools that you may find useful for particular jobs. For example, one or more pairs of long handled tongs come in handy if you are tempering or annealing (softening) metal. The hollow bit, curved lip type tongs are best for general use. They will hold both round stock as well as flat bars of metal.

22
Handy-To-Have-Around Tools

There are certain types of "tools" that are handy to have around your workshop. Most people do not purchase them until the need arises. However, when that time comes you'll wonder how you ever got along without them. Described here are tools, gadgets, and accessories, many of which you will find in your workshop sooner or later.

Stud Finder

When hanging pictures, wall plaques, and at other times when you need to locate the 2 x 4 studs beneath a wall surface, an inexpensive **stud finder** can be helpful. This tool is a small plastic case with a magnet inside. As the stud finder is moved slowly across the wall paneling, plaster, sheet rock or other covering, the magnet is attracted by the nails in the studs. On most models, a needle aligns with

a mark on the tool when the stud finder is directly over a nail.

"Third Hand" Holders

Several tools are made to hold nails and other objects for safety's sake or to reach into tight places. Among the handier of these tools is a cylinder about the size of a fountain pen, with a spring loaded clip on one end to hold brads, tacks and nails while you start them with a hammer.

Steel Wool

You may have some question about calling steel wool a *tool,* but this abrasive material is especially useful for scouring and polishing metal. Steel wool is made of long, hair-

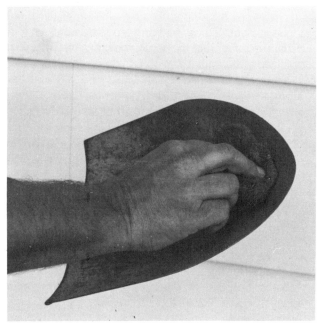

Steel wool is useful for cleaning tools, buffing metals and dozens of other chores around the home and shop.

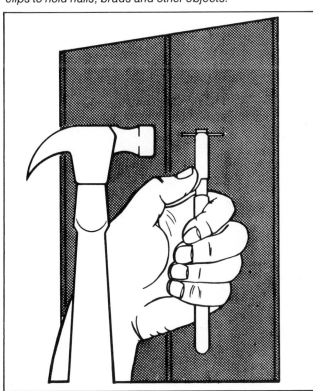

"Third hand" and "Thumb-saver" holders have spring loaded clips to hold nails, brads and other objects.

like steel fibers, and earns a place in most home tool kits. The table below lists some uses of various grades of steel wool:

Number (size)	Grade	Uses
000	Extra Fine	Super smooth finishing; rubbing down final coat of a finish.
00	Fine	Buffing brass, copper, and aluminum for soldering; finishing materials for lacquer or enamel.
0	Med. Fine	General auto and kitchen uses; scouring cookware and buffing floor tile (don't use it on "no-wax" floors); cleaning and removing stains from tile, chrome, whitewall tires.
2	Med. Coarse	Buffing floors; removing old wax; preparing surfaces for smoother finishing.
3	Coarse	Removing rust, paint, dirt and soot; cleaning shovels and hoes; use with paint and varnish remover to strip for refinishing.

Tape

The more common types of tape—white adhesive tape, cellophane Scotch tape, masking tape, electrical tape—find many uses around the home and shop. Newer, more specialized tapes with which some homeowners are less familiar can also be handy for particular jobs.

Aluminum faced duct tape (sometimes called "Flashband") is a waterproof, flexible tape that can permanently seal metal flashing, ducts, gutters, downspouts, air conditioner vents and other fixtures about the house. It can be purchased in widths from two to nine inches, and in rolls of various lengths.

Thread sealing tape has been mentioned previously, in the section on plumbing, but this pliable Teflon tape has many other uses. It seals threaded hose fittings, sprinklers, sprayers and other garden hose attachments.

Electric heat tapes can be used to prevent exposed water pipes from freezing. Some heat tapes come with an incorporated thermostat and signal light. The tape is wrapped spiral fashioned around the pipe. Be careful not to lap the tape over itself when installing it. This can cause the tape to burn in two, and possibly start a fire.

Caulking Guns

For less than $2, you can buy a half-barrel type caulking gun that will perform dozens of caulking and sealing jobs, and last indefinitely. These caulking guns utilize disposable caulking cartridges, with different caulking compounds made for various jobs. The nozzle is contained in the cartridge, and is cut to apply a bead of caulking in the desired size and shape.

The basic types of **caulking compound** are:

Oil base. The standard caulking compound. It's relatively inexpensive and will adhere to most surfaces. However, it tends to dry out and crack when exposed to weather.

Silicone. This type of caulking will stand up to weather and moisture for years, and can be used on virtually all types of surfaces. It's the type used most often to caulk around bathtubs and other plumbing fixtures. However, it does not hold paint well. It's also the most expensive type to buy.

Latex. A fast drying material that adheres well to paint. Latex caulking is medium priced and cleans up with soap and water.

Butyl Rubber. This is the type of compound used mainly for caulking joints between metal and masonry surfaces, such as the joint between a brick or stone fireplace and the adjoining house siding. It's fairly expensive, but long lasting.

Caulking guns can help make your house weather tight. This type of half-barrel gun takes disposable caulking cartridges with several types of caulking compounds.

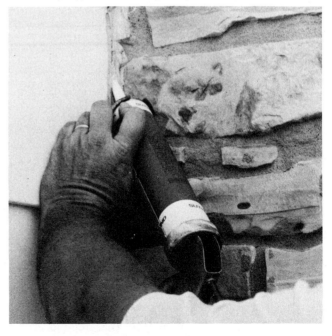

A glass cutter does not actually cut glass; rather, it scratches a line on the surface of the glass to predetermine where the glass will break. Incidentally, the glass cutter ordinarily is used with the opposite side toward the glass than that shown in this photo.

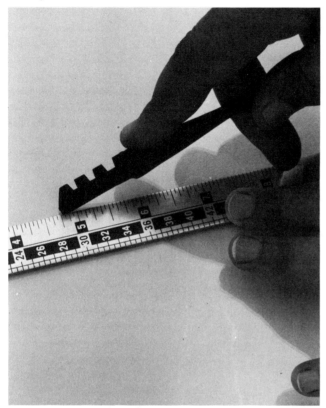

Polyvinyl Acetate. This caulking is medium in price, and can be used on most surfaces. It takes paint better than either silicone or butyl rubber, but may not last as long when exposed directly to the elements.

Cleaning up can be quite a job after caulking. These compounds are sticky and some dry quickly. Clean up tools immediately after the job is completed, and clean up any spatters on finished surfaces right away. Use mineral spirits or turpentine to remove silicone, butyl rubber and oil based caulking. Polyvinyl acetate can be wiped up with toluene solvents. Latex cleans up with soap and water.

Glass Cutters

A glass cutter is a slim iron handle with a ball on one end and a tungsten steel cutter wheel on the other. (More expensive models have tungsten carbide wheels, but you won't need one unless you plan to cut a lot of glass.)

Actually, glass *cutter* is a misnomer for this tool. The wheel is used to score a line along the surface of the glass, it does not actually cut it. Glass is an unstructured material

internally—that is, it doesn't have a definite grain or pattern. The cutter merely scores a shallow groove in the glass so that it may be broken at the desired place.

To use the glass cutter, clean the glass to be cut and wipe along the proposed cutting line with an oily rag. Use a straight edge to guide the glass cutter. Hold the tool at about a 45 degree angle, and bear down with medium pressure to make the scoring mark the full length of the glass to be broken.

Then, place the glass on a bench, table or other flat surface, with the waste end of the glass extending past the edge of the surface. Press or tap the glass lightly to break it along the scored line.

Shop Vacuums

If you're only cleaning up after an occasional job, a house sized vacuum cleaner, plus a broom and mop, may be all you'll need. But if you will be sawing, drilling and shaping wood fairly regularly, a larger capacity shop vacuum comes in handy. A steady diet of sawdust, chips and shavings can upset the digestion of a vacuum cleaner designed for household cleaning.

If you decide you need one, buy a sturdy shop vacuum with at least a one horsepower motor and wet-dry pickup features. The cannister type vacuum is most practical, and the container should have a least a 10 gallon capacity. You can buy a good, serviceable vacuum for less than $100, and the machine can save a lot of sweeping and mopping.

Air Compressor

An air compressor—one worth owning—is a fairly major investment. If you only need one for an occasional

An air compressor and tank combination represents a sizeable investment, but it's a handy machine for many uses in addition to spray painting.

painting job, you may want to rent or borrow it, rather than spend $250 or more for a tool that sees little service.

Of course, several tools other than paint sprayers can be operated with compressed air, and "packaged" air is useful for pumping up tires and toys, cleaning plugged plumbing drains and cleaning parts during auto service work.

The handier type of compressor for most homeowners is the piston-type compressor tank unit. A 12 to 15 gallon tank and a compressor with up to 100 pounds-per-square-inch capacity will be ample for most uses.

Power Polisher

You can buy a variety of polishing, buffing and scrubbing attachments for an electric drill; and still more with mandrels that fit conventional bench grinders. And, these accessories let you perform a variety of polishing scrubbing jobs.

However, for heavy duty work—such as repainting an automobile—you may want to buy a mechanic's quality polisher sander tool. These machines are built with electric motors from 1/3 h.p. to more than one horsepower. Some feature dual speeds for polishing and sanding different materials.

For lighter work, several manufacturers now make polishers and scrubbers with rechargeable battery packs that let you use the tool where electrical power is unavailable or unhandy.

Electric Engraver

An inexpensive electric engraver lets you mark your name or social security number on tools and other possessions. The primary object of such branding is to discourage theft; or at least provide a means of identifying objects if they are recovered.

Ladders

A home owner or apartment dweller can always make use of a good sturdy ladder: cats climb trees, pictures need hanging, TV antenna wires become disconnected.

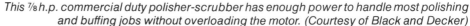

This 7/8 h.p. commercial duty polisher-scrubber has enough power to handle most polishing and buffing jobs without overloading the motor. (Courtesy of Black and Decker)

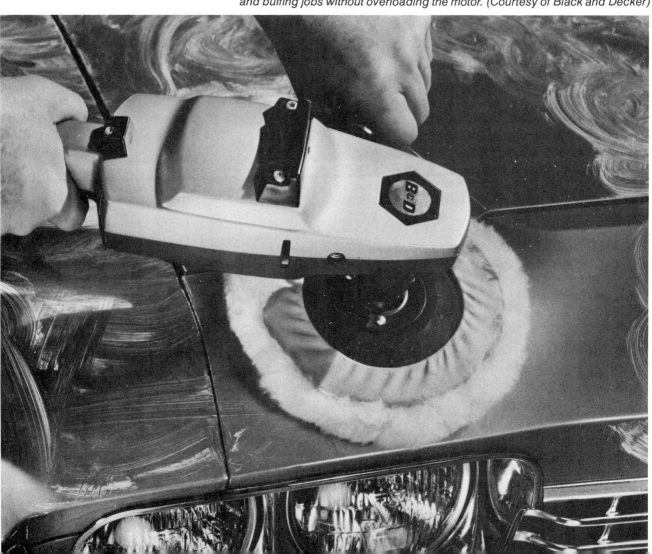

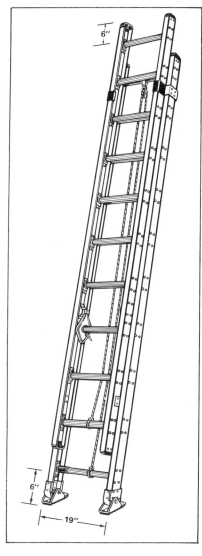

Choose a ladder that won't let you down. Features to look for in extension ladders are wide stance (18 inches or more) at the base, good tread on the rungs and non-slip shoes.

As with other tools, quality is a high consideration when choosing a ladder. When you're several feet off the ground, it's comforting to know that a sturdy, reliable ladder supports you. The price difference between a cheap, poorly constructed ladder and a good one is considerably less than the cost of re-setting a broken arm or leg.

You have a choice of materials, in both cheap ladders and well made ones. Wood is somewhat heavier than either magnesium, aluminum or fiberglass, and requires more care. However, you may want to choose a stepladder made of wood. Aluminum and magnesium ladders are lightweight (a pleasant feature when you're handling a ladder single-handedly) and virtually maintenance free, but are excellent conductors of electrical current.

Fiberglass ladders weigh in somewhere between wood and aluminum, for ladders of equal strength and quality, and fiberglass is not as dangerous to use around power lines—although you shouldn't depend on the material's insulating qualities.

When shopping for a ladder—either a stepladder or extension ladder—notice how it is constructed. A good extension ladder will cost several dollars; a poorly made one will not be much cheaper. Makers of better ladders often have their products tested and approved by Underwriters' Laboratories or the American National Standards Institute; look for their seals.

Even if the ladder carries the UL or ANSI approval, check it out. Better ladders have one rung for each foot of length. The bottom rung should be about seven inches above the base of the ladder; the top rung should be within six inches of the top of the ladder rail (the main side pieces). Choose a ladder with a fairly wide stance—17 or 18 inches wide at the base—for good stability.

The rungs should be grooved for good traction, and are more comfortable to use if the top surface is relatively flat. The locks and slides on extension ladders should operate smoothly and hold firmly.

Stepladders are made in lengths from three feet to eight feet—sometimes taller. Most homeowners need a stepladder only tall enough to let them reach the ceiling, or the soffit under the roof overhang. For higher up work, use an extension ladder or scaffold.

The main safety feature with a good stepladder is setting it up properly in the first place. Open the ladder's legs and make sure they are locked in position. Place the ladder on a level surface, or level it firmly, so that each of the four legs bears its part of the weight. Don't use the tool tray on a stepladder for a step or foot rest. It isn't meant to hold more than a few pounds of tools or paint cans.

Every homeowner should have an **extension ladder** that is tall enough to get them safely onto the roof of the house. There's a surprising number of reasons for going up there: balls and frisbees need retrieving, television antennas need to be repaired and replaced, flues need to be inspected and cleaned, gutters need cleaning, roof shingles need to be inspected occasionally.

The ladder should be long enough to extend at least three feet above the highest area you need to reach. However, you don't stand a ladder against the house in a true vertical position. The rule is: the feet of the ladder should be placed away from the wall a distance equal to one fourth the eave height.

If the eaves of your two story house are 24 feet above the ground, you'll need to rest the ladder about six feet out from the wall for safety. This makes the ladder the long side of a right triangle. To reach that 24 feet and have three feet

of ladder above it, you will need a ladder that extends to about 30 feet long.

But don't run out just yet and buy an extension ladder *advertised* as 30 feet long. The stated length of an extension ladder is two times the length of one section, but the two sections must overlap at least two feet for strength. So, a 30 foot extension ladder actually is 28 feet long—or less—when fully extended.

Ladders require little care. Wood ladders should be stored out of the weather if possible. You can replace worn or cracked rungs on most wooden ladders. Make the replacement rung of hickory or some other sturdy, tough wood and fit the rung carefully in the rails. Secure the rung in place with glue and finishing nails.

On some metal ladders, the rungs are held in place with rivets and can be re-riveted to the rails. Most aluminum and magnesium ladders, however, have tubular rungs that are welded through the rails. You can use a tight fitting dowel or broomstick to temporarily reinforce a weakened metal rung.

If a ladder's side rails become cracked or buckled, buy a new ladder.

For most homeowners, a stepladder need be only tall enough for the climber to comfortably reach the ceiling inside or the soffit under the eaves outside.

23
Dressing and Sharpening Tools

The edge of a sharp cutting tool is not glass smooth, but is composed of a series of microscopic "teeth." The size of these ultra small teeth determines whether an edge is *coarse* or *fine.*

For some kinds of work, a coarse edge is better than a fine edge. Bread knives work better when sharpened to coarse edges. Wood chisels and plane irons are more useful with fine edges. Razors need very fine edges to shave whiskers cleanly with little pull.

Sharp tools are the mark of a good craftsman. The time lost struggling along with a dull tool soon amounts to more minutes and effort than it takes to sharpen the tool for faster and better work.

While it's true that not all carpenters and woodworkers sharpen their own tools, most common cutting tools are relatively easy to sharpen, given an understanding of how the tool is designed to be used and the job it is intended to do.

Besides, not every community has a competent professional sharpening shop. In fact, a growing number of handy people are developing profitable sideline businesses by equipping and operating a professional sharpening service. Such companies make a complete line of sharpening equipment and offer buyers instruction on how to sharpen a wide range of tools.

You can equip a rather thorough sharpening shop for less than $1,000. The return on your investment will depend on how much work you want to do.

For purposes of this book, however, we are talking about homeowners who want to dress and sharpen some (or all) of their own tools, rather than those who want to go into the business. Even so, to do a professional sharpening job, you need to understand the tools and equipment you will use for sharpening.

Tools for Sharpening

You can use any number of objects to sharpen, say, a knife blade: a grinding wheel, a file, an oilstone, a chunk of smooth concrete, a sheet of abrasive paper or even an electric belt sander. Knowledge of what the knife blade does, and how it does it, probably is more important than what you use to sharpen it with.

At the outside, you will need only a few special tools to keep your cutting edges keen and serviceable. Three or four files and a two grit whetstone will do a great many sharpening chores. As with other tools, buy sharpening equipment as need arises. You're more likely to acquire exactly what you need this way.

Files

A file is a useful cutting tool for a great many purposes other than sharpening. A file is a hardened steel cutting tool that has a sharp series of points or teeth on its surface.

There are literally hundreds of styles, sizes and kinds of files. Happily, a small selection of well chosen ones will meet ordinary requirements in most home workshops.

Files are sized by the length of the body, or the part with the cutting points. For most practical sharpening jobs, files range from 4 to 14 inches.

Another classification of files is by the kind of teeth the tool has. Files with one series of chisel-like teeth running at an angle across the face are called "single cut" files. "Double cut" files have a second series of teeth crossing the first

Cross sections of file shapes.

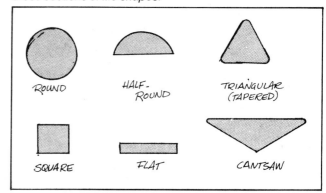

ROUND HALF-ROUND TRIANGULAR (TAPERED) SQUARE FLAT CANTSAW

A worn-out file on a battered axe is largely a waste of time. The edge of this axe should be dressed back to its original taper, either with a grinder or file, then whetted to a keen edge.

the edge on scrapers, plane irons, wood chisels, some power saw blades and similar tools that need fairly fine edge.

For filing handsaw teeth, a tapered triangular file generally is used; the size of the file depending on the number of saw points (teeth) per inch of blade. The following files commonly are used to sharpen handsaws:

Saw points	Triangular file
5 to 6	7 inch regular
7 to 8	6 inch slim taper
9 to 10	5 inch slim taper
11 to 12	5 inch slim taper
13 to 14	5 inch extra slim taper

Grinders

Sooner or later, if you do a lot of sharpening, you will want to own a bench grinder. The metal in some especially hard cutting tools cannot readily be sharpened with a file. You will need a grinder.

In selecting (or building) a grinder, the key is to get one that is sturdy and well constructed, with an adjustable tool rest. If you have an electric motor salvaged from a refrigerator or washer, you may build your own belt drive grinder.

The grinding wheel (or wheels) rates careul selection. The secret of success with grinding tools and other materials is to use a grinder wheel suited to the kind of work you're doing. Better made wheels are made of abrasives manufactured in an electric furnace, with a hardness second only to diamond. Aluminum oxide and silicone carbide are among the more widely used abrasives for grinders. It's economical to buy only the best. Cheaper wheels made of soft or uneven sized particles do not wear evenly and become slick and glazed more quickly than those made of better materials.

You'll want to pay attention to the *grain* and *grade* of the abrasive in the grinder wheel you buy.

The coarseness or fineness of a wheel is designated by a number representing the size of the particles used in making the wheel. A 42 grain wheel, for instance, means that the finest screen through which the particles will pass has 42 meshes to the inch—or is about $1/42$ inch in size. This is a fairly coarse wheel. A medium-fine wheel, about 80 grain, is best for grinding tools such as knives and wood chisels.

The grade of a wheel refers to its relative softness or hardness. The wheel should be made of material hard enough so that particles are not shed too rapidly during grinding, but soft enough so the tool does not overheat and lose temper (hardness). A medium-soft grade wheel is preferred for most tool grinding.

at an angle. Some files—and most rasps—have raised individual teeth, rather than rows of chisel shaped teeth.

As a third classification, files are also described by the shape of a cross section of the file face: flat, square, round, half-round, triangular. Another way files often are described is by their principal use, as **mill file** and **chainsaw file.**

To complicate the nomenclature further, particular kinds of files are made with just one kind of teeth. A **mill file**, a flat shaped file, is made only with single cut teeth; whereas a **flat file** (also flat in shape) is made in double cut only.

The fineness or coarseness of the file teeth is commonly designated by a number of terms, which are in order from coarsest to finest: rough, coarse, bastard, second cut, smooth and dead smooth. These terms are relative, however, and you probably will not need to pay much attention to them. Once you understand the kind of edge you need to sharpen on a cutting tool, you'll be able to choose the correct file by sight and feel.

A 10 or 12 inch mill bastard file (flat and fairly coarse teeth) is useful for sharpening shovels, hoes, spades and scythes. It also removes metal quickly when you need to re-dress axes and hatchets, and does a good job on lawnmower blades that have strayed into rocks.

For finer work, an 8 inch mill bastard or second cut file works well. For still finer work, a mill smooth file 6 to 8 inches long serves. You'd use this type of file to shape up

A bench grinder with wheels of two different grains and grades is virtually indispensable for handymen who dress and sharpen their own tools.

Always inspect a new grinder wheel before you mount it on the shaft. Wheels can become cracked or broken during shipment. Strike the wheel a light "lick" with a hammer. If the wheel is sound, it will ring. If there are flaws or cracks, the wheel will give a dull thud.

When mounting a wheel, draw the nut up only moderately tight. Be sure that compressible washers—of paper, leather or rubber—are installed between the flanges and the wheel itself, to prevent stresses that could crack the wheel.

When you start the grinder for the first time after replacing a wheel, stand to one side until the motor has run at full speed for several minutes. If the wheel flies apart, it's best not to be in the line of fire.

Whetstones

Hand and bench oilstones are the least expensive sharpening tools to own and use, and a good stone is valuable for sharpening keen edged tools—even if the major part of sharpening is done with a grinder or file.

Stones are made of both natural and man-made materials. Most expensive are Hard Arkansas stones, mined from quartz caves in the Ozarks. Soft Arkansas stones are softer and more porous—but decidedly less expensive.

Stones made with electric furnace artificial abrasives are cheaper still, although they do not produce the keen edge of natural stones.

A combination stone, with one side of coarse abrasive and the other of finer grain abrasive, is handiest to use. The coarse side is used for faster work during the first part of sharpening; the fine side for finishing to a keen edge.

A small two-grit oilstone is one of the cheaper means to keeping a keen edge on cutting tools.

Use a light oil, such as penetrating oil or a 50-50 mixture of light engine oil and kerosene, to prevent the surface of a stone from becoming slick and clogged with dirt. Natural stones should be soaked in oil for several hours, then wiped dry before being used. Most artificial abrasive stones are filled with oil when made. All stones need oil added as sharpening is done.

Other Sharpening Equipment

You can make a reasonable temporary substitute for a whetstone by tacking a piece of abrasive cloth to a wood block. A coarse grit sandpaper may be fastened to one side of the block; finer grit carborundum cloth to the other. Use it in the same way you would use a two grit oilstone.

If you can beat the antique hunters to it, you may find an old-fashioned wet grindstone at a farm sale. If the auctioneer doesn't run the price too high, buy it. An old hand or treadle cranked grindstone, well cooled with water, can produce very keen edges. A modern day substitute is made, driven by a small electric motor.

A piece of heavy leather, fastened to the bench or a wall and oiled, makes a dandy strop for honing knives and other fine edged tools. Strop with the edge trailing, rather than with the edge digging into the leather.

A number of steel and ceramic sharpening rods are on the market, designed to keep a keen edge on knives and scissors between sharpenings. These have limited use in the workshop, but are useful in keeping kitchen cutlery in good condition.

Sharpening Specific Tools

Axes and Hatchets

If an axe or hatchet edge is blunted or nicked, grind it first on a medium or fine wheel. Don't press too much on the blade, and keep it moving so the grinder wheel doesn't grind too much in one place.

When you need to remove a great deal of metal to grind out a nick, grind well back from the edge to maintain the original taper.

If you've done a good job with the grinder, you can produce a keen, smooth edge by whetting with a hand oilstone. A mill file is useful for keeping smaller nicks worked out of the blade.

Between grindings—which will not be needed often unless your axe sees rough duty—an axe blade can be kept in good form by lightly filing, or by whetting with an oilstone. You'll want to maintain a slightly thinner edge on an axe used mainly for chopping than on one used mostly for splitting wood. When chopping green wood, it's a good idea to carry a medium-fine stone (a cheaper one bought for the purpose will do) to remove sap from the blade and keep the cutting edge keen.

Sharpening Knives

Unless a knife blade is badly nicked or extremely dull, don't grind it on an electric grinder. It's difficult not to over-

Whet a knife blade with the cutting edge pushed along the stone. Whet first on the coarse side of the oilstone, then on the fine side to finish up.

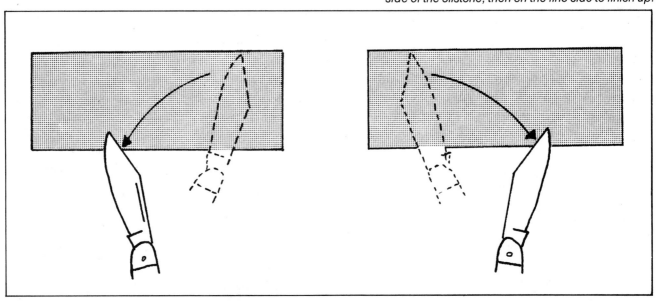

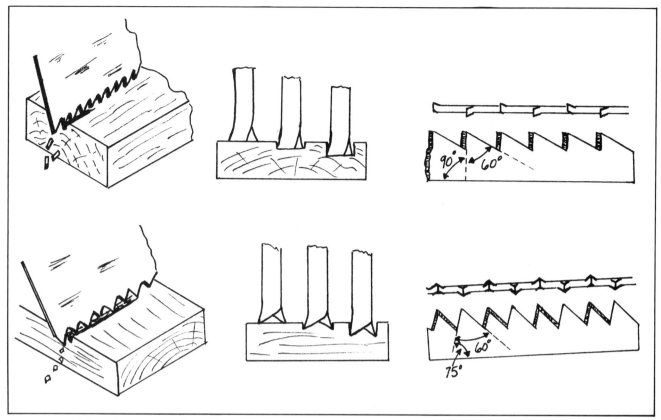

Ripsaw teeth (above) are like small chisels, severing the ends of wood fibers. Crosscut saw teeth, are shaped more like knives, to slice fibers crosswise. Notice the set or angle of both ripsaw and crosscut teeth, which makes a saw groove (kerf) slightly wider than the thickness of the saw blade.

heat the thin blade. However, if the blade has deep nicks or an edge as dull as last month's newspaper, you may have no choice but to grind the blade back to a coarse edge. If so, have a can of cooling water handy and dip the blade often.

If you do grind a knife, hold the blade so that the wheel turns against the cutting edge, not away from it. Place the blade flat against the wheel before starting the grinder, then raise the back edge just enough to make contact between the cutting edge and the wheel. This will help you judge the right angle to hold the blade when the grinder is running. Be careful not to angle the blade too much—the edge can dig into the wheel.

Most often, a knife will be sharpened when it is only moderately dull, and this is a function of the oilstone. Unless you're merely whetting a finer edge, it's faster to sharpen the knife initially by whetting on the coarse side of the stone, then finish it on the fine side.

To whet a knife, place a few drops of oil on the stone and place the blade flat against the stone. Raise the back of the blade just enough to put the cutting edge in contact with the stone, then draw the knife diagonally across the stone, cutting edge first. Turn the blade to the other side and repeat

the stroke. With practice, you'll be able to make both whetting strokes in one continuous motion.

If you need an exceptionally keen edge on a knife, strop the blade on a piece of smooth leather or ceramic rod after whetting. When stropping, pull the blade across the leather with the cutting edge trailing. With a ceramic rod, push the blade, cutting edge first, along the rod in a slicing kind of motion.

To test a knife for sharpness, run the ball of your thumb *very lightly* lengthwise along the edge. If the knife "pulls" or takes hold of the skin of your thumb, it's sharp. (Remember those microscopic "teeth" we talked about at the beginning of the chapter?) If the edge feels slick and smooth, the knife is dull.

Handsaws

Sharpening a handsaw—either a crosscut or ripsaw—can be a formidable first time experience. All those little teeth!

Before starting, you should have a clear idea of the shape of the teeth and understand the job each tooth is to

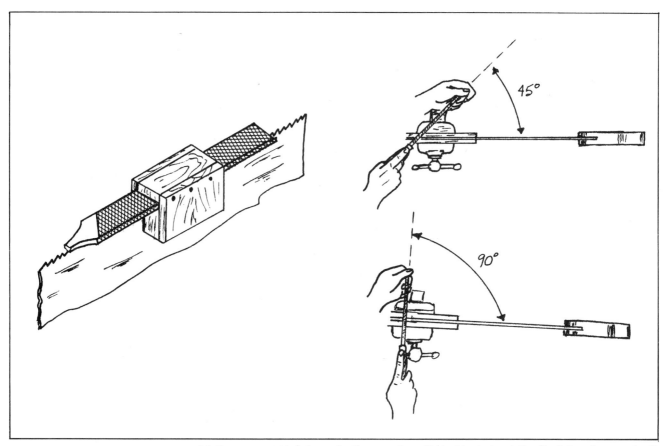

Jointing a saw, at left, is easier if you make a file holder to keep the file flat on the saw teeth. Joint (file) the teeth just enough to bring them all to the same length. At right, above, a cross-cut saw's teeth are filed at about a 45 degree angle to the plane of the saw blade, to give the knife-like edge needed for cutting wood fibers in two. Ripsaw teeth, below, are filed straight across, with the file at about 90 degrees to the saw blade.

do as the saw slices through wood. Close inspection of both types of saws reveals two principal differences in the shape of ripsaw and crosscut teeth. For one thing, the leading edge of a ripsaw tooth is perpendicular to the tooth line of the saw. The front edge of a crosscut tooth makes a 15 degree angle with the perpendicular (See illustration).

Another difference is that a crosscut saw tooth is beveled toward the point, while a ripsaw tooth is not. This is because the teeth have to perform different functions. The teeth in a ripsaw work like a series of small wood chisels to cut off the ends of wood fibers. Teeth of a crosscut are shaped more like tiny knives, to slice crosswise through the fibers.

When filing ripsaw teeth, the file is drawn straight across the blade at a right angle to the long dimension of the saw. In filing crosscut teeth, the file is held at about a 45 degree angle to the saw blade.

Notice also that the points of the teeth—on both crosscuts and ripsaws—are bent outward from the plane of the blade. One tooth is bent in one direction; the next in the

opposite direction. This alternate bending of teeth is called *set* and causes the saw to cut a kerf slightly wider than the thickness of the saw blade. This prevents the blade from binding and pinching in the kerf.

There are three major operations in filing a handsaw: jointing, setting and filing. Professional sharpeners employ a fourth operation to side dress or joint the teeth along the sides, but most home handypersons do not do this.

Jointing is done by running a flat file across the points of the teeth. This makes all teeth the same length and serves as a guide for filing. Keep the file square so that all teeth are jointed by the same amount. A homemade jointing jig can be built of scrap boards. Jointing leaves a flat, shiny surface on the point of each tooth. When this surface is just barely filed away, the tooth is sharp and has been filed enough.

After the jointing operation, saw teeth should be set, although this probably will not be needed each time the saw is filed. You can set the angle in saw teeth "by eye," by bending each tooth outward to about half the tooth's thickness. But it's more precise to use a small, inexpensive tool called a "spring saw set."

To use a saw set, clamp the saw in a saw vise or a clamp made of two pieces of 1x4 board, place the tool over a tooth and squeeze on the handle. When the handle is squeezed, a small plunger is forced against the end of the tooth and bends it against an anvil or plate to just the right angle. Don't use too much pressure on the set handle—you can mash a tooth out of shape fairly easily. Be sure to bend each tooth in the direction it was originally set, with the point of the tooth angled outward.

Most spring saw sets are adjustable. The amount of set you put in a saw will depend partly on the kind of wood you will be cutting. Green, wet wood requires a saw with more set than does kiln dried wood. Softwoods with stringy fibers require more set than most hardwoods.

Filing the teeth to a sharp point is the next step. Clamp the saw securely so that about ¼ inch of the saw teeth project above the clamp; just enough for the file to clear the vise or clamp.

A file guide which holds the file at the proper angle for the tooth bevel is a handy piece of equipment. If you use a file of the proper size, you can file the front bevel (on crosscut teeth) of one tooth and the back bevel of the tooth ahead of it on the same stroke. This takes a little practice, to adjust the file pressure to take the right amount of metal from both teeth.

File all the teeth on one side of the blade, then reverse the saw in the vise and file the teeth on the opposite side. File teeth just until the jointing marks disappear.

After jointing, setting and filing, test the saw's cutting ability on a piece of scrap wood. If the saw consistently runs to one side—strays off the line in one direction—use a fine oilstone to lightly rub the sides of the teeth on that side of the blade.

Chainsaws

Most chainsaws are equipped with chipper type cutting chains. These have round hooded cutters mounted on

To file a chainsaw's chipper cutters, hold the file level and file the hooded cutters at about a 35 degree angle.

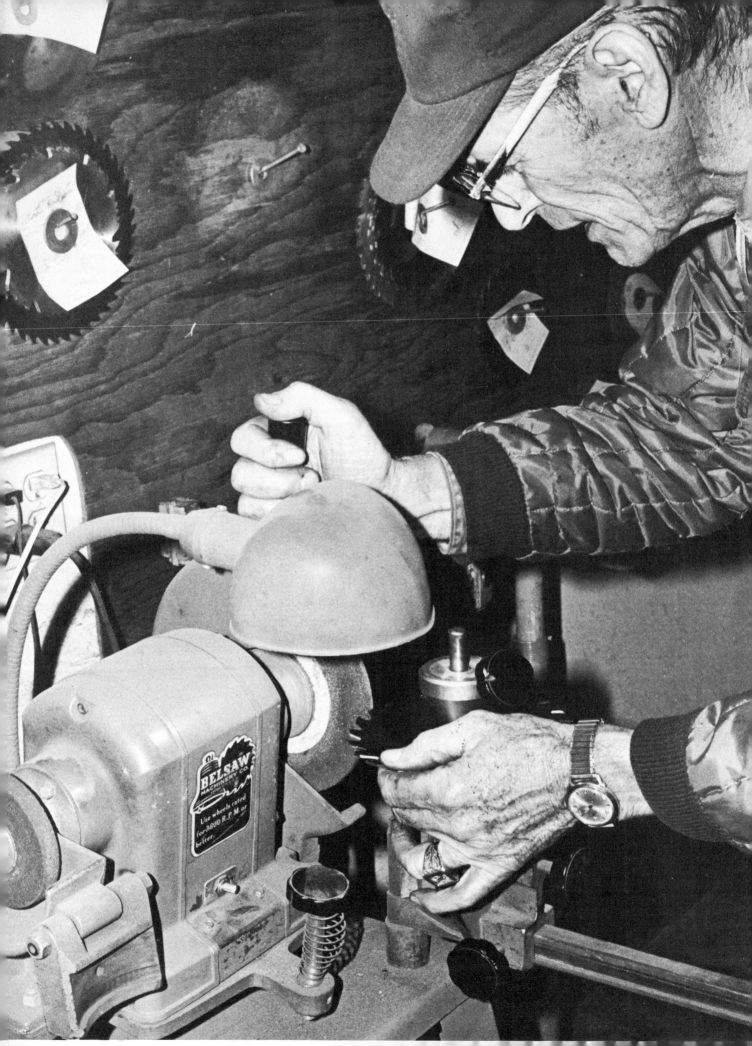

◄ *Gumming a saw, or removing metal from the deep grooves that must carry away the sawdust, is easier with a special gumming wheel on the grinder. (Courtesy of Belsaw)*

toothed flat file are used to file each depth gauge to about .025 inch below the cutter teeth.

Circular Saws

The operations in sharpening a circular saw blade are similar to those in fitting a handsaw: jointing, setting and filing. In addition, some circular saws occasionally need *gumming*, or filing down the gullets between the teeth. In circular saws, the gullets or spaces between teeth carry away the sawdust made by the teeth. If the gullets become too shallow (through filing of the teeth) in relation to the saw teeth, the gullets should be filed or ground deeper.

A circular saw is jointed by turning it backwards against a file held firmly in position to joint all teeth to the same length. With a table saw, you can adjust the saw so the teeth barely protrude through the slot in the table and hold the file flat on the table. Portable saw blades can be reversed so that the blade turns backward against the file, but be very careful when jointing a saw in this manner.

Teeth of a circular saw can be set with a hammer and a special setting block, but it's easier and more precise to do with a larger version of the spring saw set described

both sides of the drive links. Sharpen them with a special round file made to fit the exact curve of the chipper tooth. Make sure you use the right file for your chain.

Hold the file level and file at 35 degrees across the chain. Most saw manufacturers make filing guides that simplify filing each tooth at the proper angle. Use long filing strokes and file each cutter to the same length.

It's easier to file a saw chain after it is removed from the bar and clamped in a vise. However, this is not always practical. To file the chain on the saw, cut a groove with the machine in a log or stump to hold the cutter bar steady while you are filing. Then, tighten the chain tension so the chain doesn't wobble.

Most cutter teeth on saw chains have a depth gauge just ahead of the tooth. These will occasionally need to be filed down; but probably not every time cutters are sharpened. A depth gauge (for that particular type of chain) and a fine

Wood chisels and plane irons are ground to about a 25 degree angle. Set the tool rest so that the cutting edge is ground to a distance equal to twice the thickness of the chisel or plane blade. Then, whet the edge on an oilstone to about a 30 degree angle. Lightly rub the flat side of the blade along the stone to remove the wire edge produced by grinding and whetting the beveled side.

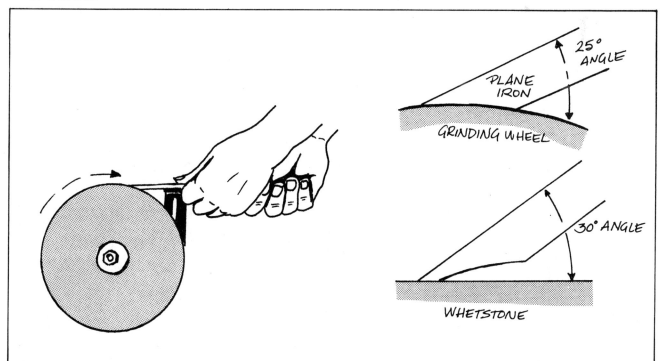

When sharpening auger bits, file the spurs (left) only on the side next to the lead screw—never on the outside. File cutters, right, only on the beveled side and remove the same amount of metal from both cutters. Don't let the file hit the lead screw.

above. Judge the amount and kind of set in much the same way you would with a handsaw.

For filing, the kind of file to use depends on the shape and size of the saw teeth. A crosscut circular saw can be filed with a 7 or 8 inch triangular file. For a ripsaw blade, it may be handier to use an 8 inch flat file. Be sure to maintain the original bevel of the teeth.

You can gum a saw blade with a round file, but it makes for long, hard work if you have much metal to remove. It's much easier to use a special saw gumming wheel on an electric grinder. Fine toothed crosscut circular saw blades do not need gumming, of course.

Chisels and Plane Irons

The method of sharpening wood chisels and plane irons (removed from the plane body, of course) is much the same.

Both tools require grinding angles of 25 to 30 degrees, and whetting angles of 30 to 35 degrees; although you may want to depart from the standard for specific jobs. Generally, the length of the bevel will be twice the thickness of the blade on these tools. Or, you can buy an inexpensive plane iron bevel gauge to check for the proper angle when grinding.

Badly dulled or nicked tools will need to be ground back to shape, but you will whet or hone cutting tools much more often than you grind them. A honing jig, such as the one manufactured by Miller Falls, clamps the tool at the proper angle for whetting on a flat oilstone.

Auger Bits

Some auger bits probably see more of the file than is good for them. Because of the designed relation of

On twist drills, the cutting lip at the point should be higher than at the trailing edge, by about 12 degrees.

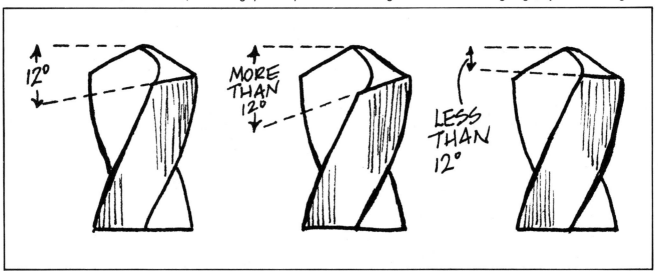

the parts of a quality bit's boring head, filing away too much metal from any part can interfere with the tool's boring efficiency.

But a bit will need light filing occasionally, to sharpen the spurs and cutters. *Never* file the lead screw of an auger bit.

To file the spur, rest the bit on a board or bench with the screw pointing up. Draw an auger bit file, or a small flat file lightly on the *inside* of the spur. Don't file on the outside—this will change the designed clearance of the bit.

To sharpen a cutter, place the bit with the screw down and file the cutters on the upper, beveled edge only. Take the same amount of metal from both cutters, so they will cut chips of equal thickness.

Twist Drills

You can go one of two ways with twist drills: either buy inexpensive drills and toss them when they become dull, or buy quality drills and sharpen them. Most workmen elect the former—except for a few favorite drills—and some of them never know how it feels to make holes with a good cutting drill.

The reason is that not all twist drills—and most especially not all cheap ones—are sharp when new.

A good twist drill, like a quality auger bit, is designed so that the various parts function in concert to do an efficient hole boring job. A twist drill should have cutting lips ground off behind the leading edge to allow the drill to bite into the work. The correct clearance is about 12 degrees.

The cutting edges should be exactly the same length and make the same angle with the central axis of the drill. If they do, the drill point is centered. If the point is not centered, one lip does more than half of the cutting and the drill will make an oversized hole.

The lip clearance and angle of the cutting edges will be properly matched in a quality drill. A simple, inexpensive grinding gauge can help you maintain this relationship during grinding and sharpening. Or, if you will be doing a great deal of twist drill sharpening, you may want to buy a sharpening jig, to assure that both cutting edges are ground to exactly the same angle and both to the same length.

To grind a twist drill freehand, steady the drill on the tool rest at the proper angle and slowly push the cutting end against the wheel. Then, raise the point of the drill in a sort of prying up motion. When one lip is ground, rotate the drill 180 degrees and repeat the process for the other lip. It's a bit tricky to get the proper angle, so you'll want to check the length and angle of cutting lips frequently.

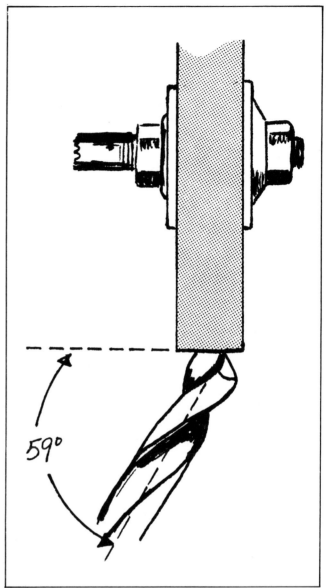

Grind the lip angle of twist drills so that it makes about a 59 degree angle with the long dimension of the drill. This angle is much easier to grind if you use a sharpening jig.

Sharpening Other Tools

There is seldom a time around the house when some tool does not need sharpening: mower blades, hoes, shovels, shears, scissors, cold chisels, punches, screwdrivers or something always seems to need attention. With a good idea of the tool's design and intended function, you can sharpen most of these implements handily.

Power mower blades need frequent attention during grass cutting season. Fortunately, mower blades are easy to sharpen with a flat file.

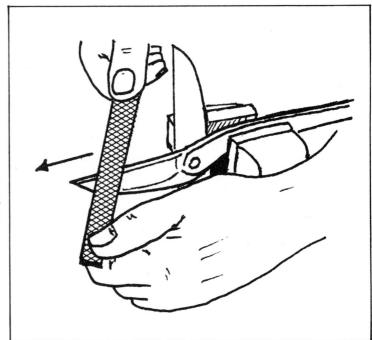

Scissors, snips and shears should be sharpened on the bevel only. If you must remove a wire edge from the flat side of the blades, do it carefully so as not to file away any clearance between the blades.

Before removing a blade from the mower, disconnect the spark plug wire and bend it back so that it cannot touch the plug. Better yet, remove the spark plug and check it each time you remove the blade. This way, you know the engine will not start accidentally when you turn the blade.

File the blade with long, slow strokes and count the number of strokes so that both edges of the blades are filed the same amount. On small power mowers, the blade doubles as a flywheel; therefore, balance is very important. After filing, place the blade over a marble on a smooth surface. Make sure the marble is centered in the hole in the center of the blade. If the blade balances, fine. If not, file away some more at the heavy side.

If a mower blade is badly nicked, as is likely to happen if the blade strikes a rock or piece of metal, grind the edge smooth on an electric grinder. But remember to take an equal amount of metal from the other side, for balance.

Cold chisels and **punches** need occasional sharpening and this is most easily done on the grinder.

For general cutting, a cold chisel should be ground with bevels on both sides making an angle of about 70 degrees at the cutting edge. If the chisel is to be used to cut light or soft metal, you may want to grind a thinner edge.

Center punches and drift pins can be ground back to their original conical shape. Hold the punch against the wheel at about a 30 degree angle and roll it slowly.

When grinding chisels, punches and other such tools, move the tool from side to side of the grinding wheel, to avoid grooving or wearing the wheel unevenly.

Screwdrivers should be ground to a blunt end, and the two flat sides should be straight and very nearly parallel at the tip. The end should be square and slightly narrower than the thickness of the screw slot it is to fit into.

Shears, scissors and snips can be sharpened with a file, or on a grinder if the cutting edges are badly nicked. Some scissors are made of such hard steel that they can be sharpened only by grinding. Key points in sharpening these tools are that they be ground or filed only on the beveled edge. Any wire edge produced by grinding or filing can be taken off by lightly whetting the flat side of the blade.

Hoes, shovels and spades are easily sharpened by filing. Generally, a super sharp edge is not needed on these tools. Be sure to maintain the original angle of the cutting edge. If much material must be removed to restore the edge, draw file (push the file sidewise) to take the metal down in a hurry. Because of the angle of the cutting edge in relation to their long handles, these tools are fairly awkward to sharpen on a grinder.

Making Your Own Tools

Chances are, you will think of tools you need for a specific job, but be unable to find exactly what you want at the hardware store. If you are interested enough in tools and their uses to have read this far, you probably can design and make some tools you will need.

Old files and saw blades, annealed (softened) by heating, can become gouges, knives, lathe tools, scrapers and similar implements. Once re-shaped into different tools, the metal can be re-hardened and tempered.

Tempering and hardening metals is a subject beyond the scope of this book, but a good text on metal working can give you pointers. It's a good way to turn one worn out tool into a brand new tool for another purpose.

Old files, saws and other tools can become new scrapers, routers and knives. This three edged scraper was made from a triangular file.

APPENDIX
Tool Safety

Opportunities for serious injury exist in any home or workshop, but they should not be literally lying around. There are many fewer chances to get hurt with tools that are used, maintained and stored properly. You have only one life, two eyes and 10 fingers: you cannot afford to lose any of them prematurely.

Safety with tools is mainly a matter of common sense. But is must be *your* common sense. Tools are woefully ignorant. Chisels and knives cut flesh as well as wood. Electrical current doesn't know that your body is not the conductor it is supposed to travel. Flying particles from a grinder wheel do not make detours around your eyes.

The Work Area

A clean, well organized shop or work space contributes to safety as well as to efficient work. Wipe up oil or grease spills right away, before you have a chance to slip and fall. Store lumber and other materials where they will be accessible, but out of the work area proper.

Have a definite place to store each tool, and return the tool to its resting place after use. If you have to rummage through a jumble of tools on a shelf or in a drawer, it doesn't help the condition of either the tools or your fingers.

Bandaged fingers.

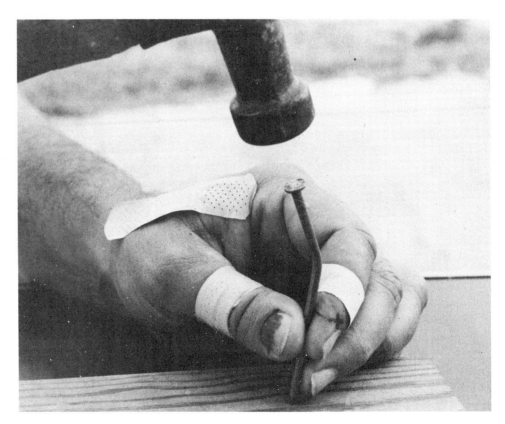

Give some thought to tool safety as you design the workshop and tool storage. The first time you cut yourself on one tool while reaching across it for another, this lesson will come home to stay.

Be alert for fire hazards. Clean up sawdust and shavings often. A pile of oily rags and a floor covered with sawdust are a spontaneous arson waiting to do you in. The electrical circuits that power the shop should be grounded and ample to carry the load.

Hot tools—propane torches, soldering irons, glue guns—can deliver painful burns, or even start fires, if carelessly used. When using these tools, set them on non-flammable surfaces between operations. Turn a torch off after each operation and re-light it for the next. That way, you aren't likely to walk off and leave it burning. In daylight, you may be unable to see the flame at the nozzle.

Tools with cutting edges must be sharp to perform their functions. This makes them potentially dangerous to handle and use.

However, a *dull* cutting tool is more hazardous than a sharp one. That sounds contradictory, but it's really true. A cutting tool with a sharp edge requires less force and pressure to slice through wood and other materials. You can control it more readily than you can a dull tool; it's less likely to slip and cause an injury.

Work being shaped with a chisel, gouge, plane or scraper should be securely clamped or supported, so you can guide the tool with both hands. Be sure the handles on these tools, as well as on files and rasps, are tight and in good condition. The pointed tang on a file is not a handle—it's where a handle is to be attached.

Struck tools—chisels, punches, steel wedges, brick sets, etc.—should have a struck face in good condition. Discard or re-dress these tools if they become cracked, chipped or mushroomed. Also, never use a claw hammer

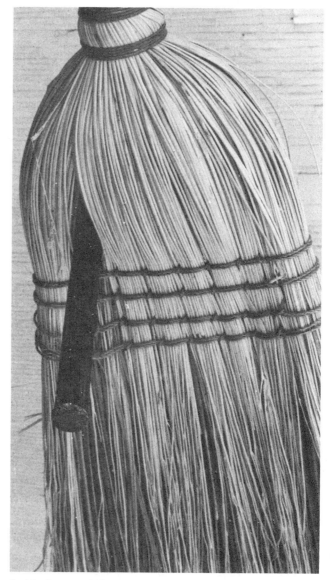

A chisel or star drill can be held by a straw broom to save wear and tear on the holder's fingers. Or, a locking plier-wrench can be used to hold struck tools while they are being struck.

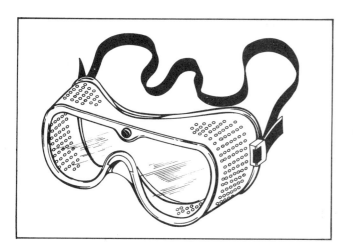

Safety goggles.

to strike these tools. A "mash" hammer, or hand driller's sledge, is the proper tool for this purpose.

Electrical power tools have a great deal of potential for serious injury, and should always be treated with respect. If you saw into your finger with a handsaw, you automatically stop sawing immediately. A power saw doesn't know it is severing your finger—it keeps turning.

The place to start safety checks with power tools is the power supply itself. As mentioned above, wiring for tool operating circuits should be grounded. Plugs and cords should be in good condition, not cracked or frayed. It's good back-up safety to have a central switch or circuit breaker that shuts off power to all tools in case of an emergency.

Keep a rubber mat on the floor in front of stationary power tools, and wear rubber soled shoes. If possible, buy only portable power tools with double insulated housings and grounded three prong plugs. And *use* the ground plugs in grounded outlets.

Don't wear neckties, scarves or loose-fitting clothing when working with power tools. It may not be high style, but a shop apron of duck or denim protects both clothing and its wearer.

When grinding, drilling metal or turning metal on a lathe, wear high-impact safety goggles. If you normally wear eye glasses when you work, you can buy safety goggles made to fit over them. Or, if this is not comfortable, use a hood with a flip-down face shield. A steel particle that spins off a grinder wheel turning 3,600 revolutions per minute can do a lot of damage to eyes.

Power woodworking tools are not so likely to fling off hard, hot chips as are grinders and lathes. The main safety consideration here is to keep fingers away from fast moving cutting edges and to hold work securely so that it isn't thrown or or kicked back by the moving blade or knives. A router bit turns at something like 20,000 r.p.m. at full speed. Shaper, molder and planer knives spin nearly that fast. Circular table saws and radial-arm saws whirl fast enough to amputate a finger at the lightest touch.

Keep all guards and shields in place and in good working condition on power cutting tools. Clamp work securely when working with portable power tools. Use a push-stick to feed smaller workpieces to a table saw, shaper or molder. If you are careless around these tools, you may loose your fingers.

When working with any tool, plan well and take your time. A good many accidents happen when the operator gets in a hurry. Don't work with power tools when you are tired or under the influence of alcohol. Take "coffee" breaks occasionally to fight fatigue when you are working. Watching a spinning blade or stock in a lathe can have an almost mesmerizing effect at times; keep your mind on what you are doing.

As a final word on safety, teach young children early that tools are not to be played with—any tools. It is not good for the kids or the tools. As youngsters grow older and show more interest in working with tools, take the time to teach them the proper way to use and care for tools. IT'S WORTH THE TIME IT TAKES!

Understanding Power Tools For Safety

(Extracted from: *Woodworking Directory and Handbook,* Hitchcock Publishing Co., Wheaton, Illinois.)

While portable electric tools are and should be powerful, cost-saving extensions of your hands, they often become costly gadgets for the indifferent. An understanding of a few general principles will help you plan, purchase, provide proper facilities and maintain a profitable variety of these modern labor-expediting devices called portable electric tools.

The motor. False economy will lead some buyers to purchase a portable electric tool on a price basis, then overload the nearly-burn-out-proof motor to incur hidden costs far greater than initial savings. The speed and current demand of this universal-type motor depends upon the load. As an overload occurs, the speed tends to slow down, higher torque is developed, the motor demands more current from the line and, as a result, overheating will cause serious trouble.

Because the high-heat resistant insulation materials built into modern motors make them nearly-burn-out-proof, operators often take their light-weight, high-powered abilities for granted. But, since overheating is not likely to burn out the motor, a whole series of other change reactions may develop. The control switch may go pffft-and, perhaps, the operator will, too!.

If the switch remains, it may be the tool cord, the extension cord, the connector plug, the conduit line or fuses and circuit breakers behind that. False economy in the purchase of a poor quality or inadequate tool may be the most costly error made all year. It could cost you a burned-down plant.

Speed control for some motors may be simple rheostats or resistance switches, as with many home appliances, merely to put back power made available to the motor.

Therefore, while the typical universal-type motor usually is applicable with AC or DC current, some portable electric tools may employ control systems which require AC only. Damage to the controls will occur if DC is used, although the motor may remain unharmed. You may remove all doubts of such a nature by proper study of the operating manual which accompanies all tools.

Whether the current is AC or DC, it is important to see that the motor capacity is adequate for the job to be done and particularly that sufficient power is fed to the motor.

Grounding. Most electric tools of reputable manufacture have provisions for grounding. Every tool should be properly grounded during operation to protect the operator against shock hazards. Accepted standards sponsored by the Electric Tool Institute, required by the U.S. National Electric Code, approved by Underwriters' Laboratories and the Canadian Standard Association, make modern tools equipped with a three-wire cord and grounding plug mandatory.

The cord has two power leads, the third wire having no effect on the normal operation of the tool. The ground wire connects with the housing so that the operator will be protected in case the tool should become internally grounded. This wire must be connected to a suitable ground for protection, although the tool will operate just as satisfactorily without it.

Do not permit the ground plug or prong to be damaged, this could cause a safety hazard. If you must work in or near moisture, the ground wire is even more important. In addition, you should wear protective gear such as rubber gloves and footwear.

If the tool needs to be disassembled for service or the cord replaced, be sure that the ground wire is connected to the tool housing and not to the switch. A continuity checker will prove out the circuits.

Extension cords. For extension of power from a distant outlet to reach a work area, the correct cord must be used to avoid safety hazards and possible damage to the tool. First, the cord should be a three-wire type, the same as the tool cord, so that proper grounding is automatically provided. Second, the wire size must be large enough to carry the necessary current.

All wire conductors have some amount of resistance and are rated on the basis of current-carrying capacity. The larger the wire and the shorter the length, the more current it will carry. Conversely, when the extension must be longer, the wire size must be larger to carry the same amount of current demanded by the tool.

Motor damage may occur should the power supply drop 10 percent or more below the values shown on the nameplate. ETI standards permit a voltage variation of plus-or-minus 6 percent with rated voltages of 115 and 230 as standard for direct and alternating current.

Drill and driver chucks. The most common chucks made to accept a wide variety of drill bits and other round shank straight tools are the three-jaw geared key types. These rather expensive, high quality components are precision machines in themselves and demand careful treatment to preserve their quality, accu-racy and useful life. Too many people give chucks improper treatment and destroy their characteristics almost before a tool has been broken in on the job. The following rules should be followed for correct treatment.

1. Open jaws wide enough to take desired bit. Clean bit shank of all foreign matter. Insert in chuck as far as it will go.

2. Close jaws by hand only, rotating the bit slowly to assure proper alignment and maximum contact between the chuck jaws and bit shank.

3. Insert key in one hole and turn to make snug fit, but not as tight as the chuck jaws may go.

4. Use other holes in sequence, tightening the key in each one as much as possible, remembering that when the key is returned to the first hole, there still may be some slack to take up. All three holes should be used to give maximum tightening pressure, to prevent slippage in operation which may damage the chuck jaws or the bit shank, and to make certain that all jaws have pressure evenly distributed. Otherwise, uneven wear can occur and eventually a bit will not run true. Excessive runout will produce oversize holes in drilling, or other kinds of sloppy and inefficient work.

5. Chuck may be released by using only one hole for the key. Keep chuck clean and free of dirt.

6. Apply a thin film of oil regularly to prevent rusting and to encourage good operation, but avoid too much oil which will tend to collect dust.

7. Store chucks with jaws open.

Tool maintenance. Regular inspection and routine protective measures should be automatic with any portable electric tool to make your investment pay out, to maintain efficiency, to obtain quality performance, and to provide safety.

The universal motor is a delicate instrument. Although its wiring and insulation will withstand high temperature operation, satisfactory running conditions depend upon adequate ventilation engineered into its design. The vent slots, fan blades and armature must be kept clear of an accumulation of dust or dirt to avoid overheating and excessive power demands. Remove such accumulations as frequently as they appear.

Lubrication. Some tools will have "lifetime" ball or roller bearings which are replaced only after long use, but never lubricated. Others may have oil-soaked porous bronze bearings which require periodic replenishment of the oil. Proper lubrication of a tool is a science, not a routine maintenance problem. If one drop of oil of a certain viscosity on a felt pad is required, you do not merely grab the nearest oil can and squirt. You may damage expensive parts or ruin a motor. Check the maintenance manual or supplier of every electric tool to determine what proper lubrication means. Make sure no tool is purchased or operated without full information.

Minimum Cord Wire Sizes
(Electric Tool Institute Standards)

Full-load Ampere Rating of Tool		Amps 0–2.0	Amps 2.1–3.4	Amps 3.5–5.0	Amps 5.1–7.0	Amps 7.1–12	Amps 12.1–16
Length of cord							
115v.	230 v.						
25 ft	50 ft.	18	18	18	16	14	14
50 ft.	100 ft.	18	18	18	16	14	12
75 ft.	150 ft.	18	18	16	14	12	10
100 ft.	200 ft.	18	16	14	12	10	8
200 ft.	400 ft.	16	14	12	10	8	6
300 ft.	600 ft.	14	12	10	8	6	4
400 ft.	800 ft.	12	10	8	6	4	4
500 ft.	1000 ft.	12	10	8	6	4	2
600 ft.	1200 ft.	10	8	6	4	2	2
800 ft.	1600 ft.	10	8	6	4	2	1
1000 ft.	2000 ft.	8	6	4	2	1	0

Note: If voltage is already low at the source (outlet), have voltage increased to standard, or use a larger cord than listed in order to prevent any further loss in voltage.

DISTRIBUTORS AND MANUFACTURERS OF TOOLS

Arrow Fastener Company
Saddle Brook, NJ 07663
Staplers; fasteners

Belsaw Machinery Company
315 Westport Road
Kansas City, MO 64141
*Power shop tools; power
sharpening equipment*

Bernzomatic Corp.
Rochester, NY 14613
Propane torches

Black and Decker Mfg. Company
701 East Joppa Road
Towson, MD 21204
Power tools

Bostik Consumer Division
USM Corporation
4408 Pottsville Pike
Reading, PA 19605
Staplers, riveters, glue guns

The Brookstone Company
Peterborough, NH 03458
Mail-order tools; equipment

The Carborundum Company
Consumer Products Division
P.O. Box 337
Niagra Falls, NY 14302
Sandpapers; abrasives

Channellock, Inc.
Meadville, PA 16335
Adjustable pliers

Disston, Inc.
601 Grant Street
Pittsburgh, PA 15219
*Hand saws; wood-shaping
tools; cordless power tools*

Dremel Manufacturing
Racine, WI 53406
Power model tools

Garrett Wade Company
302 Fifth Avenue
New York, NY 10001
Power saws, jointers

The Irwin Company
Wilmington, OH 45117
Auger bits; twist drills

J. C. Penny Company
1301 Avenue of the Americas
New York, NY 10019
*Mail-order hand and
power tools*

Millers Falls Company
Greenfield, MA 01301
Power woodworking tools

Nicholson File Company
Providence, RI 02904
Files; rasps

Power Tool Division
Rockwell International
6263 Poplar Avenue
Memphis, TN 38138
*Power tools; radial-arm
saw*

Sears, Roebuck and Company
Sears Tower
Chicago, IL 60684
   *Mail-order hand and
   power tools*

Shopsmith, Inc.
750 Center Drive
Vandalia, OH 45377
   Combination power tools

Skil Corporation
Chicago, IL 60630
   Power tools

S-K Tools
Dresser Industries, Inc.
Franklin Park, IL 60131
   Wrenches; socket sets

Stanley Tools
Division of Stanley Works
New Britain, CT 06050
   *Power; hand woodworking
   tools; measuring tools*

Swingline
3200 Skillman Avenue
Long Island City, NY 11101
   Staplers; riveters

U. S. General
100 General Place
Jericho, NY 11753
   *Mail-order hand
   and power tools*

Index